Praise for *Teaching the Dinosaur to Dance*

"Beyond the author's incredibly wide range of experiences, what makes this book different is the force and clarity with which it delivers a powerful case for change—and explains why incremental change just will not do for this time we're in. It's an elegant dance, made easier by practical tools for both organizational change and personal leadership that are brought to life with honest and powerful storytelling."

— *Chad Park, Vice President, Sustainability & Citizenship, The Co-operators Group Ltd., and Founding Director, Energy Futures Lab*

"Donna brings a wealth of diverse experiences to the table, from growing up on her family farm, to operating in the boardrooms of Canada's biggest oil companies and the halls of political power, to her leadership in the non-profit sector in Canada and the Middle East. She weaves these experiences into a practical and grounded set of insights and challenges to the status quo, providing readers with a thoughtful and measurable framework on how to assess the state of their current enterprise, and adapt and even re-invent it in the face of a rapidly evolving new world."

— *Reg Manhas, Global Fellow, Canada Institute at the Wilson Center*

"*Teaching the Dinosaur to Dance* provides the playbook for leaders and organizations on how to remain relevant. Whether you're a new builder or a rebuilder, Kennedy-Glans teaches us how to use corporate integrity tools and stakeholder engagement strategies to become more current and relatable to future generations."

— *Darren Sweeney, President, CF Construction Services & Alberta Construction Rentals*

"*Teaching the Dinosaur to Dance* is a mirror to the inner workings of our decision-making processes. It's a spark that can force us to rethink what we think we already know. It's a map through the fog of uncertainty, if not to a better tomorrow, then to a place where we can feel more certain in taking the right step toward a better tomorrow. But most importantly, *Teaching the Dinosaur to Dance* is a reminder to never stop trying—no matter the circumstances, no matter the challenges. And to remember that, when we try, we demand and achieve better—in ourselves, in our work and in our communities."

— *D. Simon Jackson, Founder, Spirit Bear Youth Coalition and Co-Founder, Nature Labs*

"*Teaching the Dinosaur to Dance* offers a cohesive, practical roadmap for a different business future. The chapters, with intriguing titles like 'Go for the Moon Shot' and 'Move Beyond Polarity,' cover central issues of change, such as: broadening perspectives, integrating generational expectations, addressing fairness gaps, and redefining and generating value. With Donna's lively writing style, it offers a stimulating read for boards of directors, CEOs, executives and employees, as we all dance towards the future."

— *Daryl Fields, Chair, Strategic Initiatives Committee, BC Hydro Board of Directors; World Bank Senior Water Specialist (retired)*

"This book is a powerful and insightful spark for leaders across all sectors to reflect on the evolving definition of sustainability, strategic foresight and—most importantly—leadership that will be helpful in our current and post-pandemic contexts. Despite the often polarizing nature of these terms, and their sometimes clichéd application, it's important—now more than ever before—to understand their true relevance and value in shaping the future of the organizations and communities we work for."

— *JS Ryu, President and CEO, National accessArts Centre*

"*Teaching the Dinosaur to Dance* provides great insight into the challenging world of leadership, including examination of the character, values, curiosity and skill sets required to be a successful leader. The leadership evaluation tools included in the book are among some of the most useful I have encountered in close to two decades as a senior leader in the public service. They are incredibly helpful to me in evaluating the kind of leader I am and where I need to grow; they also provide me with the practical questions I need to support leaders on my team to develop, and to better assess leaders I wish to recruit."

— *Justin Riemer, Assistant Deputy Minister, Alberta Region, Prairies Economic Development Canada, Government of Canada*

"This thoughtful book on leadership and its challenges presents a path to successful re-emergence. Offering guidance through experience and foresight, *Teaching the Dinosaur to Dance* suggests effective ways to evolve and adapt in the paradoxical dance of change and resilience."

— *Aritha van Herk, Award-winning Novelist and Essayist; Professor of Canadian Literature and Creative Writing, Department of English, University of Calgary*

"How we listen to stories is just as important as how stories are told. *Teaching the Dinosaur to Dance* is a relevant and timely read, mixing politics, universal crisis and the needs of humanity. Stories shared by the author about her life work experiences from Yemen to the family farm in Southern Ontario while providing lessons from multinational firms gave me a dance map for how I want to move in the world as a leader and fellow human. I am left with a renewed energy to think like an activist and the tools to embody a commitment to stewardship by actively and continuously filling the gap between my values and practice."

— *Yasmin Dean, Dean, Education and Social Work,*
  Thompson Rivers University

"I first met Donna Kennedy-Glans many years ago during some of my first steps in an unfamiliar and often less-than-friendly environment that she was well entrenched in. She, too, was a minority . . . Donna presented tobacco to me one day; and it wasn't the usual store-bought organic tobacco. She gifted me with attractively offered tobacco leaves from her very own family farm several thousand kilometers away that came with a beautiful story, some of which you will find within the pages of this book. In that moment, I knew that I could trust this woman to always be respectful and honest, and to go above and beyond the typical in her efforts to support her objectives.

"We are at a critical juncture in our evolution, and we must all learn some new behaviors if we are to survive. It's not easy to do and it can often seem that in a world that is largely focused on economics and profit, the quality of humility is not valued. This important book shows us what can happen when we get out of our heads and into our hearts: long-term, future-focused thinking that will be of tremendous benefit to those who engage their organizations and teams in this work."

— *Sandra Sutter, Cree Métis Singer-Songwriter;*
  Aboriginal Partnerships Manager, PTW Energy and
  CGT Industrial; President, Board of Directors,
  Circle for Aboriginal Relations Society

TEACHING
THE DINOSAUR
TO DANCE

Moving Beyond Business as Usual

DONNA KENNEDY-GLANS
With Contributions from Andre N. Mamprin

MILNER &
ASSOCIATES INC
· EDITING · PUBLISHING · COMMUNICATIONS · CONSULTING ·

ISBN 978-1-988344-34-8 (hardcover)
ISBN 978-1-988344-35-5 (e-book)

Production Credits
Editor and project manager: Karen Milner
Copy editor: Lindsay Humphreys
Interior design and typesetting: Adrian So, AdrianSoDesign
Cover design: Adrian So, AdrianSoDesign
Printer: Friesens
Published by Milner & Associates Inc.
www.milnerassociates.ca

Printed in Canada
10 9 8 7 6 5 4 3 2 1

FSC
www.fsc.org
MIX
Paper from
responsible sources
FSC® C016245

To my granddaughter Kennedy, and to her generation

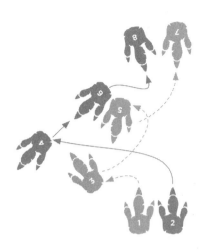

CONTENTS

INTRODUCTION

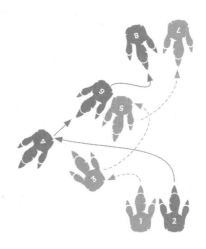

BUSINESS AS USUAL IS EXTINCT

I f your enterprise team feels like the universe is swerving, you are not alone. Disruption rules the day, and the vain hope of maintaining the status quo is, in fact, doing harm to many organizations. It's time to wake up to some tough new realities and re-invent your enterprise to not only survive, but thrive, in a very different future. The dinosaur who does not learn to evolve will die and may take much of its ecosystem down with it, even the good stuff. It's time to teach your dinosaur to dance!

Whatever kind of enterprise you are engaged in—a private-sector, for-profit business; a government or public-sector agency; a non-profit organization or a social institution—there is growing pressure to figure out new ways to make capitalism work better for more people. Issues of fairness, wealth inequality, discrimination and environmental sustainability are top of mind for many. Does this mean your enterprise has to tackle every issue that appears in the headlines? Of course not; but staying quiet during a raging conversation relevant to your sector isn't likely to land well either. Whether the issue is diversity or sustainability, people are getting called out for their silence. And it's not just that enterprises are getting called out—enterprises are losing out.

Many of these complex issues cannot be resolved through more of the same. Climate change, for example, is prone to polarized positioning if you can't find a pathway through the entanglement of objective facts and subjective values. Daunting or not, this is not the time to hide behind organizational walls and sneak wary glances at your stakeholders. It's time to evolve or else go the way of the actual dinosaurs.

If old ways of doing things are failing your enterprise, you will need to challenge embedded assumptions and ask different questions. How will you navigate changes in outsourcing and supply chains and buy-local expectations? How will you tell your enterprise story in a world of citizen journalists and social media? How will you "walk your talk" on core values? How will you innovate and test new ideas? Can your collaboration with others—politicians, communities, advocates—be more than window dressing?

Dancing with a dinosaur requires great attention and intention, otherwise you may inadvertently get hurt. "Enterprising" individuals and organizations are able to navigate the risks and step beyond the status quo. And in doing so, they can create greater value. And when I speak of value, I'm not just speaking of profits; enterprise value creation can be social, cultural, economic, creative or innovative.

Teaching the Dinosaur to Dance will teach you new steps—new ways to elegantly and effectively move your enterprise from the status quo to spectacular and sustainable.

WHO SHOULD READ THIS BOOK?

If you are curious to understand what it will take to teach your dinosaur how to evolve with the changing environment and not just survive but thrive, this book is for you. If you are a decision-maker in an enterprise mired in fossilized thinking, this book can help you to steward critical conversations. If you are not the formal decision-maker but have the ability and motivation to influence your enterprise's thinking and approach on an issue, this book can likewise provide support and guidance on how to talk about sensitive questions and advance solutions that move your organization beyond the status quo.

This book is for enterprise rebuilders and new builders open to fresh ideas and willing to do the work needed to move their organization to a preferred future. What's the difference between an enterprise rebuilder and a new builder? As I see it, "rebuilders" are experienced individuals, usually with more formal authority within an enterprise and with more official power to lead and direct change. Rebuilders are most often the decision-makers who were responsible for creating the status quo in the first place. For example, choices made by energy companies, consumers and government policy-makers over the past decades have contributed to the present climate crisis, and it may now be incumbent on them to help us find a way out of it.

"New builders" may not have as much experience in enterprise decision-making but wield considerable influence, especially when they are impatient with the perpetuation of business-as-usual approaches and are keen to make change from the inside out. The growing pressure from younger generations to do something to address climate change is just one of many examples of pent-up frustration with the status quo.

New builders may lack experience, but many know they definitely won't build enterprise following the blueprint of generations before them. This generational context is important to understand. Rebuilders are more likely to be from boomer generations (born 1946–64), and new builders are more apt to be millennials (born 1981–96) or Generation Zers (born 1997–2015). Presently, Generation Xers (born 1965–80) are most often the people making formal decisions inside enterprise; they are partially responsible for decisions that created the current conditions and they are, at the same time, frequently motivated to disrupt business as usual.

"Okay, boomer," you may ask this author, "how are you qualified to teach new dance steps to rebuilders or new builders of enterprise? Aren't you a dinosaur yourself if you're partly responsible for building the status quo?"

Those are fair and relevant questions. Truth is, I have been testing dance moves inside a wide range of organizations and among different jurisdictions and generations for four decades, and so I have ample first-hand knowledge of why people get tripped up and how they succeed. The insights, anecdotes, business tools and ideas shared in this book reflect the cumulative learnings I've gleaned while on the inside of the various organizations I've been a part of.

This experience includes holding unique and substantive roles inside the global energy business; leading a non-profit in the country of Yemen; serving as an elected politician and cabinet minister; being a blogger and community champion; holding leading roles on boards of directors; and participating as a sibling in a family farm enterprise. Additionally, my experiences as a mom to three sons (all of whom are millennials) has provided lots of hands-on learning about ways to teach and model enterprising behaviours. My goal has always been to figure out how to make better decisions within organizations, and with greater agility and intention; my goal with this book is to teach you steps that you can take to do the same.

I am delighted to be supported in this work by Andre Mamprin, a Generation X colleague who has helped new builders and rebuilders implement profound organizational redesign in enterprises across North America. In this book, Andre contributes tools and perspective on the personal leadership front, pointing out what qualities individual change-makers require to teach a dinosaur to dance.

As rebuilders, Andre and I have empathy for those responsible for the decisions that created the status quo, and we both personally share in that accountability. While business as usual may be extinct, there is value in understanding how we got to this point and in discerning what to preserve and what to discard. In this particularly destabilizing time, we feel a responsibility to support the work of all enterprise builders—the new builders and the rebuilders—who seek to remain relevant and sustainable. To that end, we encourage different thinking on organizational design, stakeholder engagement and personal leadership competencies.

BUCKLE UP THOSE DANCING SHOES!

Enterprise decision-makers face new and very challenging questions, including finding fairer ways for capitalism to pull its weight, and it is this book's aim to support these important conversations and choices. The recent pandemic has only exacerbated the challenges that organizations are confronting today. The crisis has been a devastating shock to enterprise—and it is a loud alarm and opportunity to rethink the role of enterprise. Make no mistake, though, this book is not rooted in the COVID-19 crisis. Rather, it identifies the pandemic as a catalyst for the profound change that social movements have been pushing for, for some time. The conditions are ripe for an extraordinary leap forward.

One of the most daunting challenges for enterprise rebuilders and new builders is path-finding through the many, and often conflicting, perspectives on what enterprise can and should do. There are cynics who believe enterprise should not play a role outside traditional boundaries—and who bluntly accuse any socially progressive organization of virtue signalling and using woke capital. And at the opposite end of the spectrum, there are people who believe enterprise should fix all woes. *Teaching the Dinosaur to Dance* will not necessarily equip you to avoid conflicting viewpoints. As I know all too well from experience, sometimes when you are teaching the dinosaur to dance, you may get bitten. But by aligning your enterprise values and purpose, and building your capacity to engage with influential stakeholders (including those holding different belief systems or even opposing your enterprise goals), you can build more resilient and innovative organizations.

Public expectations have been shifting for some time, disrupting the status quo and manifesting in several significant social movements as diverse as MeToo, Occupy, Black Lives Matter, Arab Spring, Fridays for Future. Clearly, each of these movements is different and focused on its own set of complex issues, but they and others have put mounting pressure on organizations of all kinds for increased accountability, equality, fairness and sustainability.

For many reasons, several of which were accelerated by COVID-19, we've reached a turning point—the extinction of business as usual—and change is inevitable. In fact, it's already happening, and simply striving to maintain the status quo is causing harm to many enterprises. Continuing to tread water in a tsunami of change will prove disastrous. However, willpower and good intentions alone will not sustain your efforts to rebuild or launch an enterprise in such a changed world.

To truly redefine and rebuild enterprise, I believe leaders in every sector need to look at new models of resiliency, innovation and sustainable growth. The book aims to work with the builders and rebuilders who are open to fresh ideas and willing to do the work needed to move their enterprise to a preferred future on a sustained basis. This book is written for those enterprising individuals and organizations who are committed to teaching the outmoded, struggling dinosaur to dance.

WHAT YOU WILL FIND IN THIS BOOK

There is no perfect model and no perfect road map; but there are proven processes to follow for putting your own plan in place. Supported by the stories and real-world experiences of other change-makers, and with the help of the enterprise tools that are shared in this book, rebuilders and new builders are encouraged to design their own models, build their own tools and figure out their own way forward.

Chapter by chapter, this book will review the conundrums (and the corresponding opportunities) facing enterprise in an emerging new world, introducing fresh approaches and enterprise models that can help guide new builders and rebuilders alike. It is up to each enterprise team to design their own strategies, from the inside out, and build the organizational capacity to implement these strategies. And the issues explored in each chapter of this book will help guide that thinking, those discussions and the strategic choices that can move your enterprise beyond business as usual. The chapters probe deep into the calcified thinking that is characteristic of the dinosaur mindset, and they offer up reviving strategies that can turn that lumbering dinosaur into a nimble creature, able to dance into the future elegantly and effectively.

And I take a very practical approach. To help readers rethink, redesign and execute enterprise revitalization and possibly even transformation, two organizational tools—*A Measure of Integrity* and

The Enterprise Onion—are shared in this book and applied to the themes explored in individual chapters. *A Measure of Integrity* is an enterprise tool designed to guide organizations in their alignment of purpose, values, commitments and actions. *The Enterprise Onion* is a stakeholder tool designed to support organizations in their outreach to, and engagement with, the diverse range of viewpoints required to progress effectively and sustainably on a new path forward. These specialized organizational tools have been tested, researched and honed through fifteen years of hands-on engagement across a wide range of enterprise. You will find both tools, *A Measure of Integrity* and *The Enterprise Onion*, in their entirety (with comprehensive user guides) in the Appendix.

A Measure of Integrity guides enterprise teams in their setting of core organizational values and purpose, internally and through engagement with external stakeholders. The seven levels of positive integrity that an enterprise may choose range from strict compliance with laws to stewardship thinking. The mid-point of the ascending scale of integrity marks the point where organizations shift from compliance with laws to "beyond compliance" values. Very importantly, this tool also helps organizations to identify and manage any gaps—between values and commitments and actions. Implementing values in practice requires ongoing attention and is far more challenging than the making of bold commitments.

The Enterprise Onion is primarily an outward-facing tool, modelling how to recognize and engage with stakeholders: from the internal enterprise team, to like-minded allies, to open-minded collaborators, and even with skeptics and those who hold entirely different values. Engagement with a wide range of unique perspectives is encouraged to create the conditions for sustainable change. To be clear, the aim of engaging with a range of stakeholder perspectives is not to merge world views into one reductionist, lowest-common-denominator strategy. Watered-down consensus is not helpful to enterprise rebuilding.

In the Appendix, you will also find *The Essential Elements of Leadership*, which is a model of personal leadership competencies that was compiled and defined by Andre Mamprin through his work at The Next Institute, where they conducted more than ten years of applied research, observation and documented evidence of thousands of leaders in twenty-one different sectors. These personal leadership competencies are sprinkled throughout the chapters as *Personal Leadership Elements,* in order to draw your attention to the essential leadership qualities and competencies required to lead specific aspects of rebuilding work. Some leadership elements are referenced more than once in the chapters ahead; this recurrence is intentional.

Effective change leaders require a range of personal leadership skills and qualities; some elements of personal leadership are foundational, while others are emerging qualities observed in more effective new builders and rebuilders. For example, sense-making, assessing risk, decision-making and executing to plan are foundational leadership qualities that every leader needs. Leaders who start to break away from the pack demonstrate incremental leadership elements, including competencies like synthesizing, suspending, catalyzing and being able to deal with paradox.

You will also find narrative storytelling woven into the book's chapters; this is by design. The stories shared in *Teaching the Dinosaur to Dance* are drawn from my personal experiences in places as diverse as oil-rich Alberta and Nigeria, the farming communities of southern Ontario, and remote places in the countries of Yemen, Indonesia and Colombia. What I hope you will notice is how, regardless of their location on a map, the challenges and opportunities that are wrestled with in these stories resonate in your own context.

That's the power of storytelling: it can build powerful resonance with others. Figuring out how to align your personal values with organizational decisions, for example, is a challenge and an aim for most of us. Telling your story, and sharing doubts and learnings with others, helps to deepen your understanding of values-driven decision-making and can inspire others to do the same.

THE DANCE MOVES: AN OVERVIEW

Each chapter of the book takes you through a different challenge that I've faced in my work with other forward-looking enterprise builders. The possible solutions are not simple, and various options are explored in their complexity. New dance moves—for you and your enterprise—are shared to give you refreshed inspiration and new ideas as you buckle up those dancing shoes and get moving, beyond business as usual.

Chapter 1: Re-energize the Sustainability Dance

How can your enterprise achieve sustainability, especially in a world focused on reducing emissions? This is a complicated issue for private, public and non-profit sector leaders. Drawing on examples from the energy and agricultural sectors, this chapter will explain how enterprise teams can apply *A Measure of Integrity* tool to set their own sustainability targets. The history of corporate social responsibility (CSR) is explored; and the ESG (environmental, social, governance) approach, the latest in a series of strategies to better define enterprise purpose and values, is introduced.

Chapter 2: Go for the Moon Shot

The second chapter focuses on your enterprise's strategy for rebuilding: will you choose incremental, revitalizing or transformational change? In my experience, an incremental change approach is not adequate to rebuild enterprise. In fact, in today's environment, revitalizing change or transformational change should be the goal for any organization that hopes to survive. *The Enterprise Onion* tool is introduced to guide your organization's engagement with the range of stakeholder perspectives required, to help design and implement a more sustainable future.

Chapter 3: Move Beyond Polarity

The third chapter focuses on the vexing challenge of polarization and entrenched positioning, which creates the conditions for black-and-white thinking and sometimes conflict. Enterprise leaders have to manage many competing dualities—efficiency versus resiliency, and collaboration versus competition, to name but a few—but these aims don't have to be opposing or mutually exclusive. What this chapter recommends and explains is how to shift from making either-or binary choices to more inclusive options. If you continue to create the conditions for fragile monocultures to flourish, you are putting your enterprise at greater and greater risk of extinction.

Chapter 4: Get to a Fair Deal

Stakeholder and public calls for greater fairness are gaining traction, and enterprise is increasingly expected to play a role in closing fairness gaps of societal, ecological and geopolitical proportions, many of which were exposed and exacerbated by the COVID-19 pandemic. Chapter four will take a closer look at how enterprise leaders can navigate these emerging expectations. This is a tall order, and it is tricky. Fairness is in the eye of the beholder.

Chapter 5: Re-imagine Your Business Model

Chapter five looks at ways to redesign your enterprise processes and structures in order to enhance your organization's ability to make better-quality decisions and deliver more value to more stakeholders. This chapter encourages you to ask more critical questions about your business model. Who is really making the decisions that impact your enterprise, and how are those decisions made? How do you integrate ideas from stakeholders outside your core team? Who really has skin in the game?

Chapter 6: Make Stewardship Part of Your Enterprise Story

In this sixth chapter, I will explain why it is critical for organizations (and their people) to know and tell their enterprise story. You can try to control the messaging all you want, but media in all its forms— mainstream, social, documentaries, citizen journalism—also shapes how people perceive your enterprise. Authentic stories of enterprise that aim for multi-generational, regenerative and stewardship values are also shared in this chapter.

Chapter 7: Rebuild for the Storm After This Storm

Even organizations with state-of-the art risk-management strategies did not foresee the COVID-19 pandemic, and it's not certain that any enterprise will accurately predict the inevitable storm after this storm. What's essential for survival and enduring success is rebuilding your enterprise by imbedding practices that challenge assumptions, anticipate risks and equip the enterprise to weather future storms with resilience. This chapter explores provocative questions like: What can be left behind? When is more not better? What constitutes "value" for your enterprise? What will be different, this time?

Chapter 8: Dance Together Toward a Better Future

In the final chapter, a story about a green energy project is shared to challenge conventional thinking about sustainability as the holy grail. What might motivate you to think differently about sustainability targets, perhaps to even contemplate stewardship and reciprocity as a higher-order way of thinking? Much of this future-thinking is uncharted territory. How can you build the internal capacity required to trust your own intelligence and imagination? As I've learned, understanding how others do enterprise is useful, but shoehorning your experience into someone else's model is self-limiting.

My aim is for you to never feel like you are alone in your enterprise-building or rebuilding endeavours. To that end, in addition to the information and tools provided in this book, you will also find resources—tools, conversations, fresh ideas—available online at **www.teachingthedinosaur.com**.

Teaching the dinosaur to dance requires your active participation. This is no time to be a wallflower. So then, shall we dance?

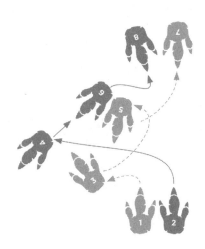

CHAPTER 1

RE-ENERGIZE THE SUSTAINABILITY DANCE

The only truly sustainable enterprise I ever encountered was the family farm I couldn't wait to run away from five decades ago. The land I grew up on in southern Ontario has been nurtured by five generations of my father's family; every critical decision made reflects the enduring values of prior generations and contemplates the impacts to future generations of the Kennedy family. My parents passed away in the last couple years, both from cancer, and in their final days this is what they wanted to talk about: how to sustain our family's farm. (Pressure to sell out farmland to industrialists isn't just a threat in Punjab, India.) It was heartening to hear what our parents had to say; my siblings and I are grateful to inherit this land, but we also feel the weight of the obligation that comes with stewardship of such a legacy.

My parents never used the word "sustainable" to describe their vision for our family farm; instead, their actions spoke of the obligations they felt to the land, the community and generations future and past. They never took more from the land than they gave back, whether that meant planting hundreds of trees to protect watersheds and halt erosion; keeping windrows and fencelines with neighbours' fields cleared of weeds; or renewing soil with cover crops and nutrients, a practice now known as soil regeneration. You might expect time on a multi-generational farm to be a simple chronological plane connecting past generations to future progeny. But, in truth, time on the farm was more circular than linear, with dips and spirals and seasons returning and regathering, like waves dancing on an ocean.

The land itself is tangible; less tangible are the values of distant generations past, handed down to each successive generation of the Kennedy family farming the soil. Those values that began more than a century ago became, like the property, central to our family enterprise and just as much a part of the legacy as the land itself, ever-present in our attitudes to the land and consistent with our daily actions. This stewardship philosophy was well-known to earlier inhabitants of this territory, nations of the Haudenosaunee Confederacy, as the "Seven Generations Principle": to this day in this tradition, decision-makers are encouraged to consider how present-day decisions might impact their descendants seven generations into the future.

Personal Leadership Element: Stewardship

Stewardship is the highest form of leadership. By its very nature, sustainable enterprise is derived from a stewardship mindset. Stewardship requires leaders to think well beyond themselves and be in service to others and the greater good. Stewardship is the art of the long view, a perspective that may span beyond a lifetime and even generations. Decisions on the family farm required stewardship.

Today, it's a rare enterprise that does not mention "sustainability" in its short list of organizational values; it's become ubiquitous in mission, vision and value statements. But what does it really mean in the context of a business or other enterprise? Can you clearly explain what being sustainable means in your company or organization? You may make assumptions, but until you talk to others—including your employees, customers and the local communities where you operate— it's impossible to know if you have a consensus on what the value of sustainability represents to the people impacted by your enterprise.

Fifty years ago, sustainability was understood in the singular language of economics. Smart enterprise heeded the wisdom of Nobel laureate and economist Milton Friedman, who famously said: "The social responsibility of business is to increase its profits." In other words, focus on keeping shareholders happy and the benefits will trickle down. In the decades since Friedman introduced his social responsibility theory in a 1970 essay for the *New York Times*, public expectations have stretched Friedman's narrow view of financial sustainability into a more expanded aspiration that brings together economic, environmental, social and governance aims.

Even American laws are being challenged by evolving public standards. In Delaware, for example, the American state where many U.S. companies are incorporated, corporate directors owe a traditional fiduciary duty to their corporation and its shareholders; however, regardless of that legislation, CEOs of 192 of America's largest businesses released a Business Roundtable statement in 2019 publicly promising to deliver value to all *stakeholders*. And in Canada, corporate directors now have a fiduciary responsibility not only to the corporation itself and its shareholders, but also to consider the interests of all corporate stakeholders and to treat them fairly. Cuddly capitalism, or sincere promises? The public is still deciding, but according to the 2020 Edelman Trust Barometer survey, the vast majority of respondents believe that CEOs should take the lead on instituting social change rather than waiting for governments to impose rules.

Over the last five decades, the evolution of public expectation has been remarkable. But these changes didn't happen overnight, and they weren't easy to navigate. (I know, as I rode many of the waves.) The 1970s and '80s brought focus on environmental responsibility and in-house verification systems, including non-financial audits; in the 1990s, we saw the emergence of corporate social responsibility (CSR) and enhanced risking models; and in the 2000s, we spoke of earning social licence, and third-party verification practices were normalized (for example, the Dow Jones Sustainability Indices and the FTSE4Good Index Series). In the last decade, we've seen ESG (environmental, social and governance) approaches take flight; evidenced, for example, by Brookfield Asset Management's deployment of a big gun—Mark Carney (former governor of both the

Bank of Canada and the Bank of England)—to lead their ESG and impact fund investment strategy.

I am very curious about where ESG will take sustainability, especially in the aftermath of the pandemic. Is this a brand-new dance score or simply a twist on earlier programs? But more on that later; we need to start at the beginning. A look back at the changes and challenges to the energy industry, where I worked for much of my career, is instructive on how the very idea of sustainability has evolved over the years.

WAVE ONE: ENVIRONMENTAL SUSTAINABILITY

Landing in Calgary, Alberta, in 1984 with a newly minted law degree, a fresh-faced husband from "the West" and buckets of ambition, I found myself working in the upstream oil and gas business where you explore for and produce the hydrocarbons. For a petroleum company in the 1970s and early '80s, being sustainable simply meant being able to find more oil reserves than you pumped out of the ground every year. Financial sustainability was largely achieved through the convenient marriage of engineers and bankers; if oil prices fell (and they did), you had to find someone (generally from "the East") to loan you enough money to keep drilling until prices rose again (and they did).

Oil and gas producers are price-takers: they must accept the prevailing prices in the market for their products. I understood what that meant from my days on the farm. I can still recall how my parents turned their ears to the radio at lunchtime, to catch market reports on prices for beef and wheat and corn. Their facial expressions were like market barometers: tensing up when prices for farm commodities or the Canadian dollar fell, and relaxing when prices were stable.

Early in my career, the idea of enterprise responsibility for environmental stewardship was gaining traction and was given a huge bump in the wake of Union Carbide's 1984 Bhopal gas disaster at a pesticide plant in India. In that moment, public opinion galvanized. The chemical industry responded with "responsible care" strategies (aligning to the "do no harm" commitments at level +4 of *A Measure of Integrity*). Given close relationships between the hydrocarbon and chemical industries, there was a natural spillover in expectations from one sector to the other. If you had a pipeline leak or an oil spill, you had to clean up your mess; yet responsibility for taking actions to prevent the risks in the first place wasn't clear-cut.

For oil companies operating in several jurisdictions (with different environmental rules in each location), the quandary was whether or not to set uniform and consistent operating standards across all operations or live with multiple standards. Not surprisingly, the communities where companies operated (especially places where the environmental rules were lax) preferred a standard operating approach. So did the advocates, who asked morally probing questions like: If you aren't allowed to flare or burn off excess gas in Alberta, why would you do so in Nigeria (even if the laws don't preclude you from doing so)?

At the time, many oil and gas companies were comfortable aiming for mere legal compliance with the rules (level +2 on *A Measure of Integrity*); and a few didn't do any more than the bare minimum required (level +1). Of course, there were rogue companies who operated at negative rungs of *A Measure of Integrity*: some did not technically comply with laws and rules (levels −1, −2); some acted illegally but not criminally (levels −3, −4); and the worst actors outsourced the dirty work (level −5), exploited and covered up violations of law (level −6), or did whatever it took to survive (level −7).

But a few were realizing that their employees and the host communities in which they operated really believed the enterprise could comply not just with the letter of the law but also with the spirit or intention (level +3). Trailblazing companies were adopting the best practices of the chemical industry, committing to doing as little harm as possible (level +4). Enterprise began to move beyond the simple fact of financial sustainability, getting comfortable with the stewardship expectations of regulators and citizens; and the employees of most companies I worked with could speak cogently and with conviction about the value of environmental sustainability.

But being a crusading environmental evangelist in an oil and gas company was not for the faint of heart in the 1980s. The only thing I recall learning about the environment in law school was in my tort law class: if there was environmental damage, your client could be sued. In those early days, I was grateful to be a lawyer, versed in the laws and rules and largely expected to guide companies to compliance thresholds. Driving change beyond that was tough; environmental stewardship was not taught to engineers as part of the standard curriculum, and trying to persuade senior management to allocate corporate funds to proactive environmental practices was daunting. Still, these values were at my core and the more I saw of our global operations, the more I began to push for constructive change.

After finishing my articling year at a law firm in Calgary (where partners assured me that the energy sector was not ready for female lawyers, and wouldn't I prefer to do family law instead?), I joined the in-house legal team at TCPL Resources, a subsidiary of TransCanada PipeLines Ltd., one of Canada's largest pipeline companies. From there, I was routinely shipped off to far-flung oil-producing countries like Indonesia, New Zealand and Australia to negotiate deals with host governments and joint venture partners. These were pre-internet days; I would send a short telex to our corporate manager in Jakarta, for instance, asking him to please meet my plane, and off I went. That was the easy part. At the negotiating table, it quickly became evident that some of our partners did not see environmental stewardship as part of their mandate.

For cash-strapped joint venture partners in places like Australia who were tiny explorers comfortable taking big risks, sustainability was still confined to the economic aim of keeping their enterprise solvent. In places like Indonesia, where I was negotiating with Pertamina (the state oil company), state-owned partners were loath to challenge President Suharto and feared reprisals if they questioned any gaps in the Indonesian government's environmental rules. It was awkward, to say the least. In the field negotiating with service providers (most often, Western drilling and pipeline construction companies), it was impossible to ignore the clear-cutting of timber by local and foreign pulp and paper companies or the cyanide pollution in the water downstream from local gold mines. On one trip to the island of Kalimantan, Indonesia, to meet with a seismic crew, our team accessed the worksite by river and then by helicopter; on a four-hour boat trip followed by a one-hour chopper ride, in the middle of the fabled jungles of Borneo, I did not see a single bird, fish or animal.

I knew that a Canadian company investing in a foreign country wasn't single-handedly going to stop this scale of environmental destruction, but I sure wasn't able to pretend it away. And that's how it all began for me. What was our role, our enterprise's sphere of influence, to do things differently on the ground in places like Indonesia, Algeria and Colombia?

I began to quietly probe my colleagues and co-workers and found that many of them were pondering the same questions. The more expedient discouraged choices that were more than strict compliance with the local laws (level +2 of *A Measure of Integrity*); but increasingly, they lost sway as our enterprise found itself in that uncomfortable place where the status quo was not acceptable to most host communities, to many employees in host countries and in Canada, and to some of our investors. Globalization, with its networks of supply chains criss-crossing the world, was creating winners and losers, with a widening gap between them, and advocates were launching powerful campaigns that moved hearts and minds to do the right thing in all places in the world where we operated, regardless of local laws and regulations.

My starting point for pushing the boundaries on how we defined our corporate values and how we thought about the sustainability of our enterprise was not tolerating dual standards for bribery and corruption, an obvious place of influence for a lawyer. It's illegal to pay bribes in Canada and in most OECD countries; why would it be okay to pay bribes in other places where we operated? No more $100 bills in your passport to get yourself whisked through immigration upon arrival at a foreign airport. Not everyone agreed with me, and it took a lot of time to explain to local employees (and not sound like I was judging their long-standing cultural practices). Eventually this way of thinking expanded to include no dual standards on lots of issues: environmental standards, sexual harassment and employment practices, reclamation of drilling sites, and safety training. Yes, our enterprise was imposing its values on joint venture partners, local employees and host governments; and that's exactly what advocates wanted. It was then that my career-long dance with sustainability began in earnest.

Personal Leadership Element: Future-Making

Future-making is birthing something that does not yet exist; having a strong vision in your mind of what a preferred future could look like. It requires vision and imagination and creativity to see what others may not yet see, and the courage to stake out the new ground. Future-making unfolds over time and requires leaders to hold the space as the process unfolds.

In my early years, I spent a lot of time in this space, connecting the dots between our Canadian enterprise and local operations on the ground in developing countries. Slowly, we inched up *A Measure of Integrity* from strict compliance (level +1), to compliance (level +2), to beyond compliance (level +3). In some parts of our business, we did commit to do as little harm as possible (level +4). TCPL Resources had to evolve or else incur the wrath of its critics, and I wanted to move the dial on our corporate purpose because it aligned with how I saw the world. It was a relief when my personal values and those of the enterprise I worked for began to converge.

In May 1989, in a wave of deregulation in Canada, TCPL Resources was spun out of the pipeline behemoth and launched as an independent oil and gas company called Encor Energy Corporation Inc. (Encor). This independent status coincided with a spectacular oil price crash, forcing the new company to sell its most valuable Western Canadian assets, an inventory of regional pipelines and petroleum reserves built up by predecessor companies including Canadian pioneers like Dome Petroleum and Hudson's Bay Oil and Gas. Overnight, sustainability in our enterprise had once again conflated to a simple calculation; it was now all about economic survival. Our wave of change crashed on the rocks of financial necessity.

WAVE TWO: SOCIAL SUSTAINABILITY

Acting as the in-house lawyer on the sale of most of Encor's North American assets was a big nine-month corporate push, at the end of which I also delivered my second son in February of 1990. (As a measure of the pace of social change, it's worth noting that maternity leave for our first son in 1987 was seventeen weeks; in 1990, following the birth of our second son, maternity leave was six months; and following the birth of our third son in 1993, I could legally take a one-year leave.) During my second maternity leave and prior to Encor being bought out by Talisman Energy in 1993, I was headhunted to work for another energy company, the Canadian subsidiary of Occidental Petroleum of California.

CanadianOxy, as the company was called, had just discovered a gigantic oil reservoir in the country of South Yemen and, according to the gruff-sounding but endearing geologist who gave this girl another chance in a male-dominated industry, the company knew how to find oil, produce oil and sell oil but didn't know how to manage the non-technical or "above-ground" risks. CanadianOxy needed someone who thought differently to tackle that job; the weathered geologist understood Diversity 101, or at least the need for it, and the benefits. In the 1990s, the driver for moving beyond compliance was all about risk and reputation management.

I worked for CanadianOxy for the next decade, negotiating their first foreign investments in jurisdictions that were newly opened for business after the fall of the Berlin Wall. That included negotiations with Rompetrol, Romania's state oil company, following the execution of their communist dictator, Nicolae Ceauşescu, and protracted deal-making with Petrovietnam (and Japanese joint venture partners) to secure coveted offshore drilling rights in Vietnam. In 1997, I was named the company's first female vice-president and by then was spending much of my time building relationships in the countries of Yemen and Nigeria and in our nation's capital, Ottawa, Canada. As a wholly owned subsidiary of a Big Oil player, figuring out what sustainability meant was sometimes a tug-of-war between thinking in California and Alberta. Pressure on extractive-sector investors operating abroad gained momentum, and CanadianOxy was frequently challenged to explain how it could possibly be "part of the solution" in places where we were operating.

Our competitors were likewise under scrutiny, in particular Talisman Energy and that company's investment in the Heglig oil field located in southern Sudan. Talisman CEO Jim Buckee would say, "We're just an oil company" and "I am a businessman and I intend to generate wealth," feeding cynical assumptions about that company's complicity in Sudan's human rights abuses. The pressure was unrelenting on enterprise to explain how the impacts of their foreign investments on social and human rights aligned to their corporate values. What did we know, or what should we have known, about misdeeds of our host governments, local partners and rogue employees? This was a wobbly time, and when employees couldn't align their personal values with the actions of their employer, they often turned to one another and to their own families and faith leaders to keep their personal moral compass pointed in the right direction, and sometimes to help make decisions about where to go next in their professional life. At times, it was still challenging for employees to feel that their values aligned with those of their employers.

In the final years of the last millennium, CanadianOxy decided to break free of its American parent and launched as an independent upstream company named Nexen Inc. (Nexen) in 2000. The corporate cultures of parent and subsidiary had diverged as CanadianOxy aspired to higher and higher levels of *A Measure of Integrity*. The final years of my career with this company were the stuff of dreams. We did bold things: partnered with Norwegian, American and West African oil producers to tackle gas flaring in Nigeria; collaborated along supply chains in our sector, with Transparency International and Nigerian President Olusegun Obasanjo, to proactively confront corruption; successfully lobbied for a state visit to Canada for the President of Yemen and the entourage of three hundred men accompanying him on a Yemenia jet (which gave President Saleh backdoor access to the American president); trained locals and indigenized our workforce; and designed and launched a merit-based scholarship program for Yemeni high school graduates to study in Canada. At this point, I finally felt that my personal values and the enterprise's values were aligning. The sustainability dance was effortless and full of life!

Personal Leadership Elements:
Decision-Making and Assessing Risk

When leading in complex high-stakes environments, leaders are required to get it right. Assessing risk and making the optimal decision are foundational to leadership. Be intentional when faced with these scenarios. As the pace and complexity of organizational life increases, so do the demands on leaders to make wise choices. Making critical decisions in real time with minimal data points in often paradoxical situations is the hallmark of a great leader.

Talisman, meanwhile, grew weary of the pressure and, in late 2002, sold its Sudan stake to ONGC Videsh Ltd., a subsidiary of India's national petroleum company, for $1.2 billion, earning a profit on the project in spite of its battered reputation. And a decade later, long after I had left the company, a financially beleaguered Nexen had exited Yemen due to political instability; bought into the oil sands business in Canada; and was acquired by CNOOC Ltd., a subsidiary of China's national petroleum company. More crashing waves that swept away those promising glimpses of genuine sustainability.

The Chinese takeover of Nexen was controversial. The American government had bristled at CNOOC's bid for an independent oil company, Unocal, a few years earlier, jittery about allowing petroleum resources to fall into the hands of a rising superpower. When Canadian Prime Minister Stephen Harper granted approval for Nexen's takeover by China's state-owned enterprise, the federal government was careful to clarify that the sale of a controlling interest in Canadian oil sands to a foreign state-owned company would, going forward, only be allowed in exceptional circumstances.

Getting permission to invest in Nexen was a diplomatic win for CNOOC. But the decision irritated the U.S. government and, ultimately, the investment proved disappointing for the Chinese too. The Long Lake oil sands project they acquired was technically challenging; CNOOC soon had to deal with an ugly pipeline spill and a deadly explosion on its project site; and oil market conditions weakened. In spite of legal undertakings made by CNOOC as a condition of securing investment approvals from Canadian regulators, CNOOC laid off hundreds of employees and diverted investment dollars elsewhere. Sustainability for CNOOC in Canada was quickly reduced to a purely economic calculus when China decided it could no longer afford to fund CNOOC's promises. The waves of change were becoming even more damaging and unpredictable, threatening to undo much of the progress made on sustainability at Nexen in the early 2000s.

Corporate social responsibility (CSR), also known as corporate citizenship, gained momentum in this same time window as a self-regulating business model to help shore up a company's ability to demonstrate social accountability to itself, its stakeholders and the public. Companies started to hire CSR directors to figure out the impact of their enterprise on society (economic, social and environmental). A commitment to CSR ambitiously aligned with values at level +4 of A Measure of Integrity (do no harm) or level +5 (create positive social, environmental and economic impacts). Self-regulation by enterprise ultimately gave way to third-party verification practices; for example, the standards set by the Dow Jones Sustainability Indices and the FTSE4Good Index Series.

From my vantage point as someone trying to move the dial on corporate values—and alignment of "talk" and "walk" on those values—CSR did not always serve enterprise well. It was a bold idea and headed in the right direction; but commitment to it was lacking at the enterprise level, limiting its ability to effect fundamental change on the sustainability front. People chosen for these roles often held very junior positions, their budgets were meagre and they had a muted voice at corporate decision-making tables.

Corporate social responsibility and earning social licence were too often conflated into boosterism, with enterprises realizing (often the hard way) that managing their values required more than public relations and marketing. For example, British Petroleum (BP) was one of the first major oil companies that purported to take CSR seriously, launching an advertising campaign to promote CSR and their "Beyond Petroleum" values; but that all looked sadly lacking in light of the Deepwater Horizon disaster of 2010. Other companies likewise adopted CSR slogans to assure stakeholders and the public that their enterprise was "doing well by doing good," but disconnects between media relations campaigns and enterprise values and actions seriously eroded public confidence in the CSR messaging.

Personal Leadership Element: Assessing Risk

When making decisions, the calculus all leaders should make is to assess what risks, hidden and obvious, are attached to the decision. Assessing risk requires knowledge and experience and intuition all being brought to bear on a financial or physical challenge. Emerging, experienced and seasoned leaders will assess risk differently. Done well, risk assessment calls on character, sound judgment and openness to input from others. Assessing and minimizing risk are essential to moving forward with strategies and decisions without peril.

WAVE THREE: ENVIRONMENTAL/SOCIAL/GOVERNANCE (ESG)

In the first decade of the twenty-first century, North American energy explorers started to flock back home to invest in their own backyard, fracking shale oil and digging into the oil sands. By 2014, Canada's number-one export market, the United States, had achieved energy independence. The Arab Spring and social upheaval in several oil-producing jurisdictions proved unmanageable for outsiders: Suncor Energy (Canada's largest energy company) exited projects in Libya and Syria; Nexen was forced out of Yemen; British Gas faced challenges operating its liquefied natural gas (LNG) facility in Egypt. By then a seasoned hand in understanding these perilous investment landscapes, I was consulted at many a decision-making table as these choices were vigorously deliberated.

The sheer scale of the oil sands in northern Alberta presented an alluring option for companies attracted to world-class reservoirs. The magnitude of these projects also attracted climate change activists, and oil sands investors committed to a litany of ESG best practices in response to pressure from advocates: reclamation, reducing water use, employment of local Indigenous communities, sharing of benefits with locals, generating electricity from excess steam and on and on and on. Notwithstanding, the vilifying of oil sands projects continued.

In December of 2015, I travelled to France to attend the United Nations Climate Change Conference in Paris (COP21) on my own dime and for the purpose of presenting ideas gathered from thousands of Albertans in response to the question: What would ordinary Albertans want to say in Paris about sustainability and Alberta's energy policy? The climate change gathering was rich in insights from governments, businesses and advocates; I chose instead to deliver the perspectives of citizens and communities, which had been gathered through the grassroots efforts of a non-partisan initiative called "Viewpoints Alberta." Citizens across Alberta were experiencing the short-term pain of energy transition, but most could see the longer-term sustainability aims; many understood that the sustainability dance had shifted.

After the conference, I flew to Stockholm, Sweden, to meet with Dr. Karl-Henrik Robèrt, the founder of a non-profit organization focused on sustainability called The Natural Step and the designer of a well-known framework for strategic sustainable development. Dr. Robèrt had read my book *Corporate Integrity* and was open to exploring the question of whether an extractive company could ever claim to be sustainable, in the most robust sense of that word. Dr. Robèrt was gracious and charming, but I left our meeting with grave doubts about the viability of a positive answer to that question.

Personal Leadership Element: Sense-Making

In order to truly understand what they are dealing with, leaders seek out many and diverse data points in order to get as accurate a read as possible on the situation before creating action. Sense-making is like radar, registering strong and weak signals from all levels of the operating environment. It is both intuitive and strategic—sensing change, spotting trends, observing what's happening. It also has a temporal quality, understanding how the past informs the future. It involves translating nuance and complexity in the environment into relevance and meaning for the organization. Sense-making requires a deep understanding of the system one operates within.

Advocacy against carbon has evolved over the last decade; the greatest influence is held by the folks with the money—the sustainable finance lenders and pension funds that have billions to invest in enterprise. Early in 2021, the world's largest asset manager, BlackRock, warned all companies they must demonstrate a game plan for surviving in a world aiming for net-zero carbon emissions by 2050. At the same time, S&P Global Ratings, an influential rating agency, warned of cuts to credit scores for Big Oil companies (including giants like Exxon and Royal Dutch Shell) due to greater industry risk associated with climate change. And although the board of Canada's third-largest pension plan, Ontario Teachers' Pension Plan, isn't threatening to immediately divest of its fossil fuel holdings, it has said that it will boost investments in climate-friendly assets. The message is clear: go carbon neutral or risk being left behind.

Now, companies from every sector are scrambling to respond. In the tech sector, for example, both Microsoft and IBM have vowed to be carbon negative by 2030 and Amazon has pledged to eliminate its greenhouse gas emissions by 2040. What does this all mean for sustainability now and in the future? No longer just a question for energy companies rooted in non-renewable fossil fuels, this is a vexing issue for all enterprise: How is it possible to re-invent organizations of all kinds to survive and thrive in the face of this latest push for social responsibility and sustainability? The status quo is not an option; enterprise must profoundly re-invent itself to thrive in a future where stakeholders expect capitalism to do things differently.

In August 2020, Brookfield Asset Management Inc., a global investment firm with US$550 billion in assets under management, hired Mark Carney, former governor of both the Bank of Canada and the Bank of England, to lead an ambitious expansion into environmental and social investing. Brookfield's CEO said he expects the new ESG group's investments in green energy, emissions reduction and other sustainable technologies—"impact funds"—could grow to the scale of Brookfield's investment in other individual business units (e.g., real estate, infrastructure and private equity). While investment firms like Brookfield see the ESG movement as a tipping point, there are skeptics who speculate that ESG-related investments are just another old-fashioned stock market bubble or a fad, with impact funds rallying simply because they invest in rising tech companies.

To access capital, integrated energy producers realize they need to keep pace with these changes, and ambitious corporate campaigns to expand into renewables and embrace ESG principles have been launched by many companies, including Suncor Energy and BP PLC. Clearly, these aims are well beyond mere compliance with rules and laws (level +3 of A Measure of Integrity), but how far up the ladder are these companies able to climb? For some lenders in capital markets, investing in carbon-emitters that do no harm (level +4) will be adequate. But most climate change advocates deride anything that doesn't get an enterprise to net-zero emissions by 2040 or 2050 as greenwashing and, no doubt, they will continue to lobby pension funds and institutional investors to divest hydrocarbon interests. Energy transitioning will inevitably lurch forward, and it could be a bumpy ride for enterprise that is out of sync with public opinion and technological progress. The definition of sustainability is no longer decided by the enterprise itself but is frequently driven by stakeholders—internal and external—other than shareholders. It's an awkward dance.

Personally, I'm of the view that there is room within ESG for carbon-emitters. Research on, and testing of, carbon capture and sequestration concepts, and the potential for carbon-free hydrogen to augment or even replace natural gas running through pipelines, is exciting and the viability of these new approaches is steadily improving. In other sectors, enterprise is using science to solve sustainability: 3M, Unilever and Tesla come to mind. In the near term, however, achieving sustainability in the fullest sense of that aim is likely to remain elusive for carbon-emitters.

Norway is one of the few carbon-emitting jurisdictions that seems to have puzzled out a strategy to square this sustainability circle, a strategy that may have appeased some climate change acolytes.

Equinor ASA (formerly Statoil and StatoilHydro) is a state-owned energy company drilling for oil across the globe and in its own backyard, the Barents Sea. The Government of Norway is comfortable granting licences to petroleum operators, even recently announcing the possibility of drilling in the remote Arctic. At the same time, Norwegians, who get 90 percent of their electricity from hydroelectricity, have embraced the electric car and targeted the phase-out of sales of all new fossil fuel vehicles by 2025. Norway's sovereign pension fund, known as the "oil fund" and modelled on Alberta's Heritage Savings Trust Fund, was created in 1990 to invest Norway's surplus oil revenues and now has over US$1 trillion in assets. (Norway's population is just over five million citizens; do that math!) In 2019, Norway's minister of finance undertook to divest fossil fuel assets from the oil fund and to double down on investments in green energy.

Personal Leadership Elements:

Designing Action and Executing to Plan

The Norwegians were focused, disciplined and steadfast in lifting this idea. Designing action is knowing the race you are going to run before you start. It requires moving from the ethereal to the concrete, from the unseen to the seen; creating the intelligent plan and articulating that plan to others. Designing action is translating a felt sense of the future into getting there.

Executing to plan is the means by which all focused action happens. It is the disciplined, measurable, results-based movement from here to there.

Is a similar strategy feasible in a country like Canada, another jurisdiction rich in hydroelectricity, oil and natural gas resources as well as renewable energy and hydrogen potential? I would like to think so. To implement this kind of plan in Canada, federal-provincial governance would require a reset; federal and provincial politicians would have to demonstrate a willingness to negotiate a fair sharing of benefits and opportunity across the country. That could mean a green hydrogen hub in Quebec, capitalizing on that province's hydroelectric power, and a blue hydrogen hub in Alberta, utilizing that province's natural gas resources. We could also re-imagine how east–west pipeline infrastructure is deployed to enable cost-effective, safe and secure hydrocarbon delivery as feedstock to regional refineries and value-add facilities, and as reliable backup to intermittent renewable energy resources.

Of course, we can't ignore the geopolitical reality that Canadian energy is tightly integrated into continent-wide infrastructure and markets; the policy choices of our American neighbours materially impact our options, as evidenced by President Joe Biden's decision to cancel TC Energy's Keystone XL Pipeline expansion on his first day in office. When investment in the oil sands in northern Alberta was initially launched by pioneering companies like Syncrude Canada in the late 1970s, politicians on the left and right aisles of the Canadian House of Commons supported the projects for their ability to "Secure Canada's Energy Future." Over the years, these oil sands investments became large enough to secure America's energy future too. Now, Canadian hydrocarbon producers face a massive marketing problem: Americans no longer need our oil. The Keystone XL Pipeline project has now been cancelled completely, a casualty of market demand as well as political tensions and pressure from advocacy groups and the public in general.

The United States is betting on lithium battery innovation, and some Western Canadians find themselves in the uncomfortable position of tilting at American windmills. Carmakers are listening to consumers who see electric cars in their future; in January 2021, General Motors announced plans to eliminate gas and diesel light-duty cars and SUVs by 2035, undoubtedly influenced by the fact that Elon Musk's Tesla Inc., the electric car pioneer, has a market value greater than all the big car companies in the world combined. Where does that leave Canada's energy companies and what does it mean for sustainability in the big picture?

Personal Leadership Element: Political Intelligence

Political intelligence is accepting that in any organization of people there are issues of authority, status and power, and that, as a result, there are politics. Understanding the consequences of America no longer needing

Canadian oil reflects an understanding of the political terrain, the climate, the power structures and the pressure points. It is choosing to be aware rather than naive. It is working with this extra layer of complexity and chaos in order to serve the organization's highest interest.

Let's return to *A Measure of Integrity* for a moment. People I mentor often ask if I've ever worked with an enterprise able to credibly target or achieve levels +5 or +6 of *A Measure of Integrity* or, its zenith, stewardship and regeneration at level +7 (leaving an enterprise better than you found it, re-instating what has been lost and making decisions focused on future generations). It's a lot of work, but some hydrocarbon producers are able to function at level +4, paying attention to economics, the environment, social impacts and governance, and doing as little harm as possible. Most companies liberally toss around the word "sustainability" but operate at level +2 or +3. Only a handful of for-profit carbon-emitting companies can leverage their investments to achieve positive social, environmental and economic impacts at level +5, and only in rare situations are companies able to create the conditions for these sustainability aims to survive beyond the life of individual projects (level +6). Sustainability is elusive. And yet, pursuing it is increasingly an imperative for the survival of today's enterprises.

BACK TO THE FARM

"Hewers of wood and drawers of water" is a pejorative shorthand for Canada's historical reliance on natural resources. The reference is Biblical but is often attributed to Canadian economist Harold Innis, from his 1930 book, *The Fur Trade in Canada: An Introduction to Canadian Economic History*. Innis grew up on a family farm in southern Ontario, just down the road from the farmhouse where my father was born. It's a sensitive point for many Canadians; we would like to shake this dependency on resources and be recognized for our value-add manufacturing and affinity for tech. Yet there is something there, in our historical experience with natural resources, that can teach us how to rebuild sustainable enterprise in the aftermath of crisis, even a pandemic. In our mad rush to move forward, let's not forget those hard-earned foundational dance steps.

When I rushed off the farm, to law school and then to work in the gleaming towers of downtown Calgary, I held my personal beliefs tight but did not ascribe much broader economic value to the enterprise models I had grown up with. Yet, after witnessing the triple whammy of an oil crisis, a crippled economy and the pandemic in Alberta, I find myself returning, again and again, to the experiences of my youth.

How did my family survive the upheavals, weather the storms and sustain the family enterprise through thick and thin? For example, when I was in law school, a large chunk of our farm, including an 800-head beef feedlot and upright silos for corn silage, was expropriated by Ontario Hydro to build a 500 kV transmission line from the Bruce Nuclear Generating Station to electricity consumers in southern Ontario. My parents vehemently opposed the takeover of their land. Raising cattle had been a passion of my grandfather and father; all of that ended with the Ontario Hydro expropriation.

Transitions didn't come easily to my parents, both of whom were born, attended primary school, went to church, farmed and were buried within a five-kilometre range of the family farm. A few years after the transmission line was built, my brother purchased back the land, and decades later, my nephew and brother re-acquired the farm buildings. How many enterprises have the capacity and fortitude to take such a long-term view?

When the beef feedlot was expropriated, my parents decided to try their hands at growing tobacco. The family farm is situated in the heart of Canada's former tobacco belt, near Tillsonburg, Ontario, a place memorialized in song by crooner Stompin' Tom Connors. When I was a teenager, tobacco was the highest income-generating cash crop in the country. Many of my classmates at Delhi District Secondary School finished grade 12 and went home to grow tobacco. Priming tobacco is back-breaking work, and growers need lots of manual labourers, especially during harvest. Migrant workers showed up at farm gates in the spring when the tobacco seedlings were ready to be pulled from the greenhouses and replanted in the fields, and they vanished after the first frost in autumn. At times, the community struggled to absorb these migrant workers—from places as diverse as Quebec, Poland, Nigeria, Trinidad and Mexico. The outsiders challenged our status quo and compromised our sense of security. But farming enterprise depended on them.

Personal Leadership Element: Adaptive Learning
Adaptive learning is real-time, continuous, lifelong learning. It is creating new maps in the middle of navigation.

In the early 1980s, tobacco was vilified as a leading cause of cancer and growers became collateral damage in anti-smoking crusades. Overnight, big banks changed their policies and decided they would no longer lend money to tobacco growers; many farmers declared bankruptcy. It was a painful time with lots of uncertainty, speculation, frustration and loss. Most tobacco growers, including members of my own family, sooner or later transitioned to other crops like vegetables and ginseng to sustain their farming enterprise. It's not illegal to grow tobacco in Canada (and interestingly, a cousin of the tobacco plant may be helpful in reducing the severity of COVID-19 symptoms), but for most farmers, it is no longer viable. At the peak, there were 4,442 tobacco farms in Canada; in 2021, there are less than a couple hundred farmers contracted to grow.

The farming life is difficult and tenuous at times. The family farm where I was raised has been able to endure through five generations not by simply focusing on this year's expenses and crop prices, or even on the changing cycles and trends imposed from outside, but by staying true to the values that have been passed down for centuries and by taking very seriously the role of being stewards of the land the family lived on and cultivated, keeping it healthy and sustainable for at least another five generations to come.

Whatever the enterprise and whatever the industry, the short-term scramble for financial survival in a crisis—be it a devastating industry change or a pandemic—draws attention away from the organizational values and business fundamentals essential to longer-term sustainability. If your enterprise survives the pandemic, hearty congratulations. Now it is time to refocus on core values and think about how to redesign and rebuild your enterprise to thrive, sustainably, in a post-pandemic world where stakeholder and public expectations of enterprise are pushing the boundaries. The dance toward sustainability is no longer solely in your control; it's not a solo performance. Achieving this elusive goal involves a new kind of thinking, a new conversation with the communities you serve and a new way of engaging with stakeholders. Your future is in their hands.

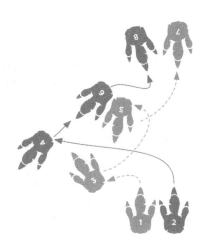

CHAPTER 2

GO FOR THE MOON SHOT

Elon Musk, founder of SpaceX, Tesla, Inc. and The Boring Company and co-founder of Neuralink and OpenAI, is the quintessential risk-taking entrepreneur. Musk is outrageous; he doesn't just shoot for the moon, his aim is Mars! And he is richly rewarded for his ambition. in January 2021, Musk surpassed Jeff Bezos to become the world's richest person. In the auto sector, he drove Tesla to become the most highly valued carmaker in the world. SpaceX has encroached into NASA's rocket technology space with visions of "building a freeway to Mars." Through a venture called Starlink, Musk is planting private satellites capable of selling internet connections to almost anyone on the planet. His Hyperloop is described as a fifth mode of transportation, "a cross between a Concorde and an air hockey table." And the province of Alberta, where I live, has invited Musk to consider the feasibility of such a link between our two largest cities, Edmonton and Calgary. Musk's The Boring Company is breaking new ground on lower-cost tunnelling "to solve the problem of soul-destroying traffic," while in health care, his company Neuralink is probing brain-machine interfaces to create futuristic humans.

Musk has very much taken to heart Buckminster Fuller's advice: "You never change things by fighting the existing reality. To change something, build a new model that makes the existing model obsolete." In every way, Musk has re-imagined what is possible in enterprise building.

MOON SHOT, REVITALIZE OR PLAY IT SAFE?

You have an important choice to make right now. If business as usual isn't working for your organization, what approach to building and rebuilding is needed in your enterprise? Is this the right time for a moon shot, for revitalization or for play-it-safer incremental change?

The COVID-19 pandemic made bold, transformational change a necessity across all kinds of enterprise: from health ministers launching unprecedented vaccine campaigns, to manufacturers repurposing facilities to make personal protective equipment, to retailers and educators going online. Non-profit enterprise did not escape the pressure to act well beyond their comfort zones either. In the 1990s, the Banff Centre (an arts, culture and education institution in Banff, Alberta) hosted entrepreneurs from major tech companies, giving these pathfinders a safe place to beta-test disruptive new concepts and push their innovative ideas to the edges; the pandemic forced the Centre and other arts organizations to innovate and push to the digital edges for their own survival.

Personal Leadership Elements: Enterprising and Adaptive Learning

Hungry, dynamic and industrious, enterprising leaders are always on the search for better or new. Even in the face of insurmountable odds, the most enterprising of leaders can make transformational change or innovation happen.

Adaptive learning is real-time, continuous, lifelong learning.

To emerge from the pandemic, or any disruptive change or crisis, *and thrive* requires momentum, agility and decisiveness. Business as usual is not a safe bet. This is not a time for drifting along or tentativeness; and even incremental, reactive change is not guaranteed to be effective. If your enterprise team went into a protective huddle to survive the pandemic or some other threat, you need to break out of that siege mentality. It can be daunting, to keep things functioning and, at the same time, design and implement fundamental change; to redesign the proverbial plane in flight. Within your organization, there will be a range of opinions on your approach to enterprise re-design. Some may prefer to settle for "generic," others will choose to cling to the safety of the status quo, and a few may even give you a defeatist shrug. Deciding your enterprise's approach to rebuilding is a high-consequence choice that should be made—deliberately and thoughtfully—by your internal leadership team, and not inadvertent-ly decided by the naysayers.

Upending the status quo brings fear, uncertainty and hesitancy. You may wonder: *How can we guarantee meaningful work for em-ployees and help fix the world's biggest problems? It's overwhelming! Where do we start? There are so many different points of view; so many expectations; so many choices!* And yet there is also something enliv-ening about this opportunity to see the world anew, re-engaging your imagination and moving toward alternative futures.

Personal Leadership Elements: Patterning and Catalyzing

Patterning requires a leader to use an array of sensory means of data collection and knowing, beyond rational thought, to gain deeper understanding of a complex situation. Heightened awareness is needed when the logical path is not clear.

Catalyzing is purposeful disruption of the status quo to provoke fresh momentum or a new direction. It requires recognition of right timing, acceptance of a lack of control, and reading feedback. Catalyzing requires the courage to act when the outcome is not clear.

Your enterprise may entirely re-imagine your reason for existing. If, for example, your business operates coal-fired electricity generators in North America, watching your competitors retire plants ahead of schedule in response to pressure from government regulators, lend-ers, customers and the public may force you to recognize that your enterprise has little choice but to figure out a new pathway forward. All carbon-emitting energy companies operating in the West face this imperative. Some are rising to the challenge, including Total, a French multinational founded in 1924 and one of seven "super major" oil and gas companies. Total has recast itself as TotalEnergies, an energy company that will deliver affordable, reliable and clean energy.

Personal Leadership Element: Future-Making

Seeing beyond the horizon; continuous renewal is a critical part of the enterprise journey and an essential capacity for leaders.

For others, such a moon shot will be a distant dimension that feels impossible; instead, rebuilding may include *revitalizing* work, changing up the scope of what's feasible but not transforming the enterprise. The arts and entertainment sector was particularly stricken by the COVID-19 pandemic, and it's worth paying attention to how these enterprise leaders revitalize for a different future.

Montreal-based circus troupe, Cirque du Soleil, did financial contortions to stay alive during the pandemic but may well emerge in more resilient shape. The enterprise hopes not only to return to business as usual, offering up live performances in Vegas and on tour, but also to follow the example set by Disney+ and become a player in streaming platforms. Forward-thinking management at museums and cultural institutions are doing the same, figuring out ways to redesign their enterprise models to leverage live experiences and performances and exhibits in the digital realm, effectively amplifying the outputs of their resources. They have figured out creative ways to teach the dinosaur to dance.

Regardless of your ultimate rebuilding strategy—moon shot or revitalization—a deliberate and proactive rebuilding plan is essential. You don't need to get things perfect, but you do need to be intentional. If your enterprise team is comfortable only with maintaining business as usual, a book on rebuilding enterprise will hopefully provide insights into why this approach may not be adequate.

The best place to begin designing a rebuilding plan is the ground on which you are standing. There has been considerable upheaval of the status quo. You may need to get your bearings. Start with your organization's identity. At its core, your enterprise needs an unwavering sense of purpose (know the reason it exists) and unambiguous values (know what level on *A Measure of Integrity* your enterprise is aiming for). For example, if it is a government-owned utility that has comfortably operated for decades at a compliance level on *A Measure of Integrity* (say, at level +2), it's honest to acknowledge upfront that it's going to require a considerable shift in thinking and in organizational culture to shutter your coal-generating plants and re-invest in clean energy.

Many private- and public-sector enterprises face unrelenting pressure to reposition to a carbon-reduced or carbon-neutral business model. Those that choose to be proactive will have to build internal support for a beyond-compliance approach (which may involve stepping up a few levels on *A Measure of Integrity* to levels +5 and +6, achieving positive social, environmental and economic impacts on a sustainable basis). Enterprise that ignores these stakeholder calls for changes in its business model, and sticks with compliance approaches, may find itself increasingly irrelevant, bypassed by competitors and peers who recognize the imperative for change. These organizations risk going the way of the dinosaur.

If your enterprise's core values are shaky or uncertain, or if core values and actions are out of alignment across your organization, it's going to be difficult to embark on a solid rebuild. You may relate to that discord's destabilizing effect if you have groups within your organization who prefer to cling to the status quo while others are keen to revitalize your purpose and key values. It can feel wobbly on the inside when an organization is indecisive about the path forward; and from the outside looking in, this lack of clarity confuses and distorts. As chapter six explains in more detail, learning better ways to understand your core values and tell your enterprise story—internally and to others—can build your organizational capacity to coax the dinosaur to dance!

Personal Leadership Element: Influencing

Influencing is the convergence of three essential Elements of Leadership: Storytelling, Aligning People, and Political Intelligence. Influencing is the art of leading without authority while having the ability to bring others skillfully and subtly to your point of view.

What does this distortion look like? An enterprise can, for example, commit in its public relations communications to "respect the rights of Indigenous peoples" either as partners in a project or as impacted communities. But how effective is the enterprise in achieving that objective through its actions? There is growing pressure on governments, private-sector companies and non-profits to recognize First Nations as rights holders and to secure the free, prior and informed consent of Indigenous peoples prior to embarking on a project that impacts their interests. (Incidentally, Clarence Louie, a First Nations leader who has been the Chief of the Osoyoos Indian Band in British Columbia and is a recognized business leader, warns us not to treat Indigenous peoples like other stakeholders; "we are rights holders, not just stakeholders!" Louie exclaims.)

Moving from this commitment to respect Indigenous peoples' rights to taking corresponding action across an entire organization requires a deliberate and intentional strategy. As the sample application of *A Measure of Integrity* depicts (shared in the toolkit at the end of this book), without the deep work required to tease out true intentions, different departments and teams within an individual organization may translate this promise in different ways. For example, some may believe the stated commitment reflects a compliance mandate to obey laws and rules at levels +1 or +2; some may interpret the promise as a commitment to achieve positive and sustainable social impacts; and a few may even believe it is a commitment to restore First Nations' heritage and cultural sites. (At the opposite, negative, end of the spectrum, a few may consider that cash payments to hereditary chiefs are acceptable to save face, even if these are inconsistent with laws and ethics policies.)

Next, look at your enterprise closely and be brutally honest. Are underlying assumptions about your enterprise's competitiveness, efficiency and resiliency sound? Do you have an up-to-date sense of your operational, governance and strategic strengths and vulnerabilities? For example, how will going digital impact your enterprise if your business is bricks-and-mortar or if your service delivery model is built on a traditional model? And be careful, the implications may not be readily discernible. Recall when Netflix launched in 1997: it wasn't appealing to most consumers who rented DVD movies from stores like Blockbuster; but when streaming video technology landed, Netflix customers gained immediate access to on-demand, high-quality, cost-effective alternatives to DVD rentals, and the video store was gone.

The impacts of digital disruption should be anticipated in any enterprise, as well as the implications of a host of other assumptions, including the consequences of protectionism on supply chains, or of cryptocurrency on traditional financial structures, and of shifting diversity and fairness expectations. This entire book will press you to test your enterprise's underlying assumptions and update your perception of risks and opportunities.

Enterprise rebuilding can deploy a range of strategic actions: changes in resource allocations; mergers or acquisitions; capital investments or divestitures; pursuit of different markets, processes or products. Operating and governance strategies may likewise need to be reshaped, perhaps to foster more agile decision-making, resiliency, talent development, succession planning and innovative thinking. If, for example, your board of directors has merely been functioning as a rubber stamp to the decisions of your organization's senior management team, what improvements could be gained by creating a more diverse and independent-thinking board that will push and challenge management? Or perhaps your talent attraction and retention strategies can be enlivened by building the capacity to train and promote internal candidates rather than always relying on external recruiting.

Throughout this book you will be invited to think differently about your enterprise redesign and to ask yourself, "what if" we did things differently? What if we taught the dinosaur to dance?

Personal Leadership Element: Developing Other Leaders

Developing other leaders is committing to the truth that leaders must beget leaders. It is holding oneself accountable for the success of one's direct reports and for the sustainability of the organization. It is mentoring and coaching and supporting. It is leveraging one's experience by building leadership capacity in others—for the present, and the future.

Designing and launching a rebuilding strategy is one of the most important decisions your organization will make. Assuming that preserving the status quo is not a desirable option—and whether change is being driven internally or by external forces or stakeholders—you may decide on revitalization with conviction or transformative change. In either case, your enterprise will need to create the conditions for innovators, disruptors, entrepreneurs, creatives and risk-takers to have a voice that can be heard. Your core team needs to be willing and able to build rapport with not only the like-minded and open-minded, but also to engage where necessary with skeptical and dissenting perspectives.

Many enterprise teams don't have the talent pool or culture required to imagine and implement transformative change. And let's be clear, that scale of innovation isn't just about tech and it isn't just about solving the problems you face today; it's about boldly breaking through barriers of any kind. Toy manufacturer LEGO is a Danish company that has been around since 1932 and it is thriving today because of its ability to transform itself, not just with innovative connectivity to digital platforms and moviemaking, but also through direct engagement with its customers—the kids who play with these mini bricks that fit together so well and come apart again with ease.

To stimulate fresh ideas, LEGO regularly reaches out to its customers. My youngest son (now an engineer) was a LEGO enthusiast, jazzed that the company hosted design contests for fans to pitch ideas. LEGO's most recent launch is the "Everyone is Awesome" set, familiar LEGO mini-figurines that are painted not only in black and brown to reflect the diversity of skin tones, but also in the colours of the rainbow flag, as well as pale blue, white and pink, to reflect the LGBTQIA+ community. Matthew Ashton, LEGO's VP of Design, explains the rationale behind the design: "Being LGBTQIA+ myself, I knew I needed to step up to the plate and make a real statement about love and inclusivity, and generally spread some LEGO® love to everybody who needs it. Children are our role models and they welcome everyone, no matter their background."

To imbed transformative change, you must lead. Many organizations are comfortable being fast followers, adopting and adapting the innovations of others to improve themselves; but if you wait too long to see how your competitors change up their business fundamentals, you are simply a garden-variety follower. Decide how you want the dinosaur to dance—as the leader or the follower?

Personal Leadership Element: Imagining

Imagining is exploring new thinking about what is possible, beyond the norm. An imaginative spark can be maverick or childlike, as a leader reaches for the ultimate "what if" possibilities.

A DELIBERATE DESIGN

A revitalizing or transformative approach to rebuilding enterprise requires your team to look deep inside your organization (to rethink values and purpose and strategies) and to be outward-facing, at the same time. During the COVID-19 pandemic, enterprise survival was paramount for many organizations; but they still had to take into account the significant social, ecological and economic problems that were exposed and aggravated by the health crisis. Whatever the catalyst for change in your organization, your enterprise should anticipate unrelenting pressure to help "fix" these problems and help make capitalism work better for more people. How will your enterprise build rapport with shareholders, workers (including retired employees), suppliers, host communities, customers and other key stakeholders to understand these evolving expectations?

Ongoing interaction with your enterprise's core team—employees, contractors, shareholders, owners and directors—is a given in this rebuilding work. And diversity of thinking within your enterprise's internal team is essential, but it's often not sufficient. Truth is, revitalizing or transformative rebuilding work requires that you be positioned to access the experiences and insights of the best and brightest minds, inside and outside your organization. If you have a complex problem to solve, or you want to create new value, it's prudent to reach beyond your internal team.

Many management teams are plagued by the presumption of uniqueness, thinking that the problems they face are unique to their enterprise or sector and that, therefore, solutions can be prescribed only by people who are part of the internal team. Yet there is a lot of upside in reaching more widely for fresh thinking. If, for example, your government agency or company is aiming to revitalize its crisis-response strategies, might fresher ideas emerge through collaboration with emergency room physicians, firefighters and cyber-security experts than with like-minded colleagues in your own business? In the case of biotech company Moderna Inc., it was positioned to act quickly with a COVID-19 vaccine in 2020 because it had already spent time bringing together tech thinkers, life scientists and experts in manufacturing facilities to pool their thinking and accelerate the development of pioneering mRNA medicines.

Personal Leadership Element: Influencing

Influencing is the art of leading without authority while having the ability to bring others skillfully and subtly to your point of view. Influencing is having confidence in your direction and crafting the conditions for others to enrol, in their own time and of their own free will, because your ideas and vision have merit. Influence is about resonance. The best leaders are skilled in influence while using it judiciously with grace and ease.

To guide enterprise rebuilders in this quest for diversity of thought and collaborative decision-making, *The Enterprise Onion* is recommended as a tool for deliberate outreach to individuals and organizations that have a strategic interest in your enterprise and can influence the path forward. Every organization has some understanding of key "stakeholders" (an over-used and sloppy term). Interest-mapping and tapping into stakeholder influence are common practice but insufficient if your enterprise wants to surface new ideas, new strategies and new value and build durable consensus on ways forward. There isn't a right or wrong way of seeing the world, but when you are rebuilding your enterprise, it's useful, at minimum, to understand how others see an issue (including those who see it differently than you do) and to consider how reaching out to these diverse viewpoints might aid your enterprise's path forward.

The Enterprise Onion is primarily an outward-facing tool, modelling how you can identify and relate to external stakeholders, from the like-minded to the open-minded to the skeptical, and perhaps even reaching out to the cynical.

The like-minded: Most of us are comfortable reaching out to "colleagues" and "allies"—perhaps supply chains or partners or independent board members with skin in the game, local community organizations or media and citizens with aligned interests. Some people refer to these kinds of allies as "like-hearted"; you may not agree on the same strategy, but your collective hearts are aspiring to achieve the same end. We expect the like-minded and the like-hearted to be positively predisposed to our ideas, and there is often a sense that the enterprise will retain a fair amount of control of the outcomes. But when we constrain our reach to the like-minded, seeking feedback or input only from those expected to confirm our beliefs and values, then echo chambers, groupthink and monocultures are predictable outcomes. (The dangers of monocultures are explored in detail in the next chapter.)

The open-minded: When you move out of your comfort zone to engage more objective (yet interested) stakeholders, your ideas are more likely to be critically evaluated. An independent technical expert may be open to analyzing your enterprise's ideas for solving a vexing environmental problem; a competitor may be open to collaborating on the redesign of an industry safety standard; a community may be open to exploring the possibility of an atypical development project. The enterprise isn't likely to retain control of the outcome of this engagement with open-minded stakeholders, but any consensus achieved is likely to be resilient.

The skeptical-minded: Reaching out to stakeholders more apt to question or challenge your enterprise is uncomfortable, and there is a risk that your idea will be rejected. Engaging the skeptical often requires trust-building. It's not easy to win back disgruntled clients with a quality assurance campaign; to persuade wary businesses that your government's new red tape–reduction strategy is sincere; or to convince climate change advocates to believe that your hydrocarbon company has had a change of heart and is going green. To the extent that this engagement with fair-minded skeptics is effective, more creative and more robust ideas are likely to be generated, and outcomes sustained.

The cynical-minded: Voluntarily reaching out to stakeholders with world views that contradict or oppose your enterprise is not for the faint of heart. But there are times when ignoring antagonistic points of view is neither possible nor recommended. If a negative social media campaign is directed at your enterprise, you can hope it all blows over or you can engage with your critics to understand their perspective, clarify any confusion and assess underlying motivations. If there is a critical incident or crisis in a local community and your enterprise is involved, you must engage. Sometimes these encounters trigger or perpetuate an antagonistic conflict between two belief systems or two cultural trends; for example, the debate between getting tough on crime versus fostering rehabilitation, or between the opposing sides in the pipeline battles. And if the power of the parties with the differing viewpoints is relatively matched, the issue can remain stuck in polarity until a new truth emerges. Engaging with the cynical-minded is uncomfortable, and possibly antagonistic, yet there can be benefits. Perceptions of facts, values and what is possible can be distorted—not just by cynics but within your own organization as well—and engaging with stakeholders who hold different views can be illuminating and productive. They can open your eyes and inform your decision-making; even just talking can clear up confusion and misperceptions on both sides. When a question or issue or enterprise is of such significance to warrant even the most uncomfortable encounters, there is indeed a lot at stake. But if you can succeed in building trust with your critics, the upside can be powerful. (More on polarized debates in chapter three.)

Some people regard stakeholder engagement as a plodding, incremental, consensus-building, risking exercise; a way to figure out what your enterprise can do without ruffling feathers. But this way of thinking is constrained. That is, lowest-common-denominator approaches to consultation can be flat, linear, two-dimensional ways of relating. If, instead, you can see this engagement opportunity as a jumping-off point into more multi-dimensional possibilities, you may find this collaboration energizing and uplifting. Diversity of perspective can help your enterprise collaborate to generate more creative ideas, identify solutions to complex problems and be more resilient.

Think of a garden design: a wise gardener plants a diverse range of seeds in case some varieties are not resistant to disease, and strategically pairs different plants as companions in the same bed to ward off insects (for example, radishes fight the flea beetles on your tomatoes, and nasturtiums growing amid your zucchini may repel squash bugs). For millennia, in Indigenous gardens they placed corn, beans and squash seeds (the "Three Sisters") in the same mound of earth, allowing reciprocity to work its magic: the corn stalks supported the beans, the beans turned nitrogen from the atmosphere into usable nutrients, and the squash vines sheltered the soil, keeping moisture in and weeds out. Collaborating with your enterprise stakeholders can help your organization to identify solutions to problems by accessing a wider range of perspectives. Likewise, this engagement can generate the conditions for more resilient and innovative strategies that ultimately yield more value for all.

A CAUTIONARY TALE

Influenced by internal and external stakeholders with a wide range of world views, your enterprise may decide to assume a role in finding solutions to pressing social and environmental issues. A decision to leap-frog your organization up the values pyramid is ambitious. While it is not my intention to dampen enthusiasm for enterprise's role in being part of the solution to pressing challenges, I encourage you to design with intention. If your organization chooses to scale two or three levels of *A Measure of Integrity* in one bold stride—and be more things to more people—that decision is akin to a moon shot. It can be that challenging.

Personal Leadership Element: Future-Making

A moon shot requires a leader to birth something that does not yet exist, initially as an idea and eventually as an extraordinary reality. Future-making requires vision, imagination and creativity, seeing what others may not see. It is a process that occurs over time, and it requires that the space be held as the process unfolds.

You may wonder, how could it *ever* be a bad thing for an enterprise to aim for higher and higher value levels on *A Measure of Integrity*? You may even think: "I want to work for that kind of organization!" So did I, but what I discovered was not quite what I expected.

As I shared in the first chapter, during my last three years working with CanadianOxy, I was given the opportunity to advance big ideas that revitalized the company's sense of purpose and moved us from "beyond compliance" to much higher value thresholds on *A Measure of Integrity*. Working with the Government of Nigeria to reduce gas flaring in the environmentally sensitive Niger Delta, and building anti-bribery coalitions along our supply chain, moved the company into the lofty realm of achieving positive social, environmental and economic outcomes at level +5 of *A Measure of Integrity*. These decisions to aim higher—to achieve impacts beyond the boundaries of our single enterprise—were made deliberately. CanadianOxy was on a trajectory to becoming an independent company and wanted to distinguish itself from its American parent, Occidental Petroleum.

By far, CanadianOxy's most ambitious project was a scholarship program for Yemeni undergraduate students to study in Canada. After discovery of the massive Masila oil field in Yemen, CanadianOxy diligently implemented a program to "Yemenize" our workforce, training locals to take over positions held by Westerners. The business case for training and employing locals is well understood; however, undertaking to select qualified Yemeni high school graduates from across that entire country and bring the chosen to Alberta for four years of post-secondary education was *not* part of our corporate business plan. It was a very innovative project and extended our corporate purpose well beyond the boundaries of our commercial investment in Yemen and, as it turned out, beyond the duration of the company's investment in the country. We were essentially attempting to demonstrate to the Yemeni elite the potential of their own citizens, if only the country would open up opportunity on the basis of merit.

How did we end up in this situation, designing and implementing a project so far beyond the boundaries of our corporate values and purpose? Like many enterprise stories, good intentions were involved. In 1997, the CEO of CanadianOxy was an accountant hailing from Hafford, Saskatchewan, by the name of Vic Zaleschuk. There are few leaders I respect more. Vic is a straight shooter who is whip smart and unquestionably ethical. One day, he took me aside and said something to this effect: "Hey, I may have created a problem for us. The Yemeni prime minister outright asked CanadianOxy to fund a scholarship program for Yemeni students to come to Alberta to study. I think I agreed. But we have to do this right." I groaned. If this amounted to footing the bill to enable the privileged sons of Yemeni government ministers to study in Canada, it would be an ethical nightmare. After exploring the possibility of backtracking on the promise (not possible), I told Vic the only way to do this would be to do it right (for example, constructing a merit-based program so the children of Yemen's elite were not given priority), and that it would be very expensive.

No Yemeni students had ever studied in Alberta in an undergrad program; there were enormous cross-cultural barriers to overcome; Yemen's elite would need to accept that their progeny would not be eligible; local communities would have to trust that our choices were based on objective and transparent criteria; and we needed assurances that the Yemeni government would welcome these students back home at the end of their education in Canada. Vic listened patiently to my litany of demands, gave me the nod and a nearly blank cheque, and off I went, shooting for the moon and maybe even touching down.

Ten years later, one hundred Yemeni students (male and female) from across that country had been selected *based on merit* to study in Alberta, and nearly all of these young people succeeded. Many people see Nexen's Yemen Scholarship Program as a shining success;

the Canadian International Development Agency even gave me an award for the initiative. My family and I stay in touch with many of these young Yemeni leaders. Their life and career trajectories are exceptional. *And yet, I still have serious reservations about this initiative.* When other companies ask me to help them do the same, in places like Libya or Colombia or Vietnam, I hesitate.

CAN YOU AIM TOO HIGH?

Why would I not encourage others to take this moon shot? There are a few reasons.

Significantly, a scholarship initiative of this scope, while creative and impactful, did not align to our enterprise values or purpose. CanadianOxy was a company that could and did operate effectively, consistently and responsibly "beyond compliance" at levels +3 and +4 of *A Measure of Integrity*. Occasionally, we chose to stretch a little, to move beyond a compliance and "do no harm" mandate to achieve non-financial returns on our investments. This ambitious scholarship program was an episodical and quantum leap to level +6 of *A Measure of Integrity*, and it confused people: our shareholders, our employees, our partners, our own government and the communities where we operated across the world. CanadianOxy personnel working in Yemen were happy to look like heroes in the eyes of the locals; but in our other projects, local employees and host governments were wondering, are we second-rate because we don't have a similar scholarship program?

As well, we underestimated the effort required to manage the outcomes of this ambitious endeavour. Without the strong and continued support of senior management and the board of directors, this project would have failed. It was audacious to assume that we had the capacity to inject our values into social realms of Yemen, well beyond the scope of our business. The Yemeni government funded their own scholarship initiatives, and by upping the game, we put pressure on that government to adopt more transparent and merit-based selection criteria. All good, from our Western perspective. We demonstrated we could be "part of the solution" to big social problems. Yet for reasons well beyond our control, the sustainability of these ambitious aims eluded us.

The ultimate goal of the scholarship program was to educate Yemeni youth who could return home and contribute to their own country. But that dream failed. In 2008–09, Al-Qaeda terrorists began to congregate in Yemen, frightening off foreign investment, and by 2014, the country was in the throes of a brutal civil war. Armed conflict in Yemen resulted in the largest humanitarian crisis in the world at that time. And still, very few of the educated Yemeni scholarship students can return home. To their immense credit, many of these young leaders contribute financially to their families remaining in Yemen and they have constructive voices as advocates for peace in their home country.

Would I think differently about CanadianOxy's bold endeavour if Yemen had remained stable and educated students had returned home to play leading roles in their country? No, I honestly believe that I would still hesitate to recommend this strategy to others. We aimed breathtakingly high on *A Measure of Integrity* and raised great expectations. CanadianOxy didn't exactly bypass Yemeni's public institutions with the scholarship initiative, but we did fill a void left by government inaction. Understandably, it took a lot of intentional effort and transparency in decision-making processes to build trust with Yemeni citizens. Any enterprise that embarks on this scale of transformational social innovation requires commensurate corporate values, purpose and capacity to sustain the work. That is rare.

What could CanadianOxy have done differently? We could have partnered with others to help build Yemen's internal education and skills-training capacity; designed short-term cultural and educational exchanges for Yemeni and Canadian students, in collaboration with public and non-profit institutions in both countries; and/or partnered with the willing within Yemeni government agencies to help design more transparent decision-making processes and support the local capacity to implement those changes.

Moon shots require inspiration, creativity and unwavering dedication to the aim. And even with the best intentions, some people will always see this as virtue signalling: enterprise simply pretending to care about more than money and power; self-interest masquerading as public interest.

At the 2020 Toronto International Film Festival, Canadian documentary film producers Joel Bakan and Jennifer Abbott launched a sequel to their 2003 film, *The Corporation.* In *The New Corporation: The Unfortunately Necessary Sequel,* the producers criticize branded companies and elites who use seduction, charm and glibness to ingratiate themselves to governments and citizens. Using the language of conscious capitalism, philanthrocapitalism and creative capitalism, for-profit companies create hope that they are more innovative than governments and therefore can solve big issues that governments can't solve. Producers of this documentary pointed to several examples: Google promises to remake education using tech, removing the need for teachers in Google classrooms; Elon Musk and other billionaires with big ideas are privatizing science; Silicon Valley decides what media we see and how election campaigns are run.

Corporate CEOs and large investors collaborating with ideological activists and non-profits to advance radical social and environmental agendas generally raises suspicion. For example, when Amazon partners with The Nature Conservancy as part of its plan to be net-zero carbon by 2040, and invests millions to restore and conserve forests in the Appalachians or in the Brazilian Amazon Rainforest, does this "moon shot" feel like an authentic commitment, or greenwashing? Until proponents of this initiative point to evidence of rigorous public debate underpinning their agenda, cynics and skeptics are unlikely to be convinced of its benevolent aims.

Similarly, when Facebook founder Mark Zuckerberg and his wife Priscilla Chan promised to donate 99 percent of their shares in Facebook to the Chan Zuckerberg Initiative in 2015, committing billions to the goal of "advancing human potential and promoting equality," critics were skeptical of their self-interested generosity. For example, when the charitable enterprise offered grants to help families facing the housing crisis in Silicon Valley, people questioned their "charitable" donation to a significant social problem that Facebook had helped create.

When the Bill and Melinda Gates Foundation applied Microsoft solutions to its activities, critics questioned their motives; this, in spite of the foundation's remarkable contributions to global health.

When billionaire philanthropist Warren Buffett responded to ideas for proposed tax reforms to place more burden on the super-wealthy, with the comment, "I believe the money will be of more use to society if disbursed philanthropically than if it is used to slightly reduce an ever-increasing U.S. debt," tax reform advocates were enraged. Earlier generations of wealthy philanthropists have been accused of the same—including the Rockefeller and Carnegie families—building corporate reputations, goodwill and even profits through seemingly charitable works and not paying their fair share of taxes.

Bakan and Abbott aren't alone in questioning the motives underlying seemingly altruistic aims. For very different reasons, politicians like American Senate majority leader Mitch McConnell are cynical about "woke capital" and companies that adopt, in his words, progressive rhetoric on social issues. Responding to corporate decisions to speak up to support voting rights in Georgia, McConnell wagged his finger: "Parts of the private sector keep dabbling in behaving like a woke parallel government . . . Corporations will invite serious consequences if they become a vehicle for far-left mobs to hijack our country from outside the constitutional order."

To repeat: It's not my intention to dampen enthusiasm for enterprise's role in attempting to advance positive social change. The world needs that spirit! What I encourage is thoughtful reflection on the *how* and *why* of these decisions, and the dynamic juggling of hubris and humility. You need more than bold statements; you need organizational competencies and capacity. You need transparent processes that demonstrate genuine public deliberation (rather than an undermining of democracy). You need to build trust with skeptics and refrain from censoring or ignoring dissenting perspectives. I spent considerable time with critics in Yemen convincing them that CanadianOxy was not investing in a scholarship initiative as a tax-reduction strategy. I got lucky with the Yemen scholarship program; most moon shots don't land. And what do you do when your bold idea fails? In some enterprises, you cringe and become conditioned to *never* do that again.

There are few places where failure is construed positively. In the military, where people truly understand the stakes, people who can design and implement a successful retreat and thus preserve their ability to fight another day, are celebrated. The tech sector, on the other hand, not only condones "failure," they plan for failure. Mark Zuckerberg attributes Facebook's success to core values that encourage employees to first, make bold decisions (even if that means being wrong some of the time) and second, move fast and break things (the idea is that if you never break anything, you are probably not moving fast enough). Failure isn't negative, it's just data. Rather than repeating their mistakes, these innovators mine their "failures" for the learnings.

A 2018 documentary called *The Magic Company* tells the story of a secretive Silicon Valley start-up named General Magic, a company spun out of Apple in 1990 to create the "next big thing." As a business enterprise the company failed, yet the "magicians" employed by General Magic had laid the groundwork for the now ubiquitous smartphones, touch screens, USB drives and emojis. After General Magic failed as a company, the talent dispersed across Silicon Valley and went on to change the lives of billions. It's a classic hero's journey, invoking hubris and humility in perfect proportions; a pathway well worth forging in other sectors. These magicians were artfully teaching the dinosaur to dance.

THE TECH SECTOR THINKS DIFFERENTLY

The tech sector is rewarded for its approach to transformative innovation, and this enterprising, risk-taking culture served the sector well during the recent pandemic. Early in 2021, 90 percent of the S&P 500's value derived from intangible assets; in Canada, 70 percent of the TSX Composite's market value derived from intangibles. By contrast, companies with tangible assets were hammered by the pandemic; hardest hit stocks of 2020 included Norwegian Cruise, Air Canada, Suncor Energy, Boeing, RioCan Real Estate and Pembina Pipeline.

We expect tech companies to push for continuous growth, take risks and be disruptive. Given the pace of change and competitiveness in the sector, we understand how their very survival can depend on that strategy. Unlike other sectors, a tech company with an incremental, step-by-step change strategy would be the outlier. To design and then rapidly implement innovative strategies, the talent inside tech companies needs to be comfortable experimenting and pushing hard against the status quo. Questioning minds are not just a nice-to-have, they are essential.

Personal Leadership Element: Experimenting

Experimenting is adopting the beginner's mindset, connecting imagination to reality, and applying and testing ideas. It requires great tolerance for risk-taking and failure; the ability to let go of what does not work, and to move along with ease.

Most of us are familiar with the enterprise organizational systems and creative cultures of the tech sector; I'm curious to learn more about what *values* lie under the hood. We can start by looking at Big Tech. All five of the largest American companies by market capitalization are in tech—Apple, Microsoft, Amazon, Alphabet and Facebook. Combined, these companies are worth more than $8 trillion. That's nearly one-quarter of the entire S&P 500 market capitalization of almost $34 trillion! We can see the value in their shareholding, but what's the values algorithm?

The world has seen a lot of change in personal computing since Apple launched in 1976 as a company committed to "one person, one computer." Its corporate vision today is "to make the best products on earth, and to leave the world better than we found it." Apple's vice-president of Environment, Policy and Social Initiatives, Lisa Jackson, elaborates: "We aim to create not just the best products in the world, but the best products for the world." Apple has supported many initiatives to foster sustainability, environmental conservation and overall improvement of the ecological impacts of their business, including, for example, a $200 million "Restore Fund" to invest in forestry projects as a way to remove carbon from the atmosphere. These impact commitments situate Apple on the higher levels of *A Measure of Integrity*. To build consensus with stakeholders on these ambitious strategies, the company is very outward-facing, engaging a wide spectrum of stakeholders, including many who think differently.

Let's compare Apple to Amazon; not exactly apples to apples, but they are both big players in the technology space. Amazon's vision is: "To be Earth's most customer-centric company, where customers can find and discover anything they might want to buy online." That Amazon pays attention to customers is something you might understand; you may have ordered a copy of this book from Amazon and had it delivered to your door or laptop. Other core values of Amazon include a bias for action, ownership, frugality and innovation and a high bar for talent. Competitors begrudgingly note Amazon's commitment to the value of "relentless efficiency." Where is Amazon on *A Measure of Integrity*? Although Amazon founder and former CEO Jeff Bezos hints at sustainability values in his musings with shareholders—telling shareholders you need to "create more than you consume" to be successful in business (or life)—for the most part, the company's actions reflect compliance values. Yes, the company pays myopic attention to customers, yet strategies responsive to the priorities of employees, competitors and the public in general are episodical in nature.

Both Amazon and Apple are enormously successful and innovative companies, but they are motivated by very different values. Does that matter? If you are a well-satisfied customer, it's easy to turn a blind eye to enterprise values. But if you are an employee or a shareholder or a supplier, corporate values will impact your day-to-day experiences. If you are a government or non-profit or even another company wanting to partner with one of these tech giants, it is easier to collaborate if values are shared.

Even people as smart as Warren Buffett, CEO of Berkshire Hathaway, discovered this the hard way. In 2018, Amazon, Berkshire Hathaway and JP Morgan Chase joined forces to reduce health care costs for hundreds of thousands of their own workers, and model what was possible for health care in America. It was a big, audacious aim, launched by the three corporate CEOs with great fanfare. But Amazon's fail-fast innovation culture and ruthless efficiency values weren't compatible with those of its partners, and COVID-19 turned up the heat. In 2020, Amazon brought on 150,000 workers and the company's U.S. workforce topped 500,000 for the first time, triple what it had been five years earlier. Amazon spent billions to set up testing sites at warehouses to screen workers for the virus; in the meantime, the hoped-for health care collaboration with Berkshire Hathaway and JP Morgan Chase fizzled.

ATYPICAL THINKING IS RARE

There are exceptional times—auspicious times—when enterprise will break through all barriers to collaborate and help to solve a problem. In times of war, private-sector resources are frequently commandeered; and in the battle-like atmosphere of a global pandemic, many businesses and non-profits volunteer their support to government and redeploy their resources to help with the logistics of caring for the vulnerable, retrofit their facilities to produce personal protective equipment, and reconfigure and fast-track supply chains for essential goods and services. In Canada, for example, twelve major companies quietly came together during the pandemic to develop a system for rapid screening of their workers. This consortium is supported by the University of Toronto's Creative Destruction Lab and promises to freely share its ideas with others, including competitors, all as part of a collaborative effort to fix a big problem by speeding up the economy's restart. The champion of this initiative is reportedly Margaret Atwood, one of Canada's leading cultural voices and a woman who has repeatedly demonstrated her ability to teach the dinosaur to dance.

Personal Leadership Element: Translating

Few leaders can take complex situations, problems or strategies and distill the essence and communicate this complexity in a simple way that is clearly understood by all. Margaret Atwood has this ability.

Times of disturbance, breakdown and constraint are undoubtedly challenging, but they can also be invigorating for enterprise; breakthrough possibilities can emerge. Standards get raised, opportunities become tougher to find and the constraint teases out the best of the best. Some remarkable new ideas can emerge from atypical collaboration, skunkworks or enterprise-wide redesign of mandate and values. Pandemic-primed people have come to expect miracles, and why not? Global collaboration on the vaccines for COVID-19 was a moon shot and it landed.

Personal Leadership Element: Emerging

Emergence requires leaders to "sit in the fire," to be comfortable with tension and ambiguity while awaiting the right direction to become clear. Emerging is holding space for new thinking or a better idea to arise. If a leader does not push too hard for closure, something better will emerge.

The pandemic created a sense of anticipation and apprehension, and many people described their enterprise as being at a crossroads; however, it's not an either-or choice. It's about balancing two seemingly contradictory attitudes. Carl Sagan, in his book *The Demon-Haunted World: Science as a Candle in the Dark,* spoke of the need for science to balance "an openness to new ideas, no matter how bizarre or counterintuitive, and the most ruthlessly skeptical scrutiny of all ideas, old and new." Sagan also observed that these contradictory attitudes—skepticism and wonder—are held in some tension. That's the kind of critical thinking that enabled a safe landing by NASA's Mars rover, Perseverance.

Your enterprise may not require a Mars landing or even a moon shot, but like Sagan, do not allow your enterprise to be intimidated into conformity or diminished by naysayers. Be, at once, imaginative and disciplined. That's how you teach the dinosaur to dance.

CHAPTER 3

MOVE BEYOND POLARITY

Former U.S. President Donald Trump did not *create* binary think-ing—humans are predisposed to see the world in either-or dichotomies and to struggle with paradox. But Trump's divisive ap-proach to governing did normalize polarization in American politics and culture. When the Iron Curtain fell after World War II and glo-balization flourished, we thought the time of clearly drawn sides was over, but here we are again.

Most of us now have an image of a left–right political scale firmly lodged in our unconscious brains. In an either-or world, people are either champions of things like gender equality, LGBTQIA+ rights, and reconciliation with Indigenous peoples—or they stand in opposition to these positions and stare down those who dare to think differently. You are either with me or you are against me! You either believe in man-made climate change or you are a climate change denier. People draw other like-minded thinkers into their echo chambers, and social media amplifies and accelerates the self-perpetuating messages and their impacts.

Breaking free of either-or thinking is challenging, especially if you stick with people who think, act and look like you. It's safer, and sometimes quite exhilarating, to pick a side in a debate; it's fun to be on the winning team, the right team, the virtuous team. We fear the dominoes that could fall if we allow even a wee crack in our uncompromising positions.

Personal Leadership Element: Paradox

Paradox is the ability to hold a split view or two perspectives simultaneously. This requires a higher order of thinking from leaders and the capacity to navigate the "middle space." Skillfully blending multiple perspectives and extremes into an "adjacent possible."

Pressure for enterprise to pick a side is unrelenting. We have seen campaign after campaign—#PublishWhatYouPay, #BlackLivesMatter, #MeToo, #Divest, #Occupy, #BIPOC, to name but a few—target public figures and disrupt the trajectories of many organizations (including government, corporate and non-profit enterprises). Opposing forces decry these campaigns as "political correctness" or "cancel culture," claiming that advocates who blacklist or shame a public figure or organization for offensive progressive orthodoxy are complicit in social engineering and seek only money and power.

Some enterprises that are targets of this advocacy respond with meek apologies and effusive promises to change; others fight back and deepen the polarity. Neither of these options works particularly well. It's futile to engage in polarized battles that have no genuine hope of dialogue; it's equally futile to pretend that flowery language and marketing slogans will instantly transform your organization's values or how the organization is perceived. If the status quo isn't working, you will have to do things differently.

Personal Leadership Element: Storytelling

Storytelling is engaging the hearts of others and bringing a living sense of the destination to the journey. It animates a vision, paints a picture, creates a myth or metaphor. Storytelling paves the long road from the brain to the heart. It evokes passion. Individual and organizational dreams are kept alive by stories told over and over again. Storytelling motivates action like nothing else.

Experts have examined this polarization phenomenon from every angle; among the more well-recognized voices are moral psychologist Jonathan Haidt, author of *The Righteous Mind: Why Good People Are Divided by Politics and Religion*, and journalist Matt Taibbi, author of *Hate Inc.: Why Today's Media Makes Us Despise One Another* and contributing editor to *Rolling Stone* magazine. In 2017, I launched a blog under the moniker *Beyond Polarity* to re-energize the Hegelian dance of thesis-antithesis birthing synthesis in Canadian life. Despite our observations and efforts, "beyond polarity" thinking remains elusive; more often, individuals and organizations alike exist in a deadlock with monocultures raging against one another.

Rather than focusing energy on breaking out of the impasse—trying to work through the differences of perspective and opinion or seek common ground—opposing sides instead gather strength and power by attracting followers to their cause. This tendency to polarize creates more rigid and inflexible boundaries around what divides, not what unites. Much to the annoyance of many citizens, partisan politics increasingly manifests this approach with limited opportunity for coalitions forming across party lines to focus on solutions to pressing problems. And make no mistake, polarity and impasse are not confined to the political realm; entrenched positions equally afflict enterprises of all kinds, often pitting organizations against their own stakeholders. Obviously, this affinity for the like-minded is not conducive to long-term sustainability.

Science warns us that monocultures can become extremely brittle. Centuries later, the Irish still speak of the harsh consequences of a potato blight and the Great Hunger that followed the failure of monoculture planting of that country's food staple. Downtown Calgary, where I live, is suffering 30 percent vacancy rates largely because it became a monoculture, an edifice to oil company headquarters. We understand the human propensity for either-or thinking and the downside of monocultures, yet what can be done? How can you teach the dinosaur to dance in order to avoid extinction?

In my mother's kitchen garden at the farm, she planted beefsteak, cherry and heirloom tomatoes, not just to give us a range of choices for cooking and canning, but also to protect against the vulnerability of relying on a single crop. My mother's diversification strategy worked, but it's not always so easy. It's human nature to be subjective and hold hidden biases, no matter how hard we try to see other points of view. The question is: How can we overcome those biases and remain open to diverse perspectives?

In his book *The Quick Fix: Why Fad Psychology Can't Cure Our Social Ills,* Jesse Singal cautions us to resist the quick fix, including for example, reliance on a test called the Implicit Association Test that promises to reveal hidden biases. Enterprises of all types—companies, universities, police departments, school boards, government agencies, social institutions—classify employees as "prejudiced" based on this computer-based test that measures associations between concepts (like "black" and "white") and words (like "good" and "bad"). The psychologists behind this test admit to half-baked research, yet thousands of employees continue to be tested and are then told of biases they supposedly have but don't feel. Of course, figuring out ways to more accurately predict and overcome biases is constructive, but we need to do this work with rigour if we want people to believe in the results.

"Pretending" to play nice in the sandbox is another option, but I don't recommend it. Taking a Pollyanna or avoidance approach isn't going to defuse tensions between people who want pipelines and people who don't, or between people who see white privilege and those who don't. We can't get beyond confrontation, inflammatory accusations and polarized dichotomy with namby-pamby. Each of us must learn how to hold the space in what can become emotional, heated, sensitive, awkward and politically charged conversations. For years, I collaborated with quantum physicist F. David Peat, who counselled me to "hold the space in creative suspension" when facing opposing forces. "True creativity appears when we stay within the tension of a question or issue and don't rush to assuage our insecurity with easy solutions."

Personal Leadership Element: Emerging

Emerging is holding space for new thinking or a better idea to arise. It requires the willingness to be comfortable with tension and ambiguity while waiting for the right direction to become clear. If one does not push too hard for closure, something better will come. Emergence requires leaders to "sit in the fire," something that may not always be intuitive or comfortable.

What does this "breathing space" look like—a place where ideas can be exchanged in a less threatening way, a "Geneva state of mind?" This space is far from Utopian; instead, it's a place marked by imperfection, tolerance and differences. It's not a place of agreement, compromise, conformity or consensus. It's a place *to be*.

You will recognize this breathing space. Maybe one of your work colleagues will scratch his head and ponder why LGBTQIA+ employees keep quitting in spite of your law firm's written policy on diversity, inclusion and access. Maybe one of your enterprise partners will muse about the scarcity of female decision-makers on your project and wonder aloud if males can exclusively decide what is best. Maybe one of your friends will innocently ask an astute question about fairness and power: "How could any investor try to advance a project if local Indigenous communities are opposed?" A breathing space is not silently acquiescing; rather, it is not remaining silent when it costs something to speak up.

When you encounter backlash or resistance, you may have to take what seem like tiny steps along the pathway, and gauge whether the breathing spaces will stay open long enough to allow you to bridge the polarities. To break down a stalemate, I try to focus on framing questions in non-judgmental language. When I was working at CanadianOxy, wanting to figure out how to entice more females into the international division, I appealed to the economic and legal motivators of my co-workers: "Our policy manual states that this company values diversity. That makes good business sense. The oil and gas sector traditionally employs more males than females. So, I'm not entirely sure where our company stands on gender diversity in this industry. Can we invite someone from Human Resources to talk about how to encourage diversity in our next department meeting? Maybe we could even talk about why our company values diversity . . . the business case?" Decades later, as the chair of the governance and board recruitment committee at the Banff Centre, I asked similar questions about ways to recruit BIPOC (Black, Indigenous and people of colour) board members to the board of governors.

What I'm encouraging here is a visual: allowing a breathing space, a gap between polarities (masculine and feminine, progressive and conservative, spiritual and secular, East and West, white and coloured, straight and LGBTQIA+, rich and poor, colonialists and Indigenous, efficiency and resilience). I'm enthralled by the vision of this space opening up—the third dimension—between the opposing forces. The first option is for the duality to collapse into *oneness,* creating the wholeness we crave. But there is a catch. With wholeness, the tensions between the two opposites fall away, and with that loss of energy, individuality, diversity and complementarity can be lost.

Twoness can opt to allow a mutually relevant third force—a reconciling force—to hold and continuously bring together the dynamic tensions between opposites. If you are lodged between two opposing polarities—patriarchy versus equality, as one example—it may seem easier to collapse the two polarities into some inert lowest-common-denominator middle ground. Yet, there is no growth with this approach; the genius is in being able to hold the dualities—and the space between them—allowing them to energetically coexist. The addition of a third dimension allows both polarities to remain whole—no denial. Denial of one position or the other, or both, in some watered-down solution, is what compromise does; which is why compromise in favour of one over the other, can never be sustainable. It is in the third dimension between the dualities where the possibility for creativity and change lies. Holding the space allows for an entirely new, third way.

It's kind of like dancing the tango, which is not the easiest dance but can be fantastic if done well. Dancing with a partner wearing sharp stiletto heels is dangerous, one slip and you both fall down! Yet when skillfully executed and in balance—one partner neither dominant nor acquiescing to the other—both participants in a perpetual creative suspension can achieve a mutually satisfactory outcome. The glorious art is the dance of opposites as equals; an algebraic expression.

Personal Leadership Element: Catalyzing

Catalyzing is purposeful disruption of the status quo to provoke fresh momentum or a new direction. It is about recognizing the right time, accepting the lack of control and reading the feedback in what happens. Catalyzing takes courage; the courage to act when the outcome may not be clear.

MONOCULTURES IN YOUR ENTERPRISE

What monocultures flourish within your enterprise? Perhaps your business attracts or requires people who have particular training, like engineers or economists, or who have unique ways of approaching problems, like analytical thinkers. That's not unusual, but has this hiring bias created a uniform world view that blocks or inhibits other ways of seeing an issue or solution? If, for example, your enterprise is all about delivering health care, how do you inject business modes of thinking into your organizational structure? Is your workforce predominantly male or female? If so, how do you ensure that decisions made reflect a broad spectrum of interests? Are there differences in the way baby boomers and younger generations are represented or heard within your organization?

While it's quite normal for monocultures to exist within an individual enterprise (or in the ecosystem of the enterprise), the aim is to ensure that relationships, communications and understandings across the various monocultures do not become blocked, creating the conditions for rigid polarities to obstruct more expansive organizational choices.

Public advocacy can powerfully influence how we think about and respond to various interests. For instance, while most organizations would say they value gender diversity, how is the #MeToo movement impacting your organization? Certainly, "male, pale and stale" doesn't cut it any longer. Diversity targets are becoming the norm on non-profit, public-sector and corporate boards, and giving women equality of opportunity at all levels of enterprise has lurched forward over the decades. But it was the #MeToo movement's outing of Harvey Weinstein as a dangerous sexual predator that may go down in history, not only as a key turning point for gender equality, but one of the patriarchy's weakest moments. Who isn't disgusted by the doling out of scarce favours—jobs, promotions, endorsements, string-pulling—in exchange for sex? The #MeToo response is a socially acceptable platform for women to tell their story. There is solidarity, and critically, there is safety.

Women around the world, including high-powered personalities from Hollywood to Bollywood, in political offices and the private sector, can now speak out frankly and openly about harassment. Yet some of the young women I mentor find the #MeToo movement increasingly hard to identify with, as it shifts from the much-needed conversation about consent and sexual responsibility into an uncomfortable territory that paints women as victims, incapable of speaking up or saying no, and paints men in our culture as toxically masculine and as potential abusers, harassers or serial predators. In your enterprise, how do you prevent #MeToo turning into a manhunt that erodes the potential for constructive relationships between men and women?

And another word of caution here: What have traditionally been recognized as individual monocultures are increasingly each being subdivided into more exclusive (therefore less inclusive) subcultures. "Feminism," for example, can be far too broad a label to encapsulate the different perspectives that exist between women of colour and white women; women who support abortion and those who don't; and straight women and lesbians (not to mention transgendered females).

The police killing of George Floyd in May 2020 unleashed a torrent of pent-up frustration and anger toward discrimination against Blacks and, in particular, Black men. The Black Lives Matter (BLM) campaigns rebuked enterprises that inadvertently or otherwise coddled white entitlement. BLM, BIPOC and other "woke" campaigns have moved well beyond the polite strategy of good intentions and patiently waiting for room at the table. There is powerful advocacy to defund the police.

And everywhere, statues of offensive historical leaders are being targeted. Monuments to Confederate generals are being decapitated across America; in Britain, the statue of Edward Colston, a slave trader, was toppled and in Canada, citizens are torn about what to do with the ubiquitous likenesses of Sir John A. Macdonald, our country's first prime minister, who was responsible for sanctioning the residential school system for Indigenous children. It's easy to lose context in these polarized, passionate debates about what's right and what's wrong, and very challenging to find higher ground.

For most organizations, making some of the changes demanded by advocacy groups and the community in general is relatively straightforward. For example, renaming the Cleveland Indians baseball team or the Edmonton Eskimos football team or rebranding Aunt Jemima pancake syrup shows some sensitivity to this advocacy and the related cultural appropriation concerns. The harder work comes in figuring out ways to influence the thinking of people in your organization who fail to acknowledge white privilege and the baked-in power of the dominant culture.

Adam Grant, author of *Think Again: The Power of Knowing What You Don't Know,* encourages us to ask ourselves: How would your stereotypes be different if you were born First Nations, Black, Chinese or Hispanic? What opinions would you hold if you were raised on a farm versus in a city? Understanding the origins of your own beliefs and asking if different circumstances could have brought you to a different set of beliefs better equips you to: understand the challenges that others face, level the playing field of opportunity, hold your enterprise to a higher standard and do something concrete to right the wrongs of the past—and be part of building for a better, more sustainable future.

As chair of the governance and recruitment committee on the board at the Banff Centre, a non-profit dedicated to arts and creativity in Canada, it was daunting to keep pace with the changing expectations of communities we served. For example, with so many people grabbing the microphone in social media space to declare the imperative for Black, Indigenous and people of colour candidates to be offered positions of authority, our merit-based board recruitment strategy was turned on its head. The Banff Centre needed someone with accounting skills, but foremost, that person had to be BIPOC.

And I wondered: what if that's not enough in this time of cancel culture and great purging?

In 2020, cultural institutions across Canada saw a flurry of leaders hit the exit: Within weeks of each other, the artistic director at Persephone Theatre in Saskatoon, Saskatchewan, tendered his resignation; the artistic director at the PuSh Festival in Vancouver, British Columbia, was terminated without cause; and the artistic director at Theatre Aquarius in Hamilton, Ontario, retired. And in that same time frame, several prestigious Canadian institutions were forced to respond to accusations of racism, white privilege and inequality, including the Royal BC Museum, the University of Saskatchewan and the National Gallery of Canada.

When the summer 2021 edition of *Canadian Art* magazine landed in my inbox, I gulped as I read that the board of this prestigious foundation dedicated to artists had stepped down, en masse, to "allow space for a new Board of Directors to be appointed to lead the charity going forward, in a spirit of staff self-determination and sovereignty." Diversity and representation are, of course, pressing values that I endorse, but how does any enterprise deal with them or any other emerging social expectation in a meaningful, strategic and impactful way—all the while managing business and the bottom line responsibly?

The trajectory of identity politics makes me nervous, and I'm listening closely to understand how equality and equity can reach a new equilibrium. Outspoken critics of critical race theory bemoan the indoctrination of school children and the attacks on history, and frame these movements as Marxist. One of the voices I hear through all the noise is that of Ben Carson, a Black man raised in Detroit by a single mother, who was secretary of the U.S. Department of Housing and Urban Development under President Trump. Equity's world view, posits Carson, "starts with the proposition that the White majority is guilty of bigotry and oppression, and that all differential outcomes between groups are solely the result of that bigotry and oppression." Equity actions needed to right these wrongs (for example, reparations for slavery and support to BIPOC-owned businesses) have the effect of holding people responsible for injustices that took place long before they were even born, and the redistributing of benefits (and burdens) based on race or gender is guaranteed to breed resentment.

Of course I'm supportive of inclusion; it aligns to my positive experience integrating different points of view into decision-making if you want to solve big problems or create new value. You learn more from people who aren't like you. It delights me that a large enterprise like the Coca-Cola Company has the chutzpah to launch a rigorous outside-counsel diversity program, requiring the law firms they retain to give a portion of work to Black attorneys and withholding a non-refundable 30 percent of fees from law firms that fail to meet these diversity metrics. And while I'm intrigued by boards of directors of non-profits who announce new BIPOC board slates—to great fanfare—as an ouster of old thinking and an embracer of the woke, I would applaud these headlines if they spoke of having nominated an extraordinary group of talented individuals to the board who better mirror the communities the organization serves and will thus help bring a greater understanding of diverse points of view.

Many corporate leaders of public companies are setting ambitious diversity targets. In the tech sector, Microsoft promises to try to double the number of Black employees in senior and leadership positions by 2025; and Alphabet Inc. CEO Sundar Pichai promises to hire enough Black workers to push Google's numbers to 30 percent by 2025. But not everyone is onside; some leaders of for-profit enterprises are taking a moderated approach to diversity, including Snowflake Inc., a cloud software maker. Snowflake CEO Frank Slootman explains: "We're actually highly sympathetic to diversity but we just don't want that to override merit. If I start doing that, I start compromising the company's mission literally."

Decades ago, many people responded to white entitlement with humour; remember Archie Bunker, the lovable bigot in the *All in the Family* television series who was suspicious of Blacks, Hispanics, "commies," gays, hippies, Jews, Catholics, "women's libbers" and Polish-Americans? Imagine his response if someone had told Bunker to "check his white privilege!" This kind of dark humour no longer lets people off the hook. Public advocacy is focusing increasing attention on the unfairness of white entitlement; it's no laughing matter.

Seeing issues of unfairness and inequity from the perspective of the under-represented is not difficult; what's daunting is having the capacity to perceive these weighty social questions from the perspective of the entitled. I admit to being utterly overwhelmed by the pain of Indigenous communities in Canada when hundreds upon hundreds of unmarked children's graves were discovered at the sites of former residential schools. Yet I know that to hold the space— and create a breathing space for all Canadians to come together and identify possible responses—requires enormous will and compassion, not just for the victims of these egregious acts, but also to understand how this could even have happened in the first place.

It's a precarious time. We all feel the pressure to do things differently; to defuse injustice and resentment and rebuild stronger and more equitably. And yet, the dominant culture being sensitive and silent and self-censoring isn't exactly working either. We risk replacing one monoculture with another and remaining entrenched in polarized thinking. If inclusiveness checklists come at the expense of genuine dialogue and consensus on values (achievable through the creative tension of negotiating across different points of view), we risk compromising our resiliency. As I will keep repeating, monocultures are fragile.

BEING EFFICIENT AND RESILIENT

When everyone in your enterprise thinks the same way, it's easier to be efficient. And that single-mindedness is a powerful force that is often rewarded. Who doesn't want to be more efficient: squeezing more hours out of the day, designing just-in-time supply chains, running a leaner operation, preserving resources? Government regulators can rationalize monopolies on the calculus that two companies merging will create synergies; for example, cost savings and economies of scale derived from laying off employees. When economic efficiencies are offered up, enterprise consolidation is often allowed even if consumers will be forced to pay higher prices for the most basic of goods, even commodities like propane and internet access.

Efficiency works when the going is good, but it can fail spectacularly when you encounter a crisis. What happens to the merits of efficiency when the polar vortex's blast of Arctic air delivers brutally cold weather to the central United States? The Texas power grid crashed in February 2021 because operators did not adequately prepare for cold weather and, as a result, 4.5 million Texans lost power. Freezing temperatures and power outages caused natural gas compressors to quit working and, at the same time, demand for energy rose as Texans cranked up their furnaces and heaters. Not only did the electricity grid come within five minutes of complete collapse, but the backup generators designed to restart the system after grid failure were, at times, out of commission. Rewarding operational and cost efficiencies, and discounting the value of reliability and resiliency, cost Texans dearly; some estimates assess the cost of direct and indirect economic loss to the Texas economy due to the freeze and outage at over $100 billion.

The pandemic upended efficiency in most enterprises and reminded us of the value of resiliency: the ability to withstand shocks, to identify risks and be prepared, to build local and regional durability through redundancies, to be self-reliant and to plan for failure. It's not either-or; efficiency and resiliency are not mutually exclusive, yet many of us have been trained to look at them as stand-alone priorities.

The oil companies I worked with in the 1980s and '90s, which were managed by engineers and accountants, are perfect examples of this approach. In those days, nearly all of my male engineering colleagues wore khaki pants and light blue button-down shirts to work and spent their days nailing down oil reserve calculations and project timelines. They were ruthlessly focused and efficient. No knock on those ways of thinking, but in any enterprise, you can have too much of a good thing. When I spoke to them of managing "above-ground risks"—including political, reputation or litigation risks—they pressed me to assign firm probabilities and time frames. However, the issues I was raising were much fuzzier and intangible. How could you predict social behaviours in the aftermath of the fall of the Berlin Wall, with the World Bank pouring billions of infrastructure dollars into developing countries to stimulate democracy and transparency? In 1999, three countries where CanadianOxy operated—Nigeria,

Indonesia and Yemen—hosted inaugural "democratic" elections in that single year. And September 11, 2001, marked a turning point. From that day forward, the world was divided into the Muslim world and the non-Muslim world.

The dance between efficiency and resiliency is one we seem to need to relearn every time we encounter crisis. Redesigning your enterprise to consistently, and more intentionally, access different points of view, skills, talents, resources and approaches to problem-solving can help shape a more resilient strategy. And demonstrating resiliency (not just efficiency) can help to regain and restore the confidence of key stakeholders; for example, your employees, your partners and host communities where your enterprise operates.

One crisis firmly etched into my memory happened in the Latin American country of Colombia in the early 1990s. Even now, decades later, I vividly recall the call from the Ministry of Foreign Affairs in Ottawa. A long convoy of trucks carrying oil field equipment to CanadianOxy's drilling site in the Putumayo region of Colombia was torched by guerrillas, from end to end. Thankfully no one was injured, but a strong message had been delivered by FARC, the revolutionary armed forces that were active then in southern Colombia. Overnight, our company's efficiency became irrelevant. It took a lot of fresh thinking and goodwill, but the company was ultimately able to restore confidence with employees and shareholders and chart an alternative course with the Colombian government. We transferred our contractual commitments to a safer region of the country and kept drilling. Importantly, the enterprise pivoted from efficiency to resiliency, and we learned to embrace both, placing greater value on building long-term relationships of trust with the host government and with local citizens in Colombia. Communities where we operated were able to predict the movements of guerrillas and paramilitias (that is, the locals became our early warning system), and the company figured out better ways to feed this local wisdom into operational strategies.

To repeat: Enterprise needs both efficiency and resiliency. An enterprise can be efficient by remaining internally focused, but to become resilient and sustainable requires that an organization engage with other stakeholders, viewpoints and experiences outside of its walls—both the physical walls and the walls of its own thinking.

BEYOND BINARY THINKING ON CLIMATE CHANGE

Few issues these days are more polarizing than the environment. The impacts of climate change trigger raging debates between apocalyptic thinkers and climate change deniers. When Al Gore launched his "Inconvenient Truth" campaign several decades ago, he spoke of the need to "win" the conversation with climate change deniers who were at odds with the scientific consensus that human activity, largely the burning of fossil fuels that generate greenhouse gases (GHGs), drives climate change. Gore's truth contrasted science with climate denial, setting up an intractable duality.

Fort McMurray is a city in northern Alberta with a population of roughly 112,000 citizens (75,000 permanent residents and 37,000 transient workers). This remote place is the epicentre of oil sands mining and also plays host to a revolving door of non-local climate crusaders—including celebrity activists Greta Thunberg, Jane Fonda, Neil Young, Matt Damon and Leonardo DiCaprio—all declaring the continued development of the oil sands to be a certain pathway to human extinction. Artists play a critical role in society: a film, a book, a poem, a painting, a performance opens our mind to see things from a different perspective; to question and doubt our assumptions and even seek alternative answers. But these celebrities' demands for the immediate shutdown of the oil sands, while an alternative perspective to the status quo, is binary.

Climate change is a very complex question—of existential proportion—and with so much at stake, it's understandable that people get animated. But either-or thinking along the lines of, "You are either a climate change believer or a denier" or "If oil wins, climate loses," does not advance a clear understanding of the challenge or the choices. When I was an elected politician in Alberta, the mere mention of carbon tax in a newsletter or speech triggered an avalanche of reactions—both pro and con—but little interest in much-needed dialogue on effective ways to design a carbon tax to actually curb GHGs.

Bold pledges by governments, communities and companies are constructive, but enterprise also needs to design and implement concrete strategies that achieve these promised carbon reductions. Bill Gates has waded into this issue, declaring his master plan in his book *How to Avoid a Climate Disaster: The Solutions We Have and the Breakthroughs We Need*, released a month after President Joe Biden moved into the White House. Gates's insights into epidemiology were helpful during the COVID-19 crisis, but climate change is a harder problem than ending the pandemic or getting rid of malaria, says Gates. This is disquieting. Climate change has so many variables that can never be accounted for and, like chaos theory, understanding the confluence and outcomes of these vectors is nearly impossible.

In his book *Unsettled? What Climate Science Tells Us, What It Doesn't, and Why It Matters,* Steven E. Koonin (former top scientist in Barack Obama's Energy Department) echoes the complexity of the climate change question. He agrees that the globe is warming and that humans are exerting a warming influence, but he doesn't agree with climate orthodoxy on the magnitude of the impacts. And please, don't call him a "climate denier," says Koonin; he sees this label as a concocted phrase intended to shut down debate.

While there is agreement that the question of climate change is a complex one, different visionaries are taking different pathways forward. Elon Musk has already placed his bets: humanity's future is off planet. Gates is confident we can avert disaster on Earth with full-scale technological revolution being the way forward to reduce GHG emissions to zero by 2050. That means innovation must be scaled up; we need more than electric cars, lithium-ion batteries, solar panels, wind turbines and plant-based burgers. Gates is asking us to look beyond agriculture and electricity, to identify green alternatives for transportation, concrete, even green steel. There is a precedent for this scale of radical innovation by government. In 1973, the United States created the Defense Advanced Research Projects Agency (DARPA) to build out the internet. And, as a major player in Silicon Valley, Gates understandably has confidence in this approach.

The Biden administration's ambitious plan—to create a carbon-free power sector in America by 2035; to embark on an irreversible path to a net-zero economy by 2050; to set up new climate change agencies and task forces; and to recognize climate change as not just an environmental risk but a national security and foreign policy concern—sends a powerful message of transformational change that aligns to Gates's vision. President Biden's plan is described by many as a twenty-first century version of Franklin D. Roosevelt's New Deal–style presidency. Then, Roosevelt was responding to the Great Depression, trying to restore faith in government's ability to provide for citizens and defend democracy by fending off fascism; in effect, building resiliency into the government and social fabric of America.

What all these solutions have in common is that they tap into diverse viewpoints, they synthesize thinking and research from many sources and they are consultative and collaborative in their approach. They seek solutions by challenging, even disrupting, the status quo. For-profit enterprise works in conjunction with stakeholders (including governments and advocates) to come up with a more robust, resilient, sustainable way forward.

It's heartening to see enterprise leaders from all sectors lean into action on climate change with creativity and innovation—and beyond polarity. Natural gas produced in Alberta by Seven Generations Energy is certified as "responsible" by Equitable Origin (in much the same way "fair trade" coffee is certified by independent arbiters); with this certification, the company is able to secure a natural gas supply agreement with the province of Quebec's largest natural gas distributor, Énergir. Another creative design, from Europe, is the Bauhaus movement that brings together architects, artists, students, scientists, engineers and designers to make recycling, renewable energies and biodiversity nature-based and human-centred. Enterprises that can figure out ways beyond either-or thinking on climate change can help design a way forward. Those that cannot, will remain stuck in binary thinking, going nowhere. They will be at risk of extinction.

Personal Leadership Element: Experimenting

Experimenting means to adopt the beginner's mindset, connecting imagination to reality, applying and testing ideas. It requires tolerance for risk and failure. Experimenting means letting go of what does not work, and moving on with ease.

YOU NEED CRITICAL FRIENDS

In Chinese philosophy, the concept of yin and yang explains how the world is divided into pairs of opposites: darkness and light, hot and cold, masculine and feminine. Dualities plague us all, yet there can be no human life as we know it without these opposites. We are inherently conscious of the fragmentation; but we also need to be wise enough to sense life's underlying unity and the need to hold opposites in dynamic balance. Some believe unity can be fostered only by avoiding the conflicts or pretending them away. Others take the duality to extremes, relying on the catharsis of moral outrage, shame and guilt to silence people with different world views. Yet both these strategies only perpetuate polarized thinking, create fragile monocultures and increase enterprise vulnerability. Finding practical ways to embrace duality and paradox is the path to unity, not just for individuals but for enterprises as well.

Given this reality, what can your enterprise do to navigate duality, diversity and differences of opinion, and avoid entrenched polarization? There are intentional strategies that I've seen work. First, you can accept that there are people in the world who want you on their side of an issue, and you can pre-empt being co-opted and choose instead to act independently. Your enterprise is not going to wade into every polarity that crosses your path; but like the bystander in the bullying scenario, you can decide when it's necessary for your enterprise to roll up its sleeves and step in.

Second, you can intentionally build diversity. Anywhere you have differences, there's more opportunity to break out of either-or dichotomies rather than become entrenched in them. *The Enterprise*

Onion tool can help your team identify, understand and even encourage diverse perspectives, and this work can help to dislodge stuck monocultures.

Third, you can accept that living beyond duality means living with paradox. Think about times when you have dealt with opposite emotions. For me, the most poignant example occurred a few years ago when my father was diagnosed with Stage 4 lung cancer mere days after my son and his wife were married. I felt extreme joy and extreme sorrow at the same time. You don't stay in either of those "opposing" emotions; nor do they blend together and become muted. You feel them both intensely, joy and sorrow. Humans may be predisposed to see the world in dichotomies, but our brains are capable of handling contradictory value systems and contradictory points of view.

Personal Leadership Element: Paradox

Paradox is the ability to hold a split view or two perspectives simultaneously. This requires a higher order of thinking from leaders, confidence and the ability to navigate the dynamic energy of the "middle space."

Conflicts cannot always be avoided because people don't universally share the same view of the world. But there isn't a right or wrong way to see the world, and it is useful to be aware of the values, assumptions and world views of stakeholders, to understand how those perspectives help or hinder resolution of an issue. Differences in how people see the world can be startling.

Most readers will be familiar with Abraham Maslow's hierarchy of needs, the pyramid of an individual's progress from basic, physiological needs to the pinnacle: self-actualization. This theory of motivation shapes a lot of modern thinking. In Maslow's hierarchy, individual self-actualization is the aim; community-focused and cultural priorities are stepping stones to that aim. What many people don't know is that Maslow's hierarchy was informed by his engagement with the Blackfeet Nation in Montana in 1938—and Maslow got their model entirely backwards! In the Blackfeet world view, individuals are the base of the pyramid (individual self-actualization is the foundation upon which community is built), and the Blackfeet's ultimate aim (the top of their teepee) is sustaining the culture.

These differences in world view can create enormous chasms if they are not understood; but if we work to identify and understand them, they can be navigated. In fact, if we seek out and embrace differing world views, we can enrich our understanding; make better, more informed decisions; and build resilience into any enterprise.

Sometimes, encounters with critics can trigger or perpetuate an antagonistic conflict between two belief systems or two cultural trends; for example, between patriarchy and gender equality or between opposing sides of the artificial intelligence battles. It can be difficult to choose to hold the space, and not advocate for your point of view, when there is a marked difference of opinion on a matter of significance. To break the impasse, it is necessary to negate "absolute" thinking, which is not always possible. Consider the abortion debates as an example, or the positions of climate change deniers versus those who see carbon as an apocalyptic threat. If the dialectic becomes a crucible, the debate is only energized by the combatants and becomes even more polarized. There are often attempts to bring allies and others to your "side," and the grounds for compromise erode. If the power of the parties with the polarized viewpoints is relatively matched, the issue can remain stuck until a new truth emerges.

In some polarized standoffs, one party or both may grow weary of the futility of continuing to do battle in an attempt to move to resolution. More often, the energy of the polarization ultimately fades, in entropy. Feeding the polarity will sap your energy, and it can erode the solution space available by dampening curiosity. What then can you do to hold the space and keep dancing?

You can attempt to reframe the debate and clarify the boundaries of the issue in question. By defining the scope of the engagement too broadly, you may never be able to progress a challenging issue; by defining the scope too narrowly, you may succumb to reductionist thinking about a situation. As demonstrated in a case study shared in *The Enterprise Onion* tool and user guide located in the toolkit at the end of this book, proponents of the Keystone XL Pipeline attempted to limit the scope of the pipeline discussion to infrastructure and the economy and jobs; their opponents refused to have this discussion constrained and demanded that the pipeline's implications for climate change and the environment be incorporated. To bridge this wide a chasm, there are practitioners who are expert at building containers for difficult conversations and who can be called upon to define the boundaries of the question at issue by making a subjective and purposeful judgment as to what's in and what's out.

You can also choose to refer the debate to an independent third party for adjudication; for example, a mediator or a judge. Again, as the Keystone XL Pipeline example in the toolkit demonstrates, this option can be very unsatisfactory, as it requires that you give up control of the solution and therefore may not be satisfied with the decision made by a regulator or court—or in the case of that particular pipeline, by a newly elected American president. Ultimately, the pipeline proponent, TC Energy, gave in to vehement opposition and gave up on the project; the détente ended with a whimper, with one side of the duality removing itself from the situation completely.

Another alternative is to expressly acknowledge the potential for the difficult engagement to give birth to a new value or truth that either "side" in the debate wouldn't readily recognize or advance on their own. With this frame of reference, you can reach out to "critical friends" for a different perspective and to catalyze new thinking. But you have to remember, it's not easy to be a critical friend when an enterprise is powerful and has a significant vested interest or self-interest; it's like speaking truth to power, and sometimes people don't want to hear the truth. Some dinosaurs aren't interested in learning how to dance, and the ornery ones may even bite!

If your enterprise pathway continues to be blocked by opposition, despite attempts to engage, you can "agree to disagree" and continue to hold the space in dynamic tension until different possibilities emerge. In the case of the Keystone XL Pipeline, the conditions for a revived approach may at some point in the future be catalyzed by external factors—perhaps a severe shortage of domestic energy supplies or a public advocacy against shipping oil by rail. Possibly, the pipeline in question may ultimately be rethought as necessary infrastructure to support the safe transport of hydrogen and other greener sources of energy.

Personal Leadership Element: Emerging

Holding space in dynamic tension for new thinking or a better idea to arise is daunting. It's not comfortable. But sometimes, it's a better option than entropy or feeding a polarity.

Across the globe, and in every type of enterprise, I've had similar conversations with people extremely frustrated by polarized positioning: senior executives of North American pipeline companies when projects were blocked by protestors; female doctors and midwives in remote hospitals in Yemen constrained by authoritarian patriarchs; senior citizens and First Nations elders who opposed new development in their communities; and regulators in government agencies tasked with implementing unpopular policies. Of course, every enterprise will have a unique set of facts and stakeholders, and a unique *Enterprise Onion*. (Again, I point you to the toolkit at the end of the book for insights on how to apply this tool in your organization.)

The Enterprise Onion tool helps to conceptualize and constructively navigate diversity in perspectives. It is a simple tool to use, but very effective. Many times, I've taken a pen and sketched an onion on the back of a paper napkin while having a coffee with someone frustrated by a polarized debate that is blocking their organization's way forward. I start with the enterprise team at the onion's core and then add the layers of the onion: the like-minded, the open-minded, the skeptics, the cynics. I then talk about how the enterprise can begin to understand and engage with other world views, especially the more resistant ways of thinking that reside in those layers of the onion closer to the surface.

Typically, the pipeline executives I have met with enthusiastically flesh out the like-minded and open-minded layers of their onion, rhyming off supportive industry allies and unions who wanted to see their pipelines built, as well as pro-pipeline scientists and economists and experts. However, it takes some nudging for them to understand how their enterprises are viewed by, and/or can constructively relate to, skeptics and critics. The executives understand that some citizens in local communities are leery of pipeline leaks, and trust-building efforts are made on an ad hoc basis, but these layers of engagement are thin. The executives know their critics—American presidents (Democrats) and anti-pipeline advocates (including David Suzuki) among them—and they describe their encounters with these opposing points of view as "futile."

While most enterprise leaders prefer to seek allies, if you truly wish to break through barriers and move well beyond business as usual, *The Enterprise Onion* is a highly effective tool that can be used to facilitate engagement at all levels and turn vehement opposition into a powerful and constructive force.

BUILDING RAPPORT

Engaging with external stakeholders to evoke fresh ideas and solutions is anathema to people who prefer efficiency, order and predictability. Even more frightening is the notion of opening up decision-making to outsiders! Yet there is wisdom in reaching beyond the relative safety of your core team for insight. Be intentional and strategic. And tailor your outreach to the purpose of the engagement. For example, when does your enterprise need face-to-face dialogue with a stakeholder group and when will online surveys work? Should the questions to launch a dialogue be open-ended or prescriptive? You will need quantitative and qualitative data and methods to help you develop an empathetic understanding of the views and priorities of others. How do you create the conditions for an external stakeholder—a community, for example—to feel like a project is happening "with" them rather than "to" them? Think about what's worked in your enterprise and build on those experiences; to be entirely honest though, in my experience, I've learned more from my failures.

As an energy nerd, and having been trained as a lawyer, I am easily energized about technical facts—even the idea of how electricity systems function is of great interest to me. But when I'm engaging with citizens in a community and using the language of science or economics or law, eyes will glaze over if I don't realize I'm communicating at cross-purposes. Many citizens don't want to know the details of how the new pipeline or electricity transmission line will be constructed; what they care about is how they will be compensated for potential harm and whether or not they can stop the project. What they care about is similar to what my parents cared about when Ontario Hydro showed up to expropriate their farm. Communicating to help "make sense" of the scientific, economic and legal facts—in ways that relate to the values and priorities of the people I'm meeting with—can build trust.

Sense-making requires a flow of dialogue in two or more directions, not just a one-way communication. For that reason, I prefer to participate in back-and-forth dialogue rather than appear as a talking head on an expert panel. Even TEDx talks, while invigorating, aren't two-way. In the absence of intentional space for dialogue, these formats don't allow the opportunity to co-create. If you can, try to design and participate in engagement formats that are more amenable to dialogue than positioning; although sometimes this can be very difficult to do. It doesn't help that news media sets a poor example by preferring to set up contradictory perspectives and will purposely solicit opposing viewpoints. As a government minister responsible for electricity and renewable energy, I was often "squared off" against anti-coal activists, including medical doctors dressed in lab coats who were part of the Canadian Association of Physicians for the Environment. To the extent feasible, I asked different questions and resisted the temptation to use declaratory statements, to try and set a less combative tone; for example, asking how scientists could better quantify the health impacts of coal use in electricity generation or how stranded coal plants should practically be phased out.

When I was in Nepal working with female lawyers and judges in that country as part of a Canadian Bar Association capacity-building team, I was invited to share technical best practices for legal mediation in a formal space; but the real value in the engagement was listening to the participants' questions and quickly adapting the conversation to the local women's context. As primary care providers in a very patriarchal society, females in Nepal's legal profession were keen to figure out ways to balance commitments to their extended family and to their profession. In fact, their positive experiences "mediating" between home and office proved to be relevant building blocks for enhancing their skills and legitimacy as trusted legal mediators.

Deep and intentional listening is required to pick up the signals about what people in the room hear and what they want to talk about; this requires listening to others more than you talk! Preparation is also necessary to develop a deep, empathetic understanding of the needs, desires and aspirations of those with whom you are engaging. Like a dance with a partner, healthy engagement—even on topics that are controversial—often has a pulsing feel, reflecting an iterative cycling between divergence and convergence.

Personal Leadership Element: Sense-Making

Sense-making is the radar, registering strong and weak signals from all levels of the organizational environment. It is both intuitive and strategic—sensing change, spotting trends, observing what's happening. Translating nuance and complexity in the environment into relevance and meaning for the organization.

Another thing I learned—as a corporate executive, then as director of a non-profit, and most recently as an elected politician (you would think I'd have gotten it sooner!)—is the danger of hosting town hall gatherings with vague expectations. It can all start out with good intentions: gracious invitations offering up a "transparent sharing of information to support citizens' informed participation" in the design of a new pension or mental health policy or training initiative. There is a temptation to simply celebrate everyone's good work and avoid controversy. But reality can be anything but gracious when participants misinterpret the invitation as a right to exercise a veto or when they claim to speak for others not in the room. I have learned the hard way that the purpose of your engagement with stakeholders should be crystal-clear and honest. For example, are you reaching out on a voluntary basis or to comply with a law or rule or statutory mandate, and will participation by others lead to shared decision-making? If you do not want to be accused of window dressing, be explicit and explain very honestly how this engagement will influence your policy design and decisions.

Politics is particularly tricky. Having been an elected politician, in the trenches, I believe strongly in the imperative for citizens to better understand how it all really works. From the outside looking in, politics is opaque. There are vested interests; there are good intentions; there is the need for long-term strategic thinking; and there are short-term decisions influenced by election cycles and partisanship. It's a daunting mix, and cynicism is a given if these various aspects and interests aren't unspooled, named and clearly understood. As with most things, trade-offs must be negotiated across a spectrum of interests; the more people affected can understand the process and their voice in decision-making, the better the outcome and its implementation.

Politicians are expected to put forward policies that reflect the will of the people, yet they are sometimes accused of being held hostage to well-funded interest groups that do not represent the wider electorate. Plebiscites, referendums and other direct democracy tools are used to "return power to the people" and build trust in government. In Canada, referendums have been used to put very big questions directly to citizens; for example, a 1980 referendum in Quebec asked if that province should secede from Canada (the question was posed again in 1995). Figuring out when and how to integrate direct democracy methods into government process isn't clear-cut: citizens expect to have meaningful input into political decisions that affect them and the right to hold decision-makers accountable, yet politicians are elected to make decisions in the public interest.

And the most essential lesson I learned is this: Having a thoughtful and well-resourced stakeholder engagement strategy is as essential to any enterprise as an effective fiscal, operating or human resource strategy. You wouldn't design your budget on an ad hoc basis, so why approach a stakeholder engagement strategy this way? The effort and time required to restore broken trust is exponentially greater than the resources required to design and implement a thoughtful and comprehensive stakeholder engagement strategy. And sometimes, once it's lost, trust cannot be restored.

Embarking on a pathway of outreach, and then turning back, can leave a trail of distrust, unrest, inertia and cynicism. For example, the Government of Alberta released a new coal policy in the province in 2020, allowing open-pit coal mining on previously protected eastern slopes of the Rocky Mountains. The government consulted with the (very like-minded) coal industry on the new legislation, but with few others. The new policy triggered a tsunami of angry voices from the skeptical and cynical layers of *The Enterprise Onion* (citizens in local communities rose up, environmental advocates campaigned and popular country singer Corb Lund emerged to spearhead the challenge to the government policy). The beleaguered provincial government withdrew the offending policy and restarted the entire engagement process. This example highlights the mistakes of a government ministry, but I've seen companies and non-profits do the same.

It takes courage and competency to move beyond the status quo, to reach out to others who may not agree with you and build sufficient trust to generate new ideas, and to stay the course on a rebuilding effort. There is much discomfort in letting go of conventional sources of control and in shifting from one way of seeing the world to another. Holding the space in dynamic tension, and having the capacity to transcend your own world view to create a new truth or idea or value, requires courageous patience. Bringing together diverse opinions, surfacing values, tabling and weighing trade-offs, and uncovering common ground is hard work. It is very difficult to create independent space for this kind of engagement even within your own organization, but the rewards are there. Tech companies have added significant value through skunkworks, and I've seen enterprise leaders richly rewarded for creating the conditions for employees to safely share both their positive and negative perspectives.

If you truly seek to discover and understand the feelings, knowledge, inspiration and potential for change that lie in contrary views, reaching out to the critical-minded can yield enormous potential pay-offs. Outcomes include the trust, confidence and clarity generated by the dialogue and the process itself, as well as what engaged individuals do with the fruits of the dialogue. If you truly wish to signal to rebuilders and new builders inside your enterprise, and beyond, that the status quo isn't sufficient, dare to invite them as critical friends to your decision-making table. That invitation may spark an idea, concept or potential that we've all been craving. Moving your enterprise from a place where monocultures are doing battle to a space where the dynamics of diversity contribute to enriched decision-making can create an energized breathing space for innovation. It can enliven the dance of the dinosaur.

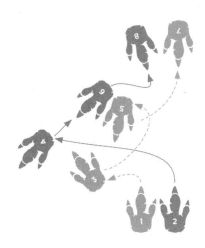

CHAPTER 4

GET TO A FAIR DEAL

In his inaugural speech on January 20, 2021, American President Joe Biden cited inequality and racism alongside COVID-19 and climate change as four of six major crises facing America (the other two being America's diminishing standing in the world and the assault on truth and democracy). To forcefully disrupt these self-perpetuating problems, Biden launched an economic plan of epic proportions for his first hundred days in office, with the intention of galvanizing Americans in a nationwide fairness recalibration. He announced that America will invest trillions into COVID relief, jobs, clean energy and infrastructure, and government money will be redistributed to the disadvantaged to restore social cohesion. It was a Sputnik moment.

Wealth imbalance, racial discrimination, even the inequitable impacts of climate change, are often discussed as theoretical or hypothetical challenges; but the COVID-19 pandemic was a publicly evident, immediate and universal crisis that upended the world as we knew it and shone a bright light on these very real injustices and disparities. Early in the pandemic, people predicted that the novel coronavirus would be the great leveller, but it wasn't; disease (like other crises) finds the vulnerable and exacerbates existing inequalities.

Arguably, the pandemic itself could be seen as a symptom; that is, its worst effects were partly due to a culmination of the social issues and challenges that have been roiling around for some time. For example, disadvantaged populations were among the hardest hit by COVID-19, and the high incidence and severity of their illness was in no small part due to the inequities these groups have lived with for so long (including poverty, crowded living conditions, limited access to health care, and lack of sick pay in low-paid, essential and front-line jobs). Female workers were also disproportionately impacted by the pandemic; more often than not, women gave up jobs to take care of children when schools and daycares closed. Small businesses owned by minorities were less confident of their ability to access loans needed to rebuild. In America, the Federal Reserve Bank found that Black and Hispanic small business owners were half as likely as their white counterparts to be approved for a non-emergency loan, despite having similar credit risk. We were all in the same storm during the pandemic, but seated in very different boats.

Mere months before COVID-19 landed in North America, the premier of Alberta, Jason Kenney, invited me to join a roster of eight fellow Albertans on a "Fair Deal Panel." Our mandate was to travel the province and listen to ordinary citizens' perspectives on whether Albertans had a "fair deal" within Canada's confederation. Driving the icy back roads of Alberta—south to Lethbridge, north to Fort McMurray, east to Lloydminster, west to Grande Prairie, with stops at dozens of places in between—the panel heard the unvarnished stories of hundreds of Albertans, and I learned a lot about fairness. Trained as a lawyer, I have a good sense of what's just, impartial and even-handed; what I relearned in these town halls is that what's "fair" lies in the eye of the beholder. The way we see the world frames our perception of not only what's beautiful, but what's fair. And what we perceive as fair can change. Designing a policy or strategy—for a nation or an individual enterprise—capable of responding to fairness expectations across a breadth of worldviews is a formidable objective and an essential undertaking.

WE AIM TO BE FAIR

Has your enterprise ever offered the assurance, "We aim to treat everyone fairly"? It's what my husband and I say to our three sons to this day; it's what my parents told me and my siblings when divvying up chores on the farm and, decades later, when drafting their wills. Of course you want to be fair, but it's a tall order when your enterprise has so many constituencies to take into account—employees, shareholders, debtholders, suppliers, contractors, customers and clients, partners, and the communities and countries where you operate—plus hundreds of advocacy campaigns aimed at delivering just and fair outcomes, like reining in CEO pay and enhancing pay equity, diversity, and women on boards.

Emerging accountability models more deliberately hold enterprise responsible to fairness expectations, and increasingly, they do this by correlating to environmental, social and governance (ESG) performance metrics. For example, Apple CEO Tim Cook negotiated an executive "bonus modifier" calculated on Apple's ESG metrics, not on corporate sales or profits. It remains to be seen whether this executive bonus calculation is fairer (and don't forget that Cook earns 256 times the median Apple employee's pay of roughly US$58,000).

In the same spirit, Canadian midstream energy company Enbridge set diversity and inclusion goals tied to management compensation. Enbridge also negotiated a $1 billion "sustainability-linked" credit facility aligning ESG performance to the cost of financing. But Enbridge's efforts to respond to evolving fairness expectations are unlikely to appease all critics. For example, the Stop the Money Pipeline movement lobbies banks, asset managers, insurance companies and institutional investors to stop funding, insuring and investing in hydrocarbon companies, no matter the ESG metrics.

ESG categories are not fixed, but to give you a sense of what can be included, here are the issue buckets: Environmental issues can include pollution, climate change, water and energy use, waste management, single-use plastics, land use and ecological sensitivity. Social issues can include employee relations, diversity and equality, health and safety, product safety, human rights, digital rights, skills for the future and trust. And governance issues frequently encompass matters like board oversight of risks, engagement and stakeholder rights, transparency, ethics and executive compensation. While Apple and Enbridge are large public companies, it's fair to say that ESG and fairness are not just big company issues; the metrics trickle down to smaller players along a supply chain, and private companies and NGOs likewise need to pay attention to their reputation, attract talent and access capital.

People often ask: "How is ESG performance different than corporate social responsibility (CSR)?" Proponents of ESG will tell you the only issues that matter to investors are those with financial materiality, and that the aim is to preserve enterprise "value." CSR performance, by contrast, can include a wider set of stakeholder issues, which are often depicted in expansive sustainability reports using the language of "values." Many CSR checklists have been generated over the last two decades independently (by a range of industry associations, stock exchanges, advocacy organizations) or collaboratively across sectors. For example, the World Economic Forum International Business Council proposes common metrics, breaking the issues down into four buckets: governance, planet, people and prosperity. The fourth category, prosperity, includes aims like wealth creation and employment (including net number of jobs created, net economic contribution and net investment); innovation in better products and services (including R&D spend ratios); and community and social vitality (including community investment and country-by-country tax reporting).

What's important to note is that CSR issues, even if largely values-based, can also be financially material (or capable of becoming so), impacting an enterprise's ability to attract talent, its social licence to operate in communities, its reputation with customers and consumers, and its access to and cost of capital. The lines between CSR and ESG are blurring; in my opinion, ESG isn't an entirely new dance, it's a variation on a theme. And materiality isn't a fixed state for either approach. Stakeholder expectations evolve, and sometimes very rapidly. Just ask fashion brands Nike, Adidas, H&M and Tommy Hilfiger, all of which are facing boycotts in China as Beijing pushes back against allegations of human rights abuses harming the country's Uighur Muslim minority; or Georgia-based businesses Coca-Cola, Delta Airlines and General Motors, which are being criticized by activists of "low-key betrayal" for not taking a harder stance against new voting laws in that American state.

The Enterprise Onion is a tool that enterprise rebuilders and new builders can use to gauge the fairness expectations of stakeholders. Build out from the core of the enterprise—starting with the internal team and working your way out, layer by layer, to the outside edge of the onion—focusing on the question of fairness. You are encouraged to sketch your own Enterprise Onion using the models shared in the user guide that accompanies this tool in the Appendix.

Begin with your enterprise's internal team—employees, contractors, shareholders, owners and directors. And remember, individuals on the team will have different ways of thinking and you are wise to encourage that diversity! Notice how these internal players interpret what's fair in your enterprise, and think about the ways their sense of fairness corresponds to overall enterprise values and actions. Ask yourself, for example, how do employees and the management team navigate the "fairness" of widening differentials in compensation and benefits between labour and senior leadership, or between employees and contractors? If your enterprise operates most comfortably in compliance modes (at level +1 or +2 on *A Measure of Integrity*), how do internal stakeholders navigate growing pressure for "beyond compliance" diversity quotas when this strategy is encouraged as a fair way to provide opportunity for those historically denied access to opportunity?

Think about "fairness" as an overlay to your entire enterprise infrastructure. Where does the alignment feel strong between "what's fair" (from the perspective of your internal team) and your organizational values and actions? And where is your enterprise exposed? Your non-profit may, for example, have experienced a nerve-rattling year of financial uncertainty, warranting payment of a contractually contemplated bonus to the hard-working executive director. Yet, there are serious reputation and talent management downsides to this decision if payment of a bonus to the leader and not the rest of the team is perceived as being "unfair" to equally deserving employees.

Once you have a sense of how your internal team incorporates "fairness" thinking into your organization's decision-making, priority-setting and operations, shift your focus to external stakeholders. As *The Enterprise Onion* model recommends, begin with the like-minded, including your suppliers and partners. What happens, for instance, when your just-in-time supply chain hits a log-jam and suppliers cut off your enterprise's allocation of toilet paper, computer chips, timber roof trusses—whatever—while your larger competitors continue to get unconstrained access to much-needed supplies? That strategy may seem defensible to your suppliers, but the impacts to smaller enterprise, including your organization, feel unfair.

As you move out into further layers of *The Enterprise Onion,* expect to encounter more and more of these dilemmas, created as a result of different perceptions and interpretations of fairness. One of the more persistent, and sometimes egregious, quandaries faced by corporate, government and even non-profit organizations that happen to be in the public eye is the heavy weight of accountability, while their counterparts operating in more private space get away with non-compliance and even bad behaviour. Former CEO of Talisman Jim Buckee often lamented the unfairness of this dual standard when critics aggressively attacked the practices of his organization, a Western oil company operating in Sudan, but would decline comment on the far less responsible and sometimes reckless practices of Talisman's competitors in that same country.

As I was reminded when participating in the Fair Deal Panel's listening tour across Alberta, what's fair can be a subjective metric. This subjectivity is what makes it so difficult to figure out what fairness means for your enterprise. Where there are gaps in what is perceived as fair—between leaders, the board of directors and the rest of your organization—stakeholders inside and outside your enterprise will be confused. When Air Canada's senior leadership team and board of directors paid bonuses to senior corporate executives in the midst of a pandemic, while rank-and-file workers were laid off and government bailouts were being paid to the airline, there was a visceral and immediate reaction from the federal government, Air Canada customers and members of the public, on the grounds that these bonuses were patently unfair.

This all begs the question as to why some organizations, leaders and stewards (boards of governors) are so out of touch with the reality of how their decisions will be perceived. Double standards and the concept of entitlement are huge issues and underlying currents in questions of fairness. To ensure that values are aligned across your organization, use your business tools: *A Measure of Integrity* is designed to help you gauge internal stakeholders' practical interpretation of your organization's core values; the tool will point to the gaps. And pull out *The Enterprise Onion*, frequently, to ask questions about how enterprise decisions are likely to be perceived by internal and external stakeholders, ahead of a decision being made rather than after the fact.

Over the years, I've seen fairness rationalized by executive leadership teams at nearly every rung of *A Measure of Integrity*. For example, shareholders, owners and other profit-takers in a company insisting they are paying "their fair share" of taxes, strictly complying with the laws but doing no more than is legislated. Even at negative rungs of *A Measure of Integrity*, perceptions of fairness can underlie situational non-compliance with laws and rules. For example, the rationale that ignoring a privacy violation is okay if it's to right a wrong or to achieve perceived fairness. And the thinking that, if others fail to comply with a law or rule, we won't put our company at an unfair disadvantage by complying. It is a standard defence in embezzlement cases for disgruntled employees to rationalize their criminal actions on the basis of feeling unfairly treated relative to others.

In the role of a board member on corporate and non-profit boards of directors, I often frame my questions using the language of fairness: How can we rationalize wage freezes for workers and bonuses for management; how will this choice be perceived by our stakeholders?

Should we be paying our front-line workers a "hero pay" supplement during the COVID-19 pandemic, in lieu of paying dividends to shareholders? Gig workers don't have access to sick days or holiday pay; is that fair when they are doing the same work as employees? The company is offering stock options to directors, possibly rewarding short-term thinking; this feels unfair and doesn't encourage sustainability. How can we ensure that conflicts of interest (and perceived conflicts of interest) are avoided? Is it fair to use government bailout dollars to add to our corporate surpluses? How do we consult with patients about their perceptions of equitable access to health care? Do people in a particular community believe our new policy is fair? Is our human resources policy fair to retired employees? Is our decision to assume such large debt fair to future generations? Is this policy equitable; does it exploit any constituency? Who is at risk of being left behind?

Not all dinosaurs want to dance, and you should expect pushback from some people when you pose these questions. But it's essential that these fairness issues be put on the table, at minimum, to put colleagues on notice of their accountabilities and the need to adapt to the changing environment.

Stakeholders' expectations for fairness deliverables will be unique to individual enterprises and will even vary between the different communities and constituencies they serve; there is no one-size-fits-all standard. How does your enterprise engage on issues where fairness is at stake; with the like-minded, the open-minded, the skeptical and your critics? How do you assure stakeholders that no interests have been unfairly disregarded, and navigate competing perceptions of fairness (for example, shareholders comfortable with short-term value extraction versus stakeholders who want to see value creation)?

"Fairness" as an outcome can be easily misconstrued and perhaps there is clearer language to explain this value: equitable, equal, impartial, even-handed. I've agonized over this question and have concluded that none of these words comprehensively captures the notion of fairness. It may require time to distill the full meaning of fairness. "Sustainability" was an aim that many argued could not be operationally defined, yet after decades of trying, we now have widely understood metrics.

Regardless of these flaws in the precise definition of "fair," your enterprise needs values and processes you can point to that demonstrate how your organization's decisions will deliver a fair deal to all. Vague statements—for example, regulators promising "to level the playing field" or educators and health care providers offering up "fair access" to services—don't suffice. Real accountability is only possible when a company, government or non-profit takes the time to explain the fairness rationale and the values underlying its decision-making, and demonstrates how it walks its talk. For example, if a lending enterprise promises non-discriminatory access to credit, stakeholders are more likely to endorse their practices as fair if lending statistics and processes for reviewing credit risk across a spectrum of demographics are transparently disclosed. Don't expect any stakeholder to be enthusiastic about your enterprise's vague promise to be fair.

Personal Leadership Element: Decision-Making

Making the optimal decision is foundational to leadership. As the pace and complexity of organizational life increases, so do the demands on leaders to make great choices. Making critical decisions reflecting values, in real time, with minimal data points in often paradoxical situations is the hallmark of a great leader.

AN ALGORITHM FOR FAIRNESS

The COVID-19 pandemic exposed and exacerbated pre-existing fairness gaps, including the wide chasm between enterprises stuck in the twentieth-century analogue world and those able to transition to twenty-first century digital. With people requiring access to broadband for education, work and leisure during lockdown, constraints on citizens' ability to log into affordable high-speed internet put pressure on politicians and business. Is there an algorithm for fairness? Elon Musk's solution—to send thousands of satellites to space and bring low-latency high-speed internet to every corner of the world—may point the way.

Personal Leadership Element: Imagining

Imagining is exploring new thinking about what is possible and beyond the norm. It requires giving up a seat in the knowable world. The spark can be maverick or childlike as one reaches for the ultimate "what ifs."

Google is the world's dominant online search-engine enterprise, now used by billions of people across the planet and accounting for about 90 percent of all search-engine traffic worldwide. Google knows where you are, who you are with and what you are doing. When Google went public in 2004, its corporate tagline was "Don't be evil"; by 2018, the company had substituted this punchy promise with a more pedestrian commitment to "ethical business conduct." At the same time, Google's own researchers were demanding the company abandon involvement in a controversial Pentagon artificial intelligence program called Project Maven (intended to improve the accuracy of drone strikes in a battlefield); and Google's ambitions in China with Project Dragonfly likewise alarmed Google employees who didn't want to be complicit in censorship. Fast-forward to 2020, and a union campaign was underway at Google. Unions aren't the norm in Silicon Valley and there had never been a union at Google, but now there are Google workers who are card-carrying members of the Communications Workers of America.

What happened? A company launched with the aspiration of doing no evil theoretically aligns with the "do no harm" values at level +4 of *A Measure of Integrity*. That aim, and Google's undertaking to forego short-term gains for the sake of innovation and public good, seemed sincere in 2004. Yet concerns raised by skeptics and critics over the past decade (the litany of allegations includes anti-competitive behaviour, dual standards, failure to protect privacy, and complicity in human rights abuses including surveillance) suggest Google operates in compliance mode. (To its credit, the company launched an initiative called Machine Learning Fairness to inject fairness into its approach; to stop, among other things, political bias in artificial intelligence.) For a leading digital enterprise dependent on attracting top talent to stay on top, failing to pay attention to the evolving expectations of employees and other key stakeholders has consequences.

CEOs of Big Tech are often described as modern-day robber barons, and people expect these powerful companies to use their market power constructively. Tim Berners-Lee, creator of the World Wide Web, is of the opinion that Google (and other tech giants) have used their access to vast troves of data to become surveillance platforms and gatekeepers of innovation. Berners-Lee believes it would be fairer to give individuals greater control of their own data—what he calls "personal data sovereignty" (even beyond their rights to preserve privacy)—and he's founded an open-source software company named Inrupt to test these ideas.

Digital companies in general are being pushed to be more transparent and more accountable, to explain how they protect individual privacy and how they apply censorship rules fairly. More and more, these companies control communications channels, private and public, including our news and commerce pathways. Given this level of domination by a sector, is it not fair that these companies bear more responsibility for ensuring equitable practices? Indeed, is it so difficult to imagine a world where antitrust legislation can be revived and people are put first; a world where tech serves us and not the other way around?

FAIR COMPETITION

The pandemic tilted the retail landscape from bricks-and-mortar to digital. But long before that, competitors were bemoaning "the Amazon Effect": Amazon's nearly magical ability to deliver on consumer demands in record time. Want the latest best-seller? Order through Amazon Prime and, abracadabra, it's at your doorstep the next day. Ever growing, Amazon purchased Whole Foods to jumpstart its place in the online grocery queue. The company is also gobbling up pharmaceuticals and shipping infrastructure. Shopify, a made-in-Canada company that helps retailers set up online, is being eyed as a takeover target by Amazon. (To give you a sense of the potential worth of these online markets, in early 2021, Shopify was valued at over $200 billion and traded at 817 times earnings despite never having paid dividends to shareholders.) Are the prices charged by Amazon "just?" Is Amazon's share of the online marketplace "fair?"

In 2017, Amazon's market share of the U.S. e-commerce retail market was 37 percent; that percentage is projected to be 50 percent in 2021. It is revealing to compare these stats to the market share of other, more traditional, companies established well before the launch of online business; for example, Procter & Gamble, the biggest consumer goods company in the world. We're all familiar with P&G's products—Tide, Mr. Clean, Pampers and Charmin toilet paper being among them—and in spite of its size and global reach, rough numbers for P&G's market share in key categories (fabric and home care at 11 percent; baby and family care at 35 percent; beauty care at 15 percent) don't touch Amazon's share of the much wider e-commerce retail business.

In his final letter to shareholders as CEO, Jeff Bezos reported: "More than 1.9 million small and medium-sized businesses sell in our store, and they make up close to 60% of our retail sales." Bezos makes no apology for creating such vast wealth for shareholders ($1.6 trillion, to be exact) and is proud of Amazon's ability to generate value for customers, through lower prices, vast selection, fast delivery and, most of all, by saving people time.

Shopify is stepping up to tell a different narrative and to dance a different dance. This for-profit company is distinguishing its merchants with the "Shopify Effect": rationalizing a difference between "consumerism" (no buyer loyalty and emphasis on price) and "shopping" (cultivating a meaningful relationship with a merchant who helps you find what you need). With "good" businesses, Shopify merchants are able to sustain healthy gross margins and support employees, their supply chain and local communities.

Amazon's culture of relentless efficiency has been challenged by antitrust agencies across the globe: European regulators charge

Amazon with violating competition law, and American legislative committees accuse the company of exerting monopoly power over sellers. Amazon's tactic of imposing unreasonable terms and conditions on vendors arguably goes beyond tough negotiating. For example, when Canadian smart-thermostat manufacturer ecobee declined to share data from its voice-enabled devices with Amazon, on the basis of privacy concerns, Amazon threatened to yank the manufacturer's access to their online retail platform. Amazon denies these claims of unfair competition, asserting "large companies are not dominant by definition," but at what point does hobbling vendors and gobbling up rivals become patently unfair?

While Amazon's competitors and vendors are wringing their hands, the company's employees are increasingly agitated. Delivery truck drivers can be expected to distribute up to three hundred packages a day on a ten-hour shift; spending time to find a bathroom isn't always an option, and there are many Reddit posts documenting the practice of drivers peeing in bottles and coffee cups in their vans. It's not just the drivers who are pissed. In 2020, Canadian Tim Bray, former VP at Amazon Web Services, quit the company and posted a personal blog explaining his reasons: "It's that Amazon treats the humans in the warehouses as fungible units of pick-and-pack potential . . . It [Amazon] has a corresponding lack of vision about the human costs of the relentless growth and accumulation of wealth and power." What snapped for Bray was the company's firing of whistle-blowing employees who lobbied for improved safety conditions.

Bray cites power imbalance as the root cause of unfairness between Amazon and its workers, and he offers up solutions: "If we don't like certain things Amazon is doing, we need to put legal guardrails in place to stop those things. We don't need to invent anything new; a combination of antitrust and living-wage and worker-empowerment legislation, rigorously enforced, offers a clear path forward." In effect, Bray is encouraging setting the compliance bar higher. Asking governments and regulators to stringently enforce rules can help to fix the problems exposed in Amazon's workplaces.

The company's corporate response to the 2020 firing of employees who spoke up to criticize working conditions reflects a compliance mindset: "We terminated these employees not for talking publicly about working conditions, safety or sustainability but, rather, for repeatedly violating internal policies." Generating fairer practices through negotiation with workers feels elusive in this situation, and unsuccessful appeals for unionization at Amazon's fulfillment centres risks deepening the divides. In his 2021 letter to shareholders, Bezos admits the company needs a better vision for employees' success and offers up a new promise: "We are going to be Earth's Best Employer and Earth's Safest Place to Work."

The world will be watching to see how Bezos and his team deliver on this bold promise. More meaningful engagement and consultation with employees would be a good place to start. But let's not stop there. Imagine what could be possible if Amazon was influenced *by its customers* to take the lead on finding solutions for recycling and reducing the use of single-use plastics and cardboard? Amazon certainly has the brainpower to tackle an environmental challenge of this magnitude, and with all its bubble wrap and cushy plastic envelopes and cardboard boxes, the company is a very big part of the problem. The company has phased out single-use plastic packaging at fifty fulfillment centres in India. Now what about the rest of the world?

ASYMMETRIC POWER

Asymmetric power has become standard operating procedure for many enterprises; it's inherent in the way that capitalism operates. Perhaps a rethink is in order, from a fairness perspective.

We've explored how asymmetric power challenges Amazon's employees and competitors, but that's just the tip of the iceberg. Entire regions and countries are being whacked. Take Canada, for example; a very large country with a relatively small population. How can Canadian enterprise (public and private sector) stand up to superpowers in the United States (by far Canada's biggest trading partner, with 75 percent of our exports heading south) and China (Canada's second most important trading partner)? Defenders of multilateralism champion global free trade, universal approaches and collaboration;

yet the recent emergence of vaccine nationalism (including, for example, efforts by the European Union to restrict exports of the COVID-19 vaccines produced in their countries) betrays true sentiment about who is the real judge of "fair" when domestic priorities come head-to-head with global collaboration. It's understandable to want to tend to one's own citizens first, before worrying about others, but the resulting inequities create suffering and disruption.

Perspectives on what's fair can shift quickly. This happens on a macro scale—with issues like vaccine nationalism and like-minded democracies figuring out how to out-compete China (for example, the Five Eyes intelligence alliance among Australia, Canada, New Zealand, the United Kingdom and the United States)—and it can happen on a more localized basis, in regions and communities and even within individual organizations.

It's easy to be an armchair critic and call out unfairness, but what can your enterprise do when fairness expectations are rapidly changing? Where there are deep divides between groups or constituencies, fiery rhetoric can stoke divisiveness; for example, populism or regionalism appeals to "ordinary people" who believe their interests are unfairly disregarded by elites or outsiders. Creating or exacerbating this kind of rift is a risk in culturally and regionally diverse countries, including Canada (and one I paid great heed to as a member of Alberta's Fair Deal Panel); it's a risk in cities like Portland, Oregon, where anti-racism protests have been unrelenting; and it's a risk in any individual organization when marginalized voices believe they aren't being heard and fear being left behind.

SETTING FAIRNESS METRICS

If your enterprise is committed to compliance levels on *A Measure of Integrity*, you are unlikely to voluntarily adopt fairness strategies that exceed legislated obligations. But nonetheless, to stay competitive and relevant you need to pay attention to shifting expectations and make sure your enterprise has a voice in policy-setting that impacts your organization; for example, changes in minimum wages, unionization rights, taxation policies, immigration strategies, automation and training, tariffs and buy-local campaigns or diversity mandates. Enterprise teams aiming for "beyond compliance" thresholds—and especially those targeting to create not just economic value but impacts at levels +5 and higher on *A Measure of Integrity*—are encouraged to be very intentional about fairness aims.

No enterprise can be all things to all stakeholders, so choose where your team can leverage the work of your enterprise, set clear fairness aims, and measure and report on your outcomes. If you are an enterprise delivering broadband internet services to customers in a region, explain how you will deliver affordable high-speed internet service to all. The "fair" strategy could involve new technology (using satellites, for example) or new business models (co-operatives or local community associations). If you want to improve diversity and inclusion, not just in your own organization but in your sector, your enterprise may choose to partner with others to launch a diversity initiative (for example, collaborating to get women or people of colour on boards). If you want to enhance fairness in a value chain, your organization may decide to initiate a public conversation on buy-local opportunities. If you promise to implement government policy to restore fairness—for example, clean drinking water and access to quality health care for First Nations communities living on reserves—then expect any platitudes, however well-intended, to generate cynicism if you don't walk your talk.

Setting the metrics for fairness, and accurately measuring fairness impacts (or any non-financial impact), can be a challenge. When you are reporting on financial indicators (for example, income and expenses, profit and losses, tax liabilities and write-offs), there are well-established and standardized accounting, tax and fiscal reporting practices in place that set clear expectations. In the last decade, improvements in reporting initiatives, codes and guidelines have evolved for non-financial indicators—championed by groups including GRI, SDG Impact, and Social Value International, to name but a few—to move enterprise reporting from anecdotal and subjective measures to more rigorous and objective standards. For example, while the use of storytelling to humanize the impacts of corporate, government or non-profit investment in youth sport can be inspiring and demonstrate alignment to enterprise values, organizations are also encouraged to measure and report on tangible results, including changes in the number and nature of the young people in that community participating in sport as a consequence of this investment.

Measuring and reporting on non-financial impacts was once the mainstay of non-profits; today, every enterprise is expected to measure and report on these qualitative and quantitative metrics. It's not difficult to measure the number of students you educate in a scholarship program or the number of people your non-profit shelters and feeds after a natural disaster. More challenging is assessing your enterprise's singular impact on finding fairer solutions to corruption or injustice or homelessness, especially when several sectors are involved. When I was leading the design and implementation of the Yemen Scholarship Program for Nexen, we understood that our aim was to improve the communities where we operated by creating merit-based scholarships and educating locals. The outcome we didn't anticipate was raising the bar on education access across the country of Yemen.

Presently, reporting on non-financial indicators is largely voluntary and individual enterprises decide what, how and when to report. But this is all changing as pressure from securities exchanges, shareholders, advocates and society in general is influencing what's required. There's a balance to strike here between what stakeholders really want to see reported about your organization and what you can realistically measure and report on. There has been considerable progress on harmonizing the ways in which social, environmental, governance and other non-financial impacts are measured and reported on, but uniformity is elusive; therefore, the ability of stakeholders to compare performance across organizations is far from perfect.

If you look up the reporting on non-financial performance indicators by competing airlines Air Canada and Southwest Airlines, for example, you will see that both carriers talk about people, planet and business/performance. Yet, their reporting styles and what's measured are very different: Air Canada separates the issues into socio-economic development, innovation, diversity and inclusion, climate action and waste management buckets; while Southwest talks of culture, diversity and inclusion, and charitable activity. Even in cases where the same reporting guidelines are applied by competitors, you can't assume that comparability will be easy. It's also worth noting that one faltering step can diminish or wipe out that ledger of positive impacts. The fact that Air Canada paid bonuses to senior management during the pandemic—all the while cashing government COVID-relief cheques—ignited customer outrage, with many declaring they were never flying with the airline again, notwithstanding that Air Canada reversed its unwise decision. This is what cancel culture looks like.

When you think about how your organization chooses to measure and report on its alignment to values and performance on non-financial measures (including "fairness" impacts), ask yourself, who is our target audience? In for-profit corporations, the focus has historically been on the shareholders or owners. In government enterprise, there is pressure to appeal to taxpayers and voters. And in non-profit organizations, reporting on outcomes is sometimes tailored to what funders and donors would like to see.

But while shareholders, owners, funders and taxpayers are all critical stakeholders of enterprise, they are not the only groups that should be contemplated in designing your metrics and reporting strategy. Supporters of cultural and arts institutions (including museums, libraries, public galleries and performing arts centres) aren't looking for these organizations to earn profits, but they do expect to see reporting on financial sustainability (and assurances that money is spent wisely). Most stakeholders also want a deeper understanding of how funds raised and dollars spent actually support the artistic and cultural communities the institutions are designed to serve. Value for money matters, whatever the organization or sector. If you want to deliver that message to stakeholders, have your CFO deliver the impact reporting.

Designing ways to account for non-financial impacts requires rigour, consistency, transparency and, often, creativity. For example, Unilever's Knorr brand is leading the way in sustainable agriculture, collaborating with stakeholders to codify gold-star metrics for agricultural producers along that company's supply chain (measurables include working conditions, biodiversity, water and fertilizer usage, soil quality and animal welfare). Highest-performing farmers are granted landmark farm status.

Considerable effort is being made by enterprise leaders seeking to commit their organizations to be carbon neutral by 2030 or 2040, a decade or two ahead of the Paris Agreement's goal of net-zero carbon emissions by 2050. The question for stakeholders is, how will this carbon-neutral pledge be credibly measured and transparently reported on by these organizations? Work is also being focused on ways to responsibly and credibly track and report on these pledges. One such initiative, The Climate Pledge, has been championed by Amazon and Global Optimism and invites organizations to commit to reaching the Paris Agreement net-zero carbon emission threshold by 2040. Signatories to the pledge agree to measure and report on greenhouse gas emissions on a regular basis; to implement decarbonization strategies in line with the Paris Agreement; and to neutralize any remaining emissions with additional, quantifiable, real, permanent and socially beneficial offsets.

The number of companies making these pledges is gaining momentum: consumer goods giant Unilever undertakes to be carbon neutral by 2039; Microsoft has committed to be carbon negative by 2030; Starbucks says it will be "resource positive" within a decade; JetBlue aims to make its domestic flights carbon neutral; Heathrow Airport in London pledges to be carbon neutral in its operations (excluding emissions from flights) by 2030. One question being asked: What happens if companies fail to meet these very ambitious net-zero emissions pledges? Legally trained people worry about legal liability, some people worry about reputations, and most people worry about the planet.

Not surprisingly, traditional oil and gas companies (the classic energy dinosaurs) are exposed to unrelenting advocacy from environmental critics, plus close scrutiny by their own shareholders, to figure out credible ways to demonstrate their commitments to emissions reduction. ExxonMobil, for example, has committed to reduce the intensity of greenhouse gas emissions by 15–20 percent by 2025 (compared to 2016 levels), supported by a 40–50 percent decrease in methane intensity and a 35–45 percent decrease in flaring intensity across global operations. Valid and probing questions are being asked about how these commitments will be measured and reported, in ways that will be trusted by stakeholders and that allow for fair comparisons across companies and sectors. People want access to trusted data so they can differentiate between the dinosaurs who are willing to learn to dance and those who refuse to change.

Proponents of ESG underscore the imperative for connections to be made between environmental, social and governance impacts and financial materiality. That should result in a high prioritization of what is measured and reported on by organizations. It's all a bit unclear right now and many public companies continue to report on financial indicators and non-financial indicators, in multiple reports citing hundreds of qualitative and quantitative metrics. Management teams assign vast resources to the assembly of these reports, preparing binders upon binders of materials tailored for boards of directors and advocacy groups and other stakeholders.

Do your enterprise a favour: Figure out what people really want and need to see measured and reported on, and then streamline the process. Be more creative in the design of tools. Maybe an app with a portal for your key stakeholders to access, and a dashboard to track performance, is easier to navigate for internal and external players. More paper isn't the fix here; it's distracting. The aim is making relevant information as accessible and transparent as possible to your key stakeholders and communities because open and transparent reporting and communication are critical to their perception of fairness.

A FAIRNESS RESET

The COVID-19 pandemic disrupted the status quo and reset expectations for fairness in many areas: compensation, safe working conditions, competition, inclusion and diversity, privacy, access to technology—and a litany of other significant issues. There will be no going back from digital; are there other transitions made by your enterprise that are likely to become permanent?

If it was feasible to accommodate working parents with unpredictable childcare demands during the pandemic, why not in the new normal? Perhaps your enterprise is transitioning gig workers to employee status. Will employees who enjoyed working from home during the pandemic want to come back to the office? Siemens is one of the largest companies in the world with over 380,000 employees. In July 2020, the CEO of this Fortune 500 company announced a new policy that would allow employees to work from anywhere they feel comfortable "for an average of two to three days a week." In its public statements, Siemens commits to a corporate culture that focuses on outcomes rather than clocked time at the office. That dinosaur is dancing!

During the pandemic, the rebuilding of less-tangible social infrastructure came in many shapes and sizes, and initiatives led by non-profits and ordinary citizens were, by necessity, dynamic and collaborative. When government or business failed them, ordinary people stepped up. Parents of school-age children collaborated to home-school their kids. Extended families offered child care to working parents and delivered groceries to house-bound seniors. Non-profit agencies capable of diffusing the risks of domestic violence, opioid abuse and suicide scaled up. Citizens cheered on nurses and doctors and other front-line workers.

This groundswell of support was heartening at a time of crisis; but, longer term, what is needed to remediate this scale of economic chaos and social disruption? Business and social agencies and billionaire philanthropists will play key roles, but governments must lead the way in this rebuilding effort.

Economically stagnant communities all want the same new businesses to set up shop in their hometown: blockchain, autonomous technology, robotics, artificial intelligence, wireless, biometrics and renewable resource technology. Yet competing with other communities or regions using public dollars (for example, tax holidays and incentives) can feel like a race to the bottom; fresh thinking is desperately needed. There isn't a surefire method for reviving struggling companies or communities suffering from industrial decline and economic transition, especially after the loss of a dominant employer or industry (for example, the Rust Belt in America, regions in northern England and southern Italy, and oil-producing communities in North America). Innovative new approaches are needed to rebuild in an equitable, sustainable way; continuing with business as usual is unlikely to deliver the required outcomes.

Personal Leadership Element: Catalyzing

Catalyzing is purposeful disruption of the status quo to provoke fresh momentum or a new direction. It is about recognizing the right time, accepting the lack of control and reading the feedback in what happens. Catalyzing takes courage; the courage to act when the outcome may not be clear.

The U.S. state of Nevada is contemplating the launch of "innovation zones" to attract technology firms. It's hardly a new idea, but their vision extends to granting businesses the same authority as local counties, including the ability to impose taxes, form school districts and courts, and provide government services. This all feels a bit back to the future, akin to the approach taken by The Hershey Company during the Great Depression in the 1930s. The company strategically kept employees on payroll by having them create their own model town, called Hershey Town, and the town itself ultimately became a tourist destination. In the midst of severe economic hardship, The Hershey Company did not lay off a single employee.

Finding that sweet spot going forward, one that is workable in the times we are in, will not be easy. In the twenty-first century, the idea of a company town in effect becoming a substitute for government is unlikely to gain traction. Enterprise playbooks from the 1930s and 1980s may contain helpful clues (for example, "too big to fail" is no longer a legitimate reason to protect a big bank), but they do not contain the answers. The work ahead—to reset after a pandemic that has asymmetrically affected populations and to respond to the expectations of social and environmental movements that were gaining momentum well before the novel coronavirus landed on the doors of enterprise—will require innovation and the space to test new ideas that are capable of recalibrating fairness.

Every type of enterprise will need to do things differently: governments, for-profit companies, even the most well-intended non-profits. For example, arts and cultural organizations will be expected to engage wider audiences (including those in smaller centres and rural areas) with upgraded digital platforms, accessible ticketing, live-streamed content, even virtual and augmented reality programming and exhibitions. Most people don't own a virtual reality headset, but lots of people own a smartphone, which means there are enormous opportunities to bring content into people's homes affordably. There is a plethora of different ideas being tested, including: Sweden's Moderna Museet's launch of "Sofa Tours" and in America, the Smithsonian museums' online exhibitions and the Cincinnati Zoo's "Home Safaris."

The Canada Council for the Arts is asking the arts sector across Canada to challenge "the choice of competition over collaboration, fragmentation over resource-sharing, and growth at all costs over sustainable development," acknowledging that to achieve these aims, the sector must innovate. Observing that some business models in the arts have reached their limits, the Council rightly cites not just creativity, but innovation, as the key to sustainable development in the arts. Innovating, in any sector, will require fresh approaches, with fairness top of mind. For example, who owns the intellectual property rights associated with art created in the digital realm, and how are costs of production shared? How much of a premium should cultural and arts audiences pay for live experiences versus digital? How can more insular and elitist institutions be given a breath of fresh air through engagement with a wider and more diverse virtual audience?

Issues of fairness are now top of mind for many; wealth inequality, inequitable treatment and discrimination rank at the top of many public opinion polls (alongside environmental and climate change challenges). In the midst of the COVID-19 pandemic, it's remarkable that people were more concerned with the rich getting richer and exacerbation of the have–have not divides than with health care and the economy. Public demands for a just transition from business as usual to a better, fairer future—from the pandemic to a new, healthy normal; from the fossil fuel economy to low-carbon energy; from unfettered global competition to inclusive growth; and through a myriad of other changes—will continue to evolve. Old bromides about "high tides raising all boats" will not appease. To avoid extinction, the dinosaurs will need to learn to dance.

Pay attention to the narratives about fairness; they may sound warm and fuzzy to you or feel like inconvenient demands on your business, but they are gaining momentum and evolving quickly, and your organization doesn't want to be caught out. Let me share just a few examples of the many stories bubbling up, framed in the language of what's fair:

- In the transition to a carbon-reduced economy, skeptics push back against net-zero emission targets for Western-based oil and gas companies on the grounds that state-directed petroleum producers in places like Saudi Arabia or Russia are not similarly motivated and that differentials in expectations unfairly place Western companies at a disadvantage.

- Buy-local programs and protectionist tariffs on imports are gaining momentum as a way to safeguard local workers' rights and push back against the inherent unfairness of laissez-faire globalization.

- And the income inequality narrative that is gaining traction goes like this: For the first time in our lifetime, kids aren't doing as well as their parents were at the same age, and this is triggering shame and rage as the rich get richer. Younger people depend on earning wages (which aren't rising) yet lost jobs during the pandemic; older, rich people own stocks and real estate and didn't suffer financially as a result of the pandemic.

It will serve your enterprise well to consider how you deliver a fair deal to your key stakeholders. The ESG approach is the latest in a series of strategies to better define enterprise values and translate impacts into measurable and transparent metrics. But to truly rebuild enterprise in ways that can deliver resilience, innovation and impactful models of sustainable growth, you will need to go beyond the usual CSR- or ESG-prescribed templates.

We are on a new journey of discovery in a post-pandemic world of social upheaval. No one can predict the future; we don't even know what enterprise will look like five years from now. But enterprises that choose to intentionally build the competencies required to walk their talk on organizational purpose and values, from the inside out, while paying close attention to evolving stakeholder expectations from the outside in, are more likely to be rewarded. That's a fair deal.

CHAPTER 5

RE-IMAGINE YOUR BUSINESS MODEL

Redesigning the business model used by your enterprise is a strategic opportunity that is often overlooked, but this exercise is critical to enhancing your organization's ability to deliver value to more stakeholders and thus remain more relevant and sustainable than under any pre-existing model. Re-imagining your business model may even be the key to your organization's survival. Building or rebuilding for a better future requires re-inventing how you do business, how you make decisions and how you serve a broader range of stakeholders. Most enterprise leaders understand the merits of evaluating new product lines or pursuing competitive opportunities; what I'm inviting you to do is to re-imagine your business model with the same rigour and sense of possibility.

Ask yourself some critical questions about your business model: Who is making the decisions that impact your enterprise? How do you integrate ideas from stakeholders outside your core team? Who really has skin in your game? Are there ways to redesign your business model to increase the number and influence of stakeholders who have a vested interest in your enterprise's long-term success? Are there ways to re-imagine your business model to create better alignment of interests and improve the likelihood for everyone to pull in the same direction?

QUALITY DECISION-MAKING

A useful place to start is to ask yourself: Who is *really* making the decisions that impact our enterprise, and how are those decisions made? These seem like obvious questions, but often the answers are not. Even as a young girl, I recall leaning back at the kitchen table when a critical choice about the family farm was being debated, to ask myself: Who is *really* making the decision here? Our family was unequivocally patriarchal—it was my grandfather's and father's name on the barn—yet I witnessed how effectively my gentle mother used her influence and how my father, the official decision-maker, factored her astute perspective into decisions made. Curiosity about this same question landed me in law school and, decades later, into politics.

My conclusions? First, there is a quality to successful decision-making that can be elusive, but we recognize it when we see it: a decision made having regard for the views of and impacts to others is more likely to be fully implemented, while a decision made using the instrument of blunt authority is more likely to be begrudged and undermined. Second, making or influencing or blocking a decision that affects others is a choice, a responsibility and a precious power. And third, while it's more efficient to be the top-down decider and hold the formal authority, decisions today are powerfully influenced by people with legitimacy and informal or "soft" power. These distinctions are important for new builders and rebuilders to keep in mind as beyond-the-status-quo decisions are being made inside enterprise. New builders may not hold formal authority, but they can wield considerable influence in choices made.

In many organizations, authority, influence, persuasion, groupthink and coercion can all rear their heads when a critical decision needs to be made. If you hold formal authority in enterprise today, it's never been harder to use. Techniques to block the use of power are gaining traction, including protests, boycotts, vetoes, diversion tactics, interference, foot-dragging and vexatious litigation. Obviously, the concentration of power in the hands of a few dinosaurs isn't good; it's called tyranny. On the other end of the spectrum, overly diffused power can lead to chaos.

How can you redesign your enterprise's business model to give decision-makers in your organization enough power to be effective, but not too much? How can you intentionally make quality decisions informed by listening to external voices—even people and groups who don't always agree with you? How do you ensure that your decision-makers focus appropriate time and effort on the important decisions? It's also essential to ensure that critical decisions are made, and not avoided; a decision not made is nonetheless a decision.

Personal Leadership Element: Decision-Making

Making the optimal decision is foundational to leadership. As the pace and complexity of organizational life increase so do the demands on leaders to make great choices. Our organizations depend on it. Making critical decisions in real time with minimal data points, in often paradoxical situations, is the hallmark of a great leader.

There is much nuance for enterprise architects to consider. There are times when shared and participatory decision-making is wise; but to manage your enterprise from the inside out, some decisions must be made internally (for example, deciding on what level on *A Measure of Integrity* your enterprise aims to operate). It's another paradox to navigate: wielding authority and influence, at the same time. I once witnessed an éxceptional example of the integration of hard and soft power. It happened in front of me in an unlikely place, on the island of Socotra, Yemen, in a military dictatorship.

I was there as part of a capacity-building team with a Canadian non-profit organization, Canada Bridges. Others present included local leaders, the Yemeni Minister of Public Health and Population and the meeting host, a local sheik. Lots of villagers, men and women and children, were also observing. The military were told to put down their guns. The minister and the local sheik sat on a blanket, face to face. After pleasantries, the crisis to be resolved was tabled: How could this remote island improve the health of young mothers and their babies? The minister leaned in, listening intently, rarely speaking. The stories of girls being married as "child brides," their undeveloped bodies unable to bear babies safely, were heartbreaking.

The Minister of Public Health and Population had the power to unilaterally set health care policy, yet he chose to travel to Socotra and listen closely. The policy decisions that were subsequently made reflected local perspectives and included several strategies that may not have come to light without the influence of the islanders: better health care during pregnancy, and education on birth-control choices. Most critically, local faith leaders undertook to use their considerable influence to condemn personal decisions by local men to marry child brides, which got at the root cause of the crisis. It's fairly easy to see how this policy decision could have unfolded in different ways, with less inclusion, less sensitivity and potentially less uptake.

Decision-making requires an intentional weighing of different kinds of power. In a time of powerful, and growing, outside influencers (including social media), it's important to be acutely aware of who is wielding power and influence in your enterprise, who should be making decisions in what circumstances, and how to design your decision-making architecture to reflect those intentions.

In standard-issue business textbooks, questions about decision-making are often framed as "governance" issues, with emphasis on formal processes such as the role of a board of directors and advisors to provide oversight and direction, the need for clear processes for signing authorities and delegation of authority to deter unilateral actions, and rules to guide decision-making when your interests are in conflict. I am encouraging you to think even more broadly about decision-making, beyond who has formal authority and the legalities of governance.

While a CEO or chair of the board of directors may have legal authority to make a decision, the second question to ask is how that decision-making authority is exercised. What is the quality of that exercise of decision-making power? Is your board of directors a rubber stamp for the decisions made by senior management (a dereliction of their authority and responsibility)? Does your CEO incorporate the perspectives of the internal team and external perspectives in decisions made? If so, how are those viewpoints engaged, considered and reflected in decisions made? If the dinosaur refuses to dance, how do you call it out? And how are the decision-making process and outcomes communicated to stakeholders, within and outside the organization?

As part of your business model redesign, consider evaluating five to ten of the most important decisions your enterprise makes (including critical decisions the organization has recently made or is currently facing); who has formal authority to make those decisions; and ways to evaluate the quality of decisions made. *The Enterprise Onion* tool can make this discussion about the quality of decision-making more explicit and intentional. When critical decisions are being made, encourage or require formal decision-makers to explain their engagement with internal stakeholders and with external stakeholders, including the like-minded, the open-minded, the questioning and the cynical. Building sufficient trust and reciprocity should be part of the engagement process; only with that foundation are you positioned to ask stakeholders to support implementation of an enterprise decision.

WHO HAS SKIN IN THE GAME?

One way to gauge the robustness of your enterprise's decision-making architecture is to ask yourself: Who has skin in this game? You know what it means to have a genuine stake in an outcome, to be at risk of losing something if a venture goes sideways or gain something if there is success. Nassim Nicholas Taleb, the "black swan" guru, released a book in 2018 titled *Skin in the Game: Hidden Asymmetries in Daily Life*. Taleb's thesis? He believes that forcing people to assume skin in the game corrects the inequality between risk and reward better than thousands of laws and regulations. Paraphrasing Taleb: Sharing skin in the game corrects the asymmetry between people who accept risk and those who get rich without owning the risk. The latter guy, with no skin in the game, is "immune to the possibility of falling off his pedestal, exiting his income or wealth bracket, and waiting in line outside the soup kitchen." Good example? Those who walked away from the 2008 bank blow-ups without scars, and some even with hefty bonuses. The heavy weight of that financial crisis fell on the heads of individuals and businesses who didn't cause the problem, whereas a number of the culpable institutions were deemed "too big to fail" and were rescued.

Your enterprise's shareholders and employees have obvious skin in the game. There's an ages-old tussle between owners and workers about the fair allocation of risks and rewards between the two stakeholder groups (triggering questions during the pandemic about COVID-premiums for front-line workers versus distribution of dividends and profits). If your enterprise is one where there are no profits per se (a non-profit enterprise, for example), ask yourself: Who gets the "benefits" if we succeed, and who gets blamed for failures? Benefits can include goodwill, prestige, reputation bumps, recognition in a community, access to funding, opportunity for continued service or work, pensions and credibility.

What about your board of directors? If your enterprise fails, directors' reputations may be bruised, but unless they are found to be grossly negligent, they walk away relatively unscathed. For-profit companies can issue stock options to their board members as a way to attract the best and brightest, but some shareholders discourage the practice because it offers upside benefit without downside risk. ATCO, a private company founded in Alberta over seventy years ago by one of Alberta's early builders, Ron Southern, and recognized among Canada's most successful multi-generational family-run businesses, requires its board members to invest their own money in ATCO shares.

Getting the right balance between independence and having a stake in the enterprise can be tricky with directors. A board needs a unique and separate mindset to optimize decision-making—sufficient independence to speak up and ask questions that need to be asked, and even make unpopular decisions—as well as having a stake in the enterprise.

Do suppliers, consumers and clients, and the local communities where you operate, have a vested interest in your enterprise's success? Supply chains are undergoing dynamic change—global reach tightening and local reach expanding—so it's an important time to revisit your assumptions. Call centres outsourced a decade ago to cities like Bangalore and Manila are being relocated back to North America, for example, to new hubs emerging in places like Texas and the eastern Canadian province of Nova Scotia. Meantime, local enterprise, in small places like Canmore, Alberta, are expanding their reach.

Canmore is a mecca for winter athletes, mountain climbers and granola-types, and it's not surprising that Cameron Baty and Karina Birch would set up shop here to launch a non-toxic line of soap. It's a nice local story, and then the pandemic strikes and everyone needs soap! The company's owners were quick to realize that people would need hand sanitizer too, and in April 2020, the company added a naturally derived hand sanitizer to their roster of products. The hand sanitizer was Health Canada–approved, "guaranteed to be antibacterial and kill 99.9 percent of germs"; exactly what virus-phobic customers wanted to hear. Online sales shot up 700 percent as the physical doors to the stores temporarily closed. Rocky Mountain Soap Company products are sought after by customers across Canada, not simply because of their quality but because the products are made in Canada. For that community-based enterprise on the eastern slopes of the Rocky Mountains, customers across Canada now have "skin in their game."

What about gig workers? Maybe your enterprise assumes millennials and Gen Zers prefer no strings attached, but is this assumption correct? Hiring freelancers on as full-time employees could fire up their motivation and productivity. Walmart Inc., the world's largest private-sector employer, decided to convert two-thirds of its U.S. hourly store roles to full-time positions in 2021 as a way to retain and attract workers in a competitive environment. The company also raised its minimum hourly wage to $16 and is creating clear training pathways so workers can advance within the company. This may mean that a whole new group of stakeholders will feel they have more skin in the game; although some retail-market analysts suggest, more cynically, that these moves by Walmart are more about heading off the kind of unionization push seen at Amazon.

And what about those outside experts and advisors you deploy? When I worked as a third-party advisor to energy companies, not accountable for decisions they made, the only skin I had exposed was my own (personal reputation, income, sense of well-being). At times, it felt a bit mercenary walking away from clients' poor decisions, which were often made despite the advice I was offering.

Outside consulting is designed with a liability firewall, to ensure that the advice offered is objective; but there can be design fails. If your external expert starts to act like a corporate executive, even making enterprise decisions, that can spell disaster. Just ask McKinsey & Company, consultant to big enterprise around the world. McKinsey was retained as an external advisor to Purdue Pharma, manufacturer of OxyContin painkiller. In 2021, McKinsey paid $573 million to settle investigations into its role in accelerating opioid sales after OxyContin was found to have contributed to the deaths of more than 450,000 people over the past two decades. McKinsey advisors had told Purdue it could "band together" with other opioid makers to head off "strict treatment" by the U.S. Food and Drug Administration.

Ask yourself: What role are external consultants and other outside experts playing in your enterprise? Have you built up false confidence in an ecosystem of third-party-generated strategies, a plan for every eventuality, designed by hired experts? Outsourcing enterprise capability and knowledge creation capacity to third-party consultants may feel safe (no one ever gets fired for hiring McKinsey), but if you are foregoing opportunity for internal capacity-building—and if you are outsourcing decision-making on big questions, like strategic plans and key values—the wrong people are making your enterprise's decisions. Relinquishing decision-making to people with no real skin in the game is not a recommended enterprise design.

What do you do when people pretend to have skin in the game, but they are faking it? Too often, outsiders intervene to "help" locals; Nassim Nicholas Taleb talks of America's role in Iraq and Libya. Yemen comes to mind for me: Saudi Arabia and Iran coming to the rescue of Yemeni citizens, triggering a humanitarian crisis of epic proportion. Who really has skin exposed in these games of war? The local citizens.

And we don't have to go to the Middle East or North Africa to find lurid examples. How many Indigenous leaders have asked outsiders to stop intervening because they are making things worse? And truly, while I respect the vast majority of civil servants I've worked with, there are a few whose clinical attitudes to the human impacts of their policy recommendations jar me. The thought bubble sounds like this: "Yes, I'm an employee in this government office. But I'm the bureaucrat, conveniently separated from the consequences of my recommendations and decisions. Whatever happens, I survive. One more pensionable day."

Manipulating politics from afar is an age-old tactic emboldened by social media. The Greeks and Romans railed against it, yet the practice remains alive and well. Australians fear Chinese influence over their political actors; there is the drama of Russian interference in the U.S. election of President Trump; in Canada, we worry about foreign fingers in our regulatory decisions. Today, Canadians question outside influence in export pipeline projects; what happens when the issue is interference in fresh water rights or development of the Arctic? Armed with the awareness of what makes people tick, powerful outside influencers have the means, motivation and platforms to exploit the rights of legitimate interests, to flood echo chambers with their position and to push citizens in one direction or another on an issue. Vote for Trump. Support unconstrained investment by China. Stop building pipelines. Yet the outside influencers have no genuine skin in the game.

And then there are issues where all of us are invested, whether or not we accept the assumption. Climate change champions tell us we all have skin in the game of protecting Mother Earth; that's hard to deny because carbon emissions and pollution do not recognize man-made or economic borders. And the COVID-19 virus, with all its virulent mutations, demonstrates that every one of us is exposed in a pandemic.

The Enterprise Onion is a tool you can deploy in the normal course of evaluating your enterprise's decision-making process, to assess and monitor not only who your stakeholders are, but how much stake and influence they have in your enterprise. As part of your routine stakeholder engagement, also ask yourself: Does this stakeholder or stakeholder group have skin in the game of our enterprise? If we succeed, how does this stakeholder share in that upside? If we fail, do they suffer any consequence?

To reiterate a point I'll make again and again, be deliberate in your engagement with external stakeholders. Design your operating and strategic processes to help you distinguish between stakeholders with skin in the game and those with no skin in the game of your enterprise. There are many stakeholders whose fates directly correlate to your enterprise—your employees, supply chain, partners, to name but a few. Engagement with these stakeholders is essential to generate more creative ideas and build rapport required for efficient and resilient implementation of enterprise strategies. You are encouraged to evaluate the merits of moving stakeholders to positions where they have more skin in the game, for example, by hiring contractors as employees or requiring board members to own shares in your company.

Equally, use *The Enterprise Onion* as a tool to keep tabs on stakeholders who pretend to have skin in the game but are faking it. Consider ways to change how decisions are made and how influence is exerted, to more positively benefit your enterprise. For example, if external experts are heavy-handed in their approach to guiding your organization's strategic choices, perhaps it's time to redefine their scope of work and role in your enterprise. And calling out stakeholders who have no skin in the game—including questioning their real motives—may be required from time to time. Make this use of *The Enterprise Onion* and its intentional approach to stakeholders a routine habit in your enterprise. Recognizing and thinking about stakeholder influence (both positive and negative) is like a dance routine that grows more elegant and powerful through use.

GAPS EXPOSED

During the pandemic, businesses, non-profits and government agencies had the rare opportunity to observe how their organizational model performed under pressure. How did your enterprise manifest core values (aims like do no harm, fairness or sustainability)? Could the organization be resilient and efficient at the same time? What gaps were exposed? Who led your enterprise through the pandemic, and how did they lead? How capably was the dinosaur able to dance a new dance?

When crisis strikes, it's human nature to access our corporate memory banks and the layers upon layers of accumulated history for guidance. But during the pandemic, past experience of enterprise rebuilders didn't offer safe passage and leaders were forced to figure out ways through the unknown and beyond; not erasing the past, but dislodging it a little to allow them to see something new. Pandemic or not, the crossroads at which enterprise finds itself now, with widespread pressure building from various social movements, necessitates this kind of self-examination and redetermination—of your purpose, values, internal structures and processes, and strategies for the way forward.

The pandemic presented some organizations fresh opportunity; for example, Rocky Mountain Soap Company was able to springboard from a local to a national stage. Other enterprises were constrained by the health crisis, including a highly efficient, super-sized American-owned meat-packing plant operated by Cargill in High River, Alberta. While provincially appointed regulators oversee food safety and worker safety in slaughter operations, owners of the meat-packing plants decide on the plant inputs (live cattle) and outputs (where the beef gets sold). American management pushed for "business as usual" during the pandemic, and if their plant workers were sick, whose problem was that? Many of the workers in this slaughterhouse are new immigrants to Canada; to make ends meet, plant workers and their extended families often live together in close quarters and cramped housing. Consequently, social distancing and isolation were next to impossible, and the risk of community COVID-19 spread was extremely high. The Cargill High River plant experienced some of the largest workplace outbreaks early in the pandemic, and that quickly became everyone's problem as the virus spread throughout the community and the dinosaur failed to dance.

The pandemic exposed a broader, longer-standing issue for Canadian business: over-reliance on American enterprise, infrastructure and markets. Re-localizing production and consumption, and rebuilding local and regional economies, is a wicked problem for government and business leaders to solve, and one that is easy to overlook when times are good. In 2004, Canada's Standing Senate Committee on Agriculture and Agri-Food was looking into bottlenecks in the Canadian meat-packing industry; then, American consumers were buying over 70 percent of Canada's exports of beef products and nearly all our exports of live cattle. Why was the Senate interested? Just days before Christmas in 2003, an Alberta-born cow residing in Washington State was discovered to have bovine spongiform encephalopathy (BSE, or mad cow disease). This single case meant that the U.S. border was closed to Canadian cattle. Senators listened to stories of ranchers losing their lifetime earnings, banks seizing cattle that farmers could no longer afford to feed, and breeding stock being lost. The senators also posed (and answered) a critical question: Why did one single case of BSE cause such havoc in the beef industry in Canada? Primarily because this industry, which generated more than $7.5 billion in farm cash receipts in 2002, was built on exports almost exclusively to one country.

The 8,891-kilometre-long border separating Canada and America is nearly invisible, until that border is shut down by a virus, a mad cow or a pipeline protest. Free trade with America has been good for Canada—we've enjoyed continuous prosperity for decades—but supply chains and our underlying assumptions about reciprocity with the United States have been rattled on many occasions. A nation's capacity to produce and distribute the necessities of life to citizens— produce, meat, medicines, vaccines, personal protective equipment, hand sanitizer—are now more meaningful than ever. "Buy America" isn't likely to wane, and we should expect leaders of most nations to focus on the most critical gaps in their own supply chains, including access to semiconductors, rare-earth metals, medical equipment and pharmaceuticals.

More than fifty years ago, Eric Newell launched Syncrude and the development of Alberta's vast oil sands. PanCanadian Energy Corporation gained access to the lucrative mineral rights granted to the Canadian Pacific Railway to become Canada's biggest independent producer of oil and gas, and Premier Peter Lougheed's provincial government drilled prolific gas reserves on federal lands in Alberta and created the Alberta Energy Company. Then, the aim was doing whatever it took to "secure Canada's energy future." But over the past two decades, Canadian enterprise has been obsessed with getting commodities to American markets and has taken for granted the value of energy security and food security to our own nation.

The pandemic reminds us of that goal, and the upside of this pandemic may be its ability to illuminate—even for a moment—the value of self-sufficiency. This doesn't require us to be inward-looking, insular or isolationist; economic sovereignty isn't the same as economic isolation. Canada does need other nations, and other nations need what Canada can provide. There's comfort in the fact that Canada can be self-sufficient in many things—in intellectual capital, food, energy, forestry products, even vaccines if we made that strategic choice. If needed, we have the means to take care of our own survival; we just need to dislodge our "business as usual" assumptions and design smarter ways to do enterprise. We can learn new dance routines.

Whether we are focusing on Canada or the economic self-sufficiency of any nation, the tectonic shift from a wide-open internationalist foreign policy to more isolationist thinking (consider Brexit, or the United States' approach to China) is reshaping what's possible for business and enterprise in general. In the agriculture sector, for example, this can include value-add opportunities to turn crops into marketable products, as is happening in the province of Saskatchewan with several multi-million-dollar canola crushing plants now being constructed to process canola into food and biofuel and thereby reduce reliance on sometimes-fickle export markets. The same can be done to add value to Canadian durum wheat, by processing the harvested yields here in Canada for export to Europe as flour, or even as shaped pasta, rather than as sacks of unprocessed grain. Relocating manufacturing jobs from sweatshops in the developing world to highly skilled and safer workshops here at home is also viable—and in the process, emissions from long-distance transportation would be reduced and jobs and tax dollars would remain in Canada (or the United States, or wherever home happens to be). But this strategy depends on the willingness of consumers to say no to cheaper imports and buy local instead.

Re-examining your business model and decision-making process-es with a critical eye can identify risks and gaps that need to be closed to safeguard the survival of your enterprise as well as identify previously unrecognized opportunities to rebuild for a better, more sustainable future.

Personal Leadership Element: Designing Action

Designing action is moving from the ethereal to the concrete, from the unseen to the seen. It is creating the intelligent plan and articulating that plan to others. It is strategy on the verge of tactics and leadership on the verge of management. Designing action is translating a felt sense of the future into getting there.

PULLING IN THE SAME DIRECTION

The Calgary Zoo is a cherished space for local families, and employees working there enjoy the zoo's hard-won status as Calgary's top tour-ist attraction. (It's worth noting: the zoo has a magnificent dinosaur collection that challenges old notions of what these massive creatures may have looked like.) When the zoo's leadership decided to pivot from its purpose as a local attraction to emphasize its role in wildlife conservation, it took time to direct employees' and visitors' attention to the conservation mission. To make sure everyone was pulling in the same direction, big decisions such as budget allocations had to be treated differently, and smaller decisions did too. Every piece of paper or information shared with visitors now explicitly references the conservation values, such that even the summer student flipping hamburgers at the snack kiosk feels galvanized in the zoo's purpose when the receipt he hands to the customer with the hamburger says, "Thank you for supporting wildlife conservation."

Building alignment in values and vision with your enterprise's key stakeholders—and improving capacity to collaborate on import-ant decisions, as well as to design and implement fresh ideas—can be achieved in many ways. One proven way to get everyone pulling in the same direction in an organization is employee ownership. The pandemic demonstrated the resilience of employee-owned companies; more jobs were retained in these organizations, and cutting salaries and hours happened at a slower pace. Often, we think small when we think of employee ownership models (for example, entrepreneurs or owner-operators), but an employee-owned company that stands tall in Alberta is PCL Construction, builder of big infrastructure such as bridges, petrochemical facilities and wastewater plants. PCL was founded in 1906 in Saskatchewan and then relocated to Alberta in 1932. The founders sold the company in 1977 to their twenty-five senior managers, and today this company with four thousand full-time staff and ten thousand hourly tradespeople is 100 percent employee-owned.

Incorporating employee ownership in an enterprise succession plan can be an effective succession and retention strategy: hand-pick your future leaders, mentor them carefully and intentionally, and create the conditions for everyone to pull in the same direction for the longer term through partial ownership or other vested interests. Banff Caribou Properties Ltd. is a hospitality and real estate company founded by Wim Pauw, who wanted to see the company stay locally rooted in Banff, Alberta. "We are at about 120 employee shareholders, out of a total workforce of about 600. I see this as a real success, particularly when you consider that we are in the service industry, and most of our workforce is young and entry-level," reports Gord Lozeman, president and CEO.

Personal Leadership Element: Developing Other Leaders
Developing other leaders is committing to the truth that leaders must beget leaders. It is holding oneself accountable for the success of one's direct reports. It is mentoring and coaching and supporting. It is leveraging one's experience by building leadership capacity in others—for the present, and for the future.

If your company's ambition is to generate positive social and environmental impacts (at level +5 and higher levels of *A Measure of Integrity*), you could follow the lead of companies like Patagonia and Danone and be certified as a "B Corporation" (shorthand for benefit corporations). B Corps, as they are known, are required to commit to explicit social or environmental missions, and they have a legal obligation to consider the interests of stakeholders (not just shareholders). Or, your organization could collaborate with others to design a "circular economy": redesigning a product's entire lifespan to be recyclable (for example, MUD Jeans leases jeans, rather than selling them, and recycles the jean fabric; Timberland partners with a tire manufacturer to use the rubber from tires to make soles for its footwear); designing zero-waste dining models to reduce food waste (for example, Too Good To Go connects restaurants and grocery stores with people who can purchase food that would otherwise go to waste); or selling your enterprise "waste" for other industrial purposes (for example, Vermilion Energy's Parentis operation in France uses waste heat to grow tomatoes via a geothermal system that allows greenhouses to be heated without carbon emissions).

One of Canada's better-known social entrepreneurs, Zita Cobb, launched a non-profit called Shorefast on Fogo Island, a remote community in Newfoundland detrimentally affected by the moratorium on cod fishing in that North Atlantic region. Shorefast built and operates the Fogo Island Inn as a community-owned asset, and profits from the business are re-invested in the community. The social venture aims to support the local economy and provide employment. Not surprisingly, Shorefast also champions the rebuilding of the Atlantic cod fisheries, the revival of a fish species that holds a mythic place in Newfoundland culture. Rather than succumbing to complacency, Cobb and her siblings saw a problem in their home community, then designed and implemented a solution based on critical insights and inputs from key stakeholders, including the local communities and businesses.

Personal Leadership Element: Adaptive Learning

Adaptive learning is real-time, continuous, lifelong learning. It is creating new maps in the middle of navigation. It is formal and informal; it must be sought; it requires humility. It closes the feedback loop by integrating experience gathered and lessons learned.

The co-operative model is an old idea that is experiencing a revival. A group of weavers and skilled tradesmen in Rochdale, England, are credited with pioneering the move toward co-operation in 1844, as a way to compete against the inferior-quality mass-produced goods that were a hallmark of the Industrial Revolution. Over the years, communities with shared needs have banded together and formally co-operated to create housing or purchasing or credit co-operatives or, informally, to set up community gardens and share meal preparation. I was familiar with agricultural co-ops in the rural community where I grew up, and when I moved to the city it seemed natural to me to purchase our family's groceries, gasoline and liquor at the Calgary Co-op. As one of that co-op's 440,000 members, it feels good knowing the enterprise is 100 percent Calgary-owned and operated.

The rural electrification and telephone co-operatives launched in the United States as far back as the 1930s, to bring reliable services to remote communities not served by mainstream enterprise, are now being restored to lay the fibre-optic cable needed to connect co-op members to the internet. Our family purchases outdoor sporting equipment—snowshoes, bike helmets, backpacks—at Mountain Equipment Co-op (MEC), a Vancouver-based retailer with stores across Canada. (Regrettably, MEC sold out in 2020 to an American private investment firm.) What's the difference between a co-operative and a typical retail enterprise? Maximizing profits isn't the primary goal of a co-op; the aim is building a sustainable enterprise and creating jobs, and in MEC's case, there was a strong environmental bent that was attractive for members.

What's worthwhile to keep in mind as you redesign the business model for your enterprise is that the processes and strategies that build alignment (in vision and values) with key stakeholders (employees or members of a co-operative, for example) will pay huge dividends. Keep *The Enterprise Onion* tool handy; it's a useful way to evaluate where your enterprise is pulling in the same direction with your stakeholders and where there are emerging or widening gaps in alignment of vision and values.

TAKING COLLABORATION TO A NEW LEVEL

Individual sectors use different language to describe their business models, but every organization is accountable to deliver something of value (for example, social impact, financial return on investment, goodwill or services to citizens). Rethinking your enterprise model—to be explicit about purpose and values, to shore up your capacity to pull in the same direction with key stakeholders, and to build for collaboration and not just competition—is as essential for non-profits and public-sector organizations as it is for the private sector.

In the aftermath of the COVID-19 pandemic, governments in many jurisdictions funded and initiated shovel-ready infrastructure projects to refurbish bridges and highways, build green public transportation and revive the economy. In Canada, the federal government began redistributing billions to communities across the country (provinces matched the investments), and local mayors and councils competed for the funding. What's the matter with spreading infrastructure dollars like a thin layer of peanut butter across an entire country? It's business as usual, for one thing, and the pandemic didn't really compromise our *infrastructure*; it was our health care, education system and seniors care that were brought to their knees. Imagine the potential if decision-makers opened up the space for dialogue about what communities really needed and invited those local perspectives and the possibility of more creative collaboration to the table.

Partnering across sectors to respond to an urgent need is not necessarily easy, but sometimes it is essential. During the pandemic, we saw business and government come together, very quickly, to test vaccines and roll out immunizations, nationwide. Everyone understood the shared imperative and made it work. Transforming other service delivery models in the future—for education, health care, energy, tech training and a myriad of other needs, even those less urgent—will arguably require hybrid models that don't fit neatly into traditional sector buckets.

What's the imperative for improvement in these business models for corporate, public and non-profit sectors, regardless of the pandemic? It's the public value of providing higher-quality products and services to more people, and with increased efficiency and resiliency. Rising to that challenge allows us to test what's possible, and now that we know there are better ways to deliver goods and services and provide public infrastructure, it would be a waste of resources and capacity to fail to set more ambitious stretch targets. Business as usual isn't maximizing the value of our corporate or public resources.

Personal Leadership Element: Collaborating

Collaborating is engaging a diverse range of people in order to enhance the possibility of traction and a better outcome. It brings together genuine curiosity and disparate or divergent points of view.

It's not uncommon today to find for-profit enterprise inside a non-profit agency. The Fogo Island Inn is designed this way, and at the Banff Centre, an arts and cultural organization, hotel and conferencing facilities provide income to help fund cultural and educational programs. Elsewhere, you can find non-profit advocacy organizations with for-profit consultancies (for example, the Pembina Institute, a Canadian non-profit think-tank focused on energy, also consults to industry players), and you can find for-profit companies with environmental and social missions (for example, out of Wim Pauw's for-profit enterprise came the Wim & Nancy Pauw Foundation to re-invest in the local communities).

There is a lot of room for creativity to happen when the edges of two or more sectors overlap; in nature, it's referred to as the "edge effect." In places of transition between two ecosystems, you find the greatest biodiversity and opportunity. This helps explain why a majority of marine species live near the shores and why more than 90 percent of Canadians live within 150 miles of the American border.

The lines between traditional sectors are blurring for enterprise of all kinds, and stakeholders can get comfortable with the ambiguity if the value ultimately delivered is enhanced and values are aligned. But there is also understandable wariness when responsibility for delivering public goods and services shifts from democratic institutions to the wealthy, with diminished transparency and accountability.

As explored in chapter two, philanthrocapitalism and other strategies deployed by the wealthy to harness the power of the market to deliver better charitable outcomes can evoke cynicism if the effect is to erode support for government spending on public services. It's even more offensive if the hidden aim is to line the pockets of crony capitalists! Key to making this kind of cross-pollination across sectors work is clear and transparent communication about shared values and expected outcomes. Understanding and trusting the motivations of all the actors is also an imperative; not an easy thing to achieve, but powerful and impactful when you find and leverage that sweet spot for the benefit of those you serve.

Most people are familiar with the concept of public-private partnerships (also known as P3s), formal partnerships between companies and government agencies that allow the public sector to shift certain risks and responsibilities to the private sector. When corporate access to capital is less expensive, it can make sense for a private company to design, build, finance and maybe even operate a public asset, for example, a highway, bridge or other large infrastructure. Highway 407 in Ontario and the Confederation Bridge connecting New Brunswick and Prince Edward Island are two Canadian examples of public-private partnering on large-scale projects. A P3 likewise makes sense when political risk on a project is material and the public sector is better able to manage those risks than the private sector, as is the case with the expansion of the Trans Mountain Pipeline that carries crude oil from northern Alberta to Vancouver, British Columbia.

Another innovative possibility is the creation of a trust or legacy fund to support future social, economic and environmental needs of a designated community. In Alberta, the government of Premier Peter Lougheed designed the Heritage Savings Trust Fund as a way to preserve some of the province's oil wealth for future generations of Albertans. This sovereign wealth trust concept was very successfully adopted by the State of Alaska and by the country of Norway. In the province of British Columbia, communities in the Columbia River Treaty directly affected by the construction of dams on that river, for hydroelectricity generation in the early 1960s, came together three decades later to negotiate a trust fund (the Columbia Basin Trust) with the Government of British Columbia. Income from the trust funds projects, designated by local residents, to support social, economic and environmental well-being in the Columbia Basin.

Personal Leadership Element: Catalyzing

Catalyzing is purposeful disruption of the status quo to provoke fresh momentum or a new direction. It is about recognizing the right time, accepting the lack of control, and reading the feedback. Catalyzing takes courage; the courage to act when the outcome may not be clear.

Although we tend to treat politics differently—and often, quite cynically—if the enterprise we are responsible for has partisan elements, we must do our best to treat it the same as any other enterprise. Be explicit about purpose and values, who you serve and to whom you are accountable. When I ran for election as a member of the provincial legislature in Alberta in 2012, our campaign team used *A Measure of Integrity* to talk through our shared values and how those values would guide our decisions, at a very early stage in the election process. This statement of values was posted on our website and taped to the walls of our campaign office:

> We live here and will continue doing so after the campaign; therefore, our conduct while campaigning should reflect the values of:
>
> 1. Community, as neighbours forging strong ties
>
> 2. Respect, for all ideas and opinions
>
> 3. Transparency, of associations and financial contributions
>
> 4. Honesty, no misleading information
>
> 5. Positive Campaigning Practices, adhere to the principles citizens expect of Canadian democracy

As a partisan, you are expected to be loyal to a political party but, above all, as a politician you are accountable to constituents on whose behalf you make decisions. The top-down authority of a political party is venerated, and reconciling your loyalties to the party and to your constituents can sometimes be tense. Our campaign team's aim—to ensure constituents' voices were heard in decision-making that affected them—added clarity. We taught the political dinosaur a few different moves.

HOLDING DYNAMIC TENSION

Moving beyond business as usual to re-invent your entire enterprise model can be exhilarating, but also scary stuff. When you are flailing in a sea of uncertainty, it's tempting for enterprise rebuilders to grasp for order and impose authoritarian top-down decision-making without engaging in much consultation. But what's often needed in times of chaos is quite the opposite: greater agility, flatter and decentralized decision-making, and permission for measured risk-taking. Not every enterprise can operate like a tech start-up, but every enterprise requires a design deliberately crafted to enable that company, government agency or non-profit to achieve its purpose and live its values, in the way that Zita Cobb did in Newfoundland.

Personal Leadership Elements: Paradox and Emerging

Paradox is the ability to hold a split view or two perspectives simultaneously. This requires a higher order of thinking from leaders.

Emerging is holding space for new thinking or a better idea to arise. It requires the willingness to be comfortable with tension and ambiguity while waiting for the right direction to become clear.

With good intention, many enterprise architects pile on more rigid structure as a means to bring stability and order to a chaotic situation. The risk is that too much order—oversteering the enterprise—will dampen an organization's sense of aliveness and exclude or discourage engagement with outside voices and influences. And trying to control the uncontrollable, with a matrix of strategies and procedures and guidelines, is often a futile waste of precious resources. Enterprise architecture needs to accommodate, even encourage, the holding of dynamic tension, giving decision-makers sufficient space to think deeply and see other options. You need to be able to combine a sense of clear direction and the flexibility to position (and reposition) as required to achieve that aim.

Clarity in your enterprise vision and values can be sustained through regular internal check-ins on your organizational values using *A Measure of Integrity* (checking alignment of your commitments and actions) and through ongoing engagement with key stakeholders by applying *The Enterprise Onion* approaches recommended in this chapter and throughout this book, to ensure that you recognize where there is alignment in values with key stakeholders and where there are gaps.

Personal Leadership Elements: Aligning People, Executing to Plan, Future-Making

Aligning people is having the right talent in the right roles. It is working to ensure everyone understands where the enterprise is going and that all are clear on what is expected from them and the situation.

Executing to plan is the means by which all focused action happens. It is building the skill and capacity to execute, and holding oneself and others accountable. It is the pivot point from leadership to management.

Future-making is birthing something that does not yet exist, initially as an idea and eventually as an extraordinary reality. It is vision and imagination and creativity; seeing what others may not yet see.

Redesigning the business model for your enterprise—to enhance your organization's ability to make quality decisions and deliver value to more stakeholders (and implicitly, to remain more relevant and sustainable than under any pre-existing models)—is a decision that is yours alone to make. Deciding to commit to manage "beyond compliance" with rules and laws, at higher levels of *A Measure of Integrity*, is a strategic choice that can be made only by your enterprise leadership team. These aren't decisions that should be outsourced to experts or to others with little or no skin in the game. You are encouraged to explore these strategic choices with key stakeholders; their viewpoints and collaboration can be very influential and instructive. But the final decisions, and the consequences of those choices, rest on the broad shoulders of enterprise rebuilders and new builders.

CHAPTER 6

MAKE STEWARDSHIP PART OF YOUR ENTERPRISE STORY

Bookton Lane is a gravelled, pot-holed back road that cuts through the fields of my youth, a shortcut between the farmhouse where I grew up and the cemetery where my parents and grandparents lay in rest. On most visits to the farm, I walk this narrow road and let the memories unspool. One of my most vivid memories is as a nine- or ten-year-old girl, riding in the backseat of our family's white Ford Galaxie on a Sunday morning in early May heading home after church service. It was a sunny, warm spring day; our Sunday-best clothes smelled freshly starched; the first shoots of green were piercing through the rich loam in their straight rows; and Dad had slowed the car down to a crawl to inspect his cornfields.

As we neared the intersection of Bookton Lane and Windham Road 5, I recall feeling an overwhelming flash of insight—it was as if the lush fields and the dusty lane and the blue sky and our shiny white Ford full of family and the songs of the red-winged blackbirds in the nearby ditches—became one. The moment may have lasted only five or six seconds, but it is seared in my memory. The feeling was akin to being fully immersed in water, all boundaries dissolved; a feeling of immense harmony and oneness and fecundity. I was awestruck.

Fragments of that same feeling of awe cause me to pause, decades later, when hiking in the Rocky Mountains or traversing magnificent wadis in the deserts of Yemen. While I respect industrial achievement and have even come to admire the power and efficiency of the 500 kV electricity transmission line constructed through the very field of my epiphany, the natural world is where I find meaning and discover hidden connections that bind all things together.

Personal Leadership Element: Enchantment

Enchantment is a deep and continuous curiosity and wonderment in the minute and the mundane. It is an insatiable quest for discovery that results in new ways of knowing or understanding.

My experience with the land where I grew up is a big part of my personal and professional story, and my sense of what "stewardship" means originates from that wellspring. Not every enterprise is one that I personally choose to steward because doing so is a significant commitment, not assumed lightly. Most enterprise is about creating employment, paying taxes and contributing to society in the here and now. The family farm is an enterprise where I feel a different accountability: an obligation to tend the resources for the long term, even a duty to leave the place better than I found it. Owning farmland is one thing; having a sense of responsibility to future generations, the local community and the land itself, is something more. This land isn't just commodified nature. Stewardship means that you don't just draw down on the fecundity of these fields and then move on, to "greener" pastures.

Fresh water is a resource people often relate to with a sense of stewardship, for example: water used for households and industry must be used responsibly and cleaned up so it can be safely returned to its source. And First Nations friends sometimes speak of feeling a sense of stewardship in relation to the entire Earth; a mighty obligation exemplified by the Seventh Generation Principle of the Haudenosaunee people. The word "stewardship" is insufficient to explain what is really a reciprocal relationship: humans are not just caretakers of Earth (in fact, Earth can take care of itself without humans or dinosaurs!), the planet provides care for its inhabitants too. It's the knowledge of this circular relationship that is at the root of values and actions that strive for stewardship, regeneration and renewal.

For many forward-thinking enterprise leaders, sustainability (as contemplated in levels +5 and +6 of *A Measure of Integrity*) is the holy grail. "Sustaining" requires that natural resources not be eroded or diminished, which is a significant challenge when Earth's human population is in a growth mode; but ultimately, sustainability is still connected to the status quo. At level +7 of *A Measure of Integrity*, the aim is of a higher order: stewardship and regeneration contemplate more than a sustaining of the way things are. These higher-order aims are grounded in a sense of reciprocity between the natural world and humanity, between the enterprise and its stakeholders—a sense of going forward together in a good way, toward a better future.

Stewardship is a big umbrella, and your specific focus will depend on the inputs your enterprise relies on, the outputs it produces, and the priorities of the communities in which you operate. Occasionally, I feel a sense of stewardship to man-made constructs, including long-standing institutions such as the Banff Centre; a responsibility to leave the place in better condition for future generations. Stewardship values, together with the regeneration aims that sit at the pinnacle of *A Measure of Integrity*, are only rarely achievable for enterprise. It is a glorious aspiration.

And it is through storytelling that your enterprise's pursuit of stewardship aims are best articulated. The telling of a heartfelt story will help others envision your aspiration and inspire them to pull in the same direction, and can build trust within the organization and in the broader community.

Increasingly, enterprise of all kinds will need to incorporate the aim, or at least the idea, of stewardship into their storytelling in order to respond to the growing pressure from stakeholders and the general public to be more transparent, responsible, fair and accountable in their actions. Focusing on short-term results and efficiencies—the status quo—is quickly becoming an unsustainable and untrusted model for enterprise. It's time to build the long view into your organization's value system, goal-setting and decision-making—and the stories you tell the world about all of that.

Personal Leadership Element: Stewardship

Stewardship is the highest form of leadership. Stewardship requires leaders to think well beyond themselves and be in service to others and the greater good. Stewardship is the art of the long view, a perspective that may span beyond a lifetime and even generations.

STORYTELLING: CONSTANT YET EVER-CHANGING

My parents never actually used the word "stewardship" in their enterprise stories, but when they made decisions about the family farm, their discourse reflected a thought process that stretched across generations. It wasn't anything like that cheesy advertisement for an expensive gold watch, the one featuring a father and son and the line, "You never actually own a Patek Philippe. You merely look after it for the next generation." The farming enterprise wasn't a superfluous luxury good or valued heirloom; it was my parents' home and a way of life that they were entrusted to sustain for the next generations.

Making and communicating decisions about risks to take—and risks to avoid—is different when you have a stewardship frame of reference guiding your thinking. If the enterprise is yours to manage and you make a poor decision, you live with the consequences. If the enterprise is yours to steward and you make a poor decision, the ramifications feel more significant.

My father was very reluctant to relinquish traditions; it took a compelling reason to motivate him to sell a purebred herd of dairy cattle inherited from his father and, instead, build a feedlot for beef cattle. Dairy quotas had not yet been put in place in Canada when Dad made this decision to sell his milking cows, and I always assumed he had made the switch due to uncertainty in the marketing of milk. Just a few months before he passed, I asked Dad why he chose to sell the dairy herd, and his story surprised me.

Dad had rented extra land to grow hay; unbeknownst to him, the rented field had been a landing strip for small planes hired to spray a poison used to control suckers on tobacco plants. The poison was laced in the harvested hay and the toxic bales dispersed throughout the hayloft in our barn. Calves started to die, frequently and without explanation, and it drove Dad nearly mad not knowing what was going on. The vet said it looked like poison. Many excruciatingly painful months later, when the connection to the sucker control spray was finally made, researchers at a local agricultural research university in Guelph, Ontario, were unwilling to pin down the cause and effect. Dad sold the dairy cattle in utter frustration and destroyed the hay in the lofts. And he started over, with beef cattle. Decades later, his voice still betrayed deep anger about the unintended consequences of this chemistry experiment gone awry.

Personal Leadership Element: Storytelling

Storytelling evokes passion. Individual and organizational dreams are kept alive by stories, told over and over and over again. Storytelling motivates action like nothing else.

Looking back, I realize that my parents survived wave after wave of change that seriously challenged their ability to steward the farming enterprise. After building up the beef feedlot—complete with upright silos and other infrastructure needed to support eight hundred head of cattle—Ontario Hydro expropriated the feedlot and farmhouse and surrounding land. Rather than cashing out, my parents moved to another house on the family farm and relaunched, in tobacco. Not even a decade later, that market turned on its head and tobacco growers became pariahs. Considerably older than standard retirement age, my parents decided to figure out how to grow ginseng on the farm's sandy loam.

Personal Leadership Element: Adaptive Learning

Adaptive learning is real-time, continuous, lifelong learning. It requires humility. It is building the plane while you are in flight. It is knowing leadership credentials are never earned; they are always being earned. It requires an integration of experience gathered and lessons learned.

They weren't the only Canadian farmers who turned to other crops after tobacco farming crashed. But my parents were among a small number of innovative farming families in southern Ontario who figured out how to cultivate ginseng, a high-risk and potentially lucrative option, and closely guarded their know-how and markets. The shade-loving plant requires four years to mature and is very susceptible to root rot and disease. In Canada, Chinese buyers mysteriously show up at your farm gate when the crop is harvested, dried, graded and stored in airtight hogsheads. Most of the crop is exported to mainland China (where ginseng root has been turned into powerful medicines for five thousand years), via Hong Kong, and the price paid to farmers for each pound of dried root has little relationship to the consumer market.

My brother has been cultivating ginseng for decades now. I asked him how he and our parents managed to establish themselves in this brand-new pursuit when the entire business is so secretive. My brother said he asked a lot of focused questions to old-timers who would share snippets of information that he would then have to piece together. No one was going to hand you a road map; you had to design your own. My brother probed scientists at a nearby experimental farm with questions about ginseng and disease control. Ginseng requires an arsenal of chemicals, and you have to keep up with the new chemistry. My parents and brother didn't go out and buy brand-new equipment; they rebuilt tobacco priming machines for use in the ginseng beds and similarly adapted tobacco kilns to dry the ginseng roots. In the early stages, they collaborated with neighbours in a joint venture to spread the risks and costs, and to combine their experience.

Personal Leadership Element: Experimenting

Experimenting is adopting the beginner's mindset, connecting imagination to reality, and applying and testing ideas. It requires real tolerance for risk and failure. Letting go of what does not work, and moving on easily, become the new norm.

Telling the story of my family's farming enterprise in this way paints a far-from-idyllic picture of pastoral complacency. My parents had to re-invent and rebuild their enterprise several times over, always while taking into account their long-held values and the long-term view. But they were grateful for their opportunities and were, for the most part, motivated and positive. Their Protestant work ethic was hard-wired, and they worked hard to design and redesign enterprise strategies grounded in their core values and the intimate understanding they had of their natural surroundings and changing conditions. Dad knew every tree, every wet spot and every person in the one-mile patch of planet Earth where he lived his entire life. The family farm existed in a relationship between the human community and the natural world. It was as if my parents had ways to listen, deeply, to the subtle messages of the land. They gave themselves to the place.

Your enterprise need not be a family farm for you to understand the depth of the relationship I'm describing here; my family's experiences with an agricultural endeavour is a metaphor for any enterprise. At the heart of the stewardship mindset is a paradox: the need to live by core values that never change, yet having to constantly adapt and rebuild in response to ever-changing conditions. The fundamental narrative remains the same even as the enterprise evolves to survive and thrive in the face of new circumstances and pressure points. The key is always to keep those changing strategies and actions in alignment with the underlying values. It's an intricate and subtle dance.

It's daunting to think about how to redesign for the family farm's future today, in ways that pay attention to the well-being of the land, the well-being of the community and the well-being of the enterprise owners—just as it's daunting for any enterprise to move beyond business as usual. But that doesn't mean you don't try, particularly if maintaining the status quo is a risk, or even harmful to the organization. The words of early conservation ecologist Aldo Leopold keep bubbling up: "A thing is right when it tends to preserve the integrity, stability, and beauty of the biotic community; it is wrong when it does otherwise."

Selling out to a multinational or to a farming conglomerate feels out of sync with my parents' approach. How can these types of enterprises be regenerative and not exploitive? How can such large actors hear the land when it speaks? Yet the opportunity is compelling.

The world needs agricultural outputs to be maximized (without increasing the land and water used). And though people often view family farms through a sepia-coloured prism, as a quaint throwback to earlier times, this nostalgia distorts reality about the past and the future. My parents, and then my brother, were forced to make very significant pivots in their not-at-all parochial enterprise. Is it time to pirouette, once again?

Many people who shop at Costco and other big-box stores have no real concept of where their groceries come from, reducing the planet to a resource base. And "feeding the world" is seen as a global endeavour largely undertaken by multinational corporations. But COVID-19 has given us all an opportunity to reconsider how we see agriculture and food supply chains. The pandemic has taught us that the job of feeding ourselves belongs to each community.

Political leaders speak of the imperative to substitute imports by purchasing homegrown and local products, emphasizing the value of farmers in keeping our grocery shelves stocked. Yet these romanticized perceptions of Canadian agriculture don't tell the true story. Agriculture and agri-food is more than a $100 billion industry in Canada; that's roughly 7 percent of the national economy and 12 percent of employment. And much of the growth in the sector is attributable to technology and innovation—for my brother and nephew, that means advanced sensors, big data, up-to-date science, progressive management of water aquifers, climate-friendly methods like cover-cropping, and the list goes on. Clinging to a parochial view of agriculture holds us back. Small can be beautiful, but does all farming enterprise have to remain small to sustain core values? The choices available are more than the binary: family farm versus factory farm.

My story is clearly tied very closely to the family farm I grew up on, and many of the lessons I learned about the need for rebuilding and reinvention—all in the context of good stewardship—began in that milieu. If you are listening, there are many enterprise stewardship stories swirling around in the current zeitgeist. What is your enterprise story? What lessons are there in your organizational history and culture, and how can you apply them to the challenges of a changed environment? How do you navigate the paradox of honouring the same fundamental core values while constantly evolving the application of these values to keep them alive in different conditions and circumstances? How will you pivot to write a new story for your enterprise, and how will you tell it? And how are others hearing your enterprise story?

TELLING YOUR ORGANIZATION'S OWN STORY

You can read hundreds of books on subjects such as management, ethics, organizational design, leadership and change leadership that suggest countless ways to redesign your enterprise for the future. And believe me, I have! My aim is not to discourage this exploration of ideas, but to encourage you to take time to reflect on your unique enterprise story as well, similar to the way I did earlier in this chapter with my family's farm operation. Reliving your story opens your imagination to fresh ways of thinking and seeing. It reconnects you to your organization's core values and mission, and it can be revitalizing and sense-making. A story about your enterprise has a different aim than a fact-filled report or a marketing brochure. Accurate facts inform and strategic marketing sells, but a meaningful story resonates.

To begin, map out your understanding of the genesis and evolution of your enterprise. Start by asking questions such as: Why was this enterprise created? Who were its founders? How have the organization's purpose and culture evolved over time? Explore key facts about the owners and the leaders, strategies deployed along the enterprise journey and the original and evolving vision for the organization. Consider the enterprise's core values as they have manifested and morphed over time: was stewardship the goal from the outset, or did something shift to create the opportunity for a higher aim?

Fill in the gaps in your personal knowledge of the enterprise by asking people inside the organization, and within the wider stakeholder community, for their understandings. Invite insights on the organization's challenges: What options were considered at pivotal moments? What trade-offs were made? And how did the strategic choices made reflect or affect the values and the purpose and trajectory of the enterprise? Inquire about relationships with key enterprise stakeholders. For example, have internal and external stakeholders always been supportive of the organization? If the answer is negative, inquire to learn how the organization navigated through these periods of distrust or disagreement. At what points in time did the enterprise thrive, and why? In the face of opportunity or distress, how were the enterprise's choices and values the same as, or different from, those of its competitors and peers?

To the extent possible, create the conditions for people to personalize the telling of these enterprise stories; there is much to be learned from both past successes and failures. Ask about the (positive and negative) emotions of those involved and impacted. How did the enterprise's ups and downs make people feel? Are there any regrets about choices not made or paths not taken? How did people inside the enterprise manage when their personal values were not aligned with the core values of the organization, and did these misalignments precipitate changes in leadership or strategies or values? There are many different pathways to alternative choices, and remembering the stories of how the work of your enterprise has been stewarded can shed light on those choices and may even transform your thinking on what's possible and what's preferred.

Telling your version of the enterprise's story is not about revisionist history, nor is it a rebranding exercise; it's about being authentic and honest, deepening your understanding of the values held dearly by the culture. Telling your enterprise story, in your own words, can serve as a compass for your organization—to communicate core values internally and to guide decisions and actions.

Some people may hear your enterprise story and may not believe it. That can be disheartening. As we explored in earlier chapters of this book, you have to accept that there are people who will, for example, always only see a for-profit corporation claiming to care about the environment and social impacts as virtue signalling. They will always interpret a company's talk of positive legacies as a way to ingratiate itself or its owners, strictly to gain reputational and financial advantage.

Storytelling is not the same as fact-based reporting or marketing campaigns. Of course, it's smart to talk about products and services and capacities in the best light possible, to convince external parties that your enterprise is a leader in a particular field—for example, the most fiscally responsible government, the most highly skilled workforce or the producer of the highest-quality widgets. But don't confuse reporting on outcomes or marketing with storytelling; storytelling has a different purpose. The positive impact of telling your enterprise story is measured by its ability to transmit values and deepen understanding of the enterprise's purpose.

And remember, you do not always tell your story for others. First, tell your stewardship story to deepen your own understanding of your enterprise purpose, values and culture. Eventually, you will want to share your enterprise story; to invite others to a new narrative, a new orientation or a new way of thinking. But begin with self-reflection.

Personal Leadership Element: Storytelling

Storytelling is engaging the hearts of others and bringing a living sense of the destination throughout the journey. It animates a vision, paints a picture, creates a myth or a metaphor.

We forget our personal and public stories at our peril. If we had remembered the stories told by people who survived the 1918 influenza pandemic, would we have been better prepared for COVID-19? If we remembered how governments and banks "too big to fail" acted in the wake of the 2008 financial crisis, would we make different choices rebuilding our economy and financial systems in the aftermath of a health pandemic? Connection to the past and to long-held values is critical to leading from a stewardship mindset, as is living those values in the present and handing them down through the enterprise. Sometimes, at points of significant disruption, it's crucial to revisit the old stories, to rediscover the core values at their heart and to rewrite the narrative to pave the way for a better, different future.

In the winter months before COVID-19 struck in the West, I had the unique opportunity to listen to many Albertans' stories as part of the Fair Deal Panel appointed by the Alberta government. Even before the pandemic, Alberta's story of being a world leader in responsible energy production, and being Canada's economic engine, had been disrupted. The future suddenly looked very uncertain. Listening to the individual stories, I was struck by their uniqueness. We often bundle stories together into statistics, but people sharing their own stories provides emotion and humanity and a sense of what survival can look like within individual families. This province-wide listening tour also afforded me and the other panellists with the unique opportunity to see how these individual narratives came together, to shape Alberta's story. Despite wide differences in personal experiences, the vast majority of Albertans we heard from saw this place as home, for themselves and their families. Through heartfelt storytelling, people were able to articulate their aspirations for the province, even beyond their local communities.

In Medicine Hat, bankers told stories of farmers crying in their offices, unable to withstand the triple whammy of drought, uncertain commodity markets (due to diplomatic tension with China) and economic upheaval in the province. In Fort Saskatchewan, a woman told me she was afraid her granddaughter, trained as a nurse, would be lured away to another province to work. A caterer in Fort McMurray lamented: "This is my home, this is where I want to be. Fort McMurray isn't just a place to make money." A fifty-year-old woman from Wainwright spoke of her daughter, forced to live at home because she can't earn enough money to pay rent; further lamenting that her "kids can't afford to have kids." In Lethbridge, old-timers spoke of history repeating itself: "Fix this, or we'll be back here again in twenty years." In Red Deer, a young person cautioned: "We can't negotiate a fair deal if we play the victim card." In Grande Prairie, a man pointed north: "Grande Prairie is a northern community, and there is opportunity with the Arctic warming."

The economic shocks of disruption are painful, but playing a role in the decarbonizing of the carbon economy is part of Alberta's survival story, ultimately a regenerative one. For those in the energy sector who see ESG as an opportunity—not just virtue signalling—stewardship of the resources can include transitioning shifts to carbon capture and sequestration, net-zero cement, hydrogen and dozens of other ideas we haven't even thought of yet. Stewardship, for others, may require transitioning from the energy sector to apply resources and skills in different enterprise. All of these transition strategies will require a renewed focus on competitiveness and a letting go of the nostalgic but self-deluding story that good jobs in oil and gas are the key to restoring our prosperity. This dinosaur will need to learn new ways to dance.

And yet, in moving forward, we cannot ignore our history—the experiences of rebuilders, good and bad. We may choose to forget, but amnesia creates unnecessary suffering. While I can keenly recall the joy of discovering arrowheads in the sandy loam of our family farm, finding morel mushrooms in the shady bush and playing in the maple sugar shanty as a child, my children do not know these things. If my siblings and I do not share the family farm stories of our parents and grandparents with the next generations, we compromise their ability to steward this enterprise.

WHO TELLS YOUR ENTERPRISE STORY?

It's essential to script and tell your own enterprise story to guide the organization, to communicate effectively with internal and external stakeholders (especially on controversial and sensitive matters) and to position your enterprise in the broader public. But be prepared. There will be many other versions of your narrative out there; the story that is heard and understood is increasingly out of your control. In addition to your own communication efforts in all channels, there are many other voices contributing to the conversation, and how the community and the world in general perceive your enterprise is becoming less about what you say and more about what you do. Your enterprise's ability to have its story heard, understood and believed is dependent on how others sift through all the competing stories to find the truth.

So, who else is telling your enterprise story? Mainstream media may tell it, but most likely they will only be reporting if your organization plunges into the deep, dark depths of the negative scores on *A Measure of Integrity*. It's far more likely that fragments of your enterprise story will be shared via social media; perhaps through Facebook posts by people in the communities where you operate, tweets about controversial decisions made by your organization, or a hashtag on a LinkedIn post. These media stories aren't really your enterprise stories; they are other people's interpretations or perceptions of your enterprise—its operations, its decisions, its values and its culture. More than ever, media in all its forms—mainstream, social, documentaries, citizen journalism—shapes how people perceive your enterprise. The court of public opinion is indeed powerful!

Activists routinely deploy social media to build momentum, very quickly and very inexpensively. A 2020 campaign aimed at the Government of Alberta, to stop coal mining on the eastern slopes of the Rocky Mountains, provides insight into how these social media campaigns can gather momentum. When families impacted by a proposed mining venture spoke up on Facebook, sharing stories of how generations before them stewarded the water resources in the very landscape targeted for open-pit coal mining by the provincial government, the public listened. An environmental advocacy organization, Canadian Parks and Wilderness Society (CPAWS), aggregated these grassroots stories and launched a targeted campaign, escalating the momentum and pressure on government to change course.

The anti-coal-mining advocacy reached another level of pitch, and influence, when Corb Lund, a musician from southern Alberta and one of Canada's pre-eminent singers about rural life and cowboy culture, released a Facebook video lambasting the province's new coal policy. After that, several groups launched online petitions, gathering thousands of signatures from angered Albertans in a matter of days. Members of the Blood Tribe in southern Alberta launched a postcard campaign, and the province's official opposition party started their own petition. The government had little choice but capitulation; they have reset the entire decision-making process.

The future of media is uncertain, but the trajectory is one of diminishing influence by conventional and mainstream media and of greater voice to citizens and advocates. Citizen surveillance is a reality; increasingly, individual storytellers are researching behind laptops and sharing stories on their smartphones. The Pulitzer Prize Board has even recognized Darnella Frazier, the teenager who used her cellphone to film the murder of George Floyd by a white police officer, with a special journalism award. And for those who wish to conduct their own investigation as to what's really going on in the world, resources offering guidance are emerging, such as Bellingcat (derived from the expression "belling the cat"), a British investigative journalism website specializing in open-source intelligence and fact-checking. At the same time, we're experiencing a data deluge, with more data available to us than we can possibly process. The question thus becomes one of truth. Which storyteller do you trust?

People used to trust the "salt of the earth" word of a family farmer. But the business of farming has become very complex and many questions are being asked about agriculture, including: How can we be sure water aquifers are protected if large-scale livestock operations are approved by municipal councils? What chemicals are safe to use to kill weeds in ditches along roadways? How is the safety of farm labourers (especially children) protected by governments? What measures can be taken to ensure livestock are treated humanely? Should we allow seeds to be genetically modified?

There are many opinions on what the "true" story is. When Epicurious, a popular food website owned by Condé Nast, announced it would no longer publish new recipes or even Instagram posts that include beef as an ingredient because "cows are 20 times less efficient to raise than beans," cattle ranchers in my home province dismissed the announcement as a virtue-signalling stunt. And yet, the discussion about how to raise more sustainable beef is an important question. Where can that relevant and public conversation take place?

Cultivating ginseng at the family farm in southern Ontario is labour-intensive. While my brother employs local labourers for most of the year-round work, he also hires three temporary foreign workers from Mexico to help on a seasonal basis. These workers have been coming to the farm for many years, and although technology has made separation from their own families a little more bearable (their first priority upon arrival is hooking up high-speed internet so they can Skype with their wives and kids at home), they get homesick. Canada's Seasonal Agricultural Workers Program was launched in 1966, and decades later, we still rely on temporary foreign workers to support the agriculture sector in this country. There are as many stories and experiences to be told as there are farms and migrant workers, but they are not the only ones telling them.

Advocates for migrants' and workers' rights want more focus on the negative mental health impacts of isolation and precarious working conditions. To help tell the stories of these temporary foreign workers, in 2016 film producer Min Sook Lee launched the documentary *Migrant Dreams*, which follows a group of Indonesian women who come to Canada to work in tomato greenhouses in Leamington, Ontario. The dark side of this work is exposed by Lee: curfews, surveillance, the realities of a commitment to one job, one location and one employer. "We have an idea of Canada, a mono-narrative, that is controlled by the media," says Lee. "We need to talk about the truth of where our tomatoes come from, and who wipes the noses of our babies."

As a counterpoint, the Canadian Horticultural Council produces professional-quality YouTube videos with titles like *Heartbeat: A Celebration of International Farm Workers*. The trailer to *Heartbeat* reads: "Most of us never think about how food gets onto our tables, or the critical role played by the men and women who work in the fields and greenhouses. It is an enormously labour-intensive and complex process. Sadly, Canadians are generally unwilling or unable to take on the rigours of farm labour, which is why many Canadian producers rely on international farm workers to help plant and harvest their crops." How does anyone objectively fact-check these competing narratives and discern the truth? And whose story is it, anyway?

Online retail giant Amazon, valued at $1.4 trillion, has the means to tell its story on multiple platforms, including the story of how Amazon CamperForce recruits van-dwellers and RVers from across America to work at Amazon warehouses during the peak holiday shopping seasons. In her book, *Nomadland: Surviving America in the*

Twenty-First Century, writer Jessica Bruder tells the grinding stories of CamperForce employees working ten- to twelve-hour shifts inside Amazon "fulfillment centres," many of them in their sixties and seventies; people who cannot afford to stop working or pay their rent and are earning little more than minimum wage. The book has been turned into an award-winning film directed by Chloé Zhao and has energized pro-union campaigns at Amazon.

People often ask what an organization can do, proactively, to avoid this sort of counter-storytelling or to control their own narrative in the face of it. Decades ago, an enterprise could control its own story with well-funded public relations campaigns. To be absolutely clear, those days are long gone. Even the most profitable companies—including Amazon—cannot stop others from telling a different version of their enterprise story, from an alternative perspective.

To be better positioned to anticipate these other takes on your company, non-profit or government agency, use *The Enterprise Onion* as a tool to engage with others (including cynics and critics) to gain a more honest understanding of how others perceive your organization. You cannot take away anyone's right to share their perspectives on the purpose, values, motives or decisions of your enterprise, but you can get ahead of derogatory or conflicting messages with your own storytelling. If, for example, you know that workers in your industry are agitating to unionize, prepare for those essential conversations with relevant stakeholders by evaluating those elements of your enterprise story that could be shared to constructively progress that dialogue. (Perhaps your organization's history of employee ownership, workplace safety or support for paying well above minimum wage for entry-level positions.)

Your enterprise has a story to tell—possibly even a tale about all the bumps in the road in the quest for that elusive aim of stewardship. It's essential to the survival of your enterprise vision and values that you write your own story, and tell that story, in ways that resonate with others. While it is very likely that you are not the only one telling the story, constructive and ongoing engagement with your stakeholders can equip your enterprise to anticipate and more fully understand the perspectives of others. Discerning when and how to weigh in to respond to conflicting narratives is a judgment call. The more you understand these counter-narratives, the better your ability to determine an effective response.

EMPOWERING OTHERS

Telling your enterprise story, and telling it well, seems like it should be a relatively straightforward thing for internal stakeholders in an organization to be able to do, and you might expect storytelling to be embraced by enterprise leaders. But storytelling is neither a simple exercise nor is it always encouraged. For the reasons explained in this chapter, individuals within an enterprise are increasingly reluctant to speak up and share their personalized version of the enterprise story (especially with external stakeholders), and organizations are increasingly encouraging this self-censoring culture and opting instead for organizational "control" of the story. Why? To protect the enterprise's reputation by reducing the risk of criticism and alternative or counter-storytelling by others. Very regrettably, these constraints and self-censoring are often detrimental to the enterprise's best interests.

Personal Leadership Element: Translating

Few leaders can take complex situations, problems or strategies and distill the essence to communicate this complexity in a simple way that is understood. Translation requires a deep understanding of all the moving parts, to connect the receiver to the higher purpose (the why) in a way that can be actioned to achieve the desired outcome.

Why would an organization prefer to constrain the telling of its own story? There are four recurring rationales. The first is a fear of being manipulated by skeptics and critics; the idea being that the more data you put out there, the more it can be turned against your enterprise and you can lose control of the message. The second rationale is that the enterprise team doesn't have a sufficiently cogent understanding of its own values or aims, and this truth would be embarrassing if exposed. The third reason has more to do with leadership style: the leader speaks for the organization, and others are only trusted to read from well-honed scripts. And the fourth reason is legal: it's okay to say "No comment" to prevent publication of statements that may prejudice court proceedings.

Over the last decade, I've observed a growing trend toward enterprise self-censorship, and frankly, it's worrying. No enterprise controls its own story in a world dominated by social media and citizen journalists; nonetheless, getting your team's perspectives into the mix, in an informed way, can be constructive. When an enterprise team doesn't have a sufficiently clear grasp of its values and aims to be comfortable sharing with others, that's a signal that more internal work is required to clarify the organization's values and it's time to pull out *A Measure of Integrity*. When only "the leader" can speak for the enterprise, I wonder about how other decisions get made and I question the organization's capacity to be flexible and agile when required. Finally, when a lawyer issues a gag order, it's prudent to ask for an explanation.

In our family farm enterprise, my parents were hard-working but generally light-hearted. They didn't oversell their experiences and stories—there was no declared ambition to inculcate in us their way of thinking—but we listened up when they spoke. Recalling these stories, now, is heartening. My parents had many reasons to throw in the towel and quit the enterprise, but they didn't. What sustained them in those dark times, when things came at them from forces well beyond their control—the weather, volatile interest rates and commodity prices, of course; but also, even more unpredictable forces like an expropriation, poisoned cattle and the decimation of the tobacco industry?

Both of my parents were born, lived and were buried within a five-mile radius of the family farm. From the outside looking in, their lives were the epitome of order, stability and predictability. Yet, if you looked closely, that was not their reality. Their ability to create order in their lives was an effective counterweight to the chaos they experienced; their capacity to be flexible, when required, allowed them to weave together the predictable and the disruptive in disciplined ways that enabled them to steward the family farm enterprise. My parents knew how to dance; when to pivot from their comfortable routine and when to embrace an entirely new dance. These are precisely the skills required to navigate any enterprise in the here and now.

My parents had the grace and humility to know they could not control everything, and the steadfast determination (and occasionally hubris) required to resist the feeling of being overwhelmed. And the stories they told were able to communicate both confidence and humility, not just one attribute or the other. They were at the same time self-assured and experienced *and* aware that they couldn't effectively steward the enterprise without reaching to others for insights, guidance and fresh perspectives. I hold these stories close as my siblings and I chart a course forward for the family farm enterprise, and I share them with my sons as they design their own pathways through the turbulence of a transforming energy sector in Alberta.

Others can do the same. Whether your enterprise is a for-profit company, a non-profit providing a service to others, or a government department or agency, you can inspire others in your organization to tell their personal version of your enterprise story, and to tell it well. We have all met rebuilders who spoke of their "work" with a gleam in their eye and were spirited in the way that they recounted stories of how they launched or became engaged in the enterprise or what they envision for its future. Inside government agencies, I have met people who were so passionate about the potential for economic diversification in Western Canada that they would go to any length to make sure that like-minded and like-hearted entrepreneurs and funders could meet to explore opportunities. The work wasn't just a well-paid and secure job to them; it was a calling, and these individuals could see what was possible if the right policies were designed and the best people collaborated. Their stories of what successful diversification looked like inspired others to take the risks required to set aside the status quo and believe in the possibility of a better future.

Visionary thinking is a hallmark of non-profit organizations; these enterprises are led by people who see their work as a means to creating the conditions for a better future for people in a community. I have sustained contact for decades with one such visionary, Dr. Ahlam binBriek, a female medical doctor in the coastal city of Al-Mukulla, Yemen. Through thick and thin, Ahlam's ability to take the most meagre of resources and figure out ways to provide life-sustaining health care to local families in that war-wracked city is beyond belief. Ahlam's storytelling—about her adventures converting a derelict abandoned building into a community hospital, convincing local faith leaders to support the role of women in medicine, and her harrowing experiences during the war and then the pandemic—sheds light on what drives her unflagging faith in a better future and her commitment to do whatever it takes to tend to her community.

Personal Leadership Element: Exerting Mature Judgment

Exerting mature judgment is knowing and doing the right thing. It is also being seen to be doing the right thing, whether or not the right thing is popular. It is holding the highest interest of others, and the organization, above self-interest. It is often an expression of character. It is what leaders get paid to do.

One absolutely essential aspect of a stewardship approach to enterprise is succession. The sustainability of any enterprise is contingent on continuity. This means that it is incumbent on you, as an enterprise rebuilder, to build other leaders; to work yourself out of a job and create the conditions for new builders to steward the enterprise.

Your enterprise may need to focus on the building of internal capacity, including redesigning and implementing a plan for new leadership. This requires an intentional mentoring strategy, and one that rebuilders are committed to every single day. Formal training is necessary, but new builders take cues from the small things too, including the stories we tell. This is how values and culture get passed down from one generation to another—whether it's within a family or an enterprise. My siblings and I represent the fourth generation on the family farm, and we were close enough to our parents and grandparents to hear their unvarnished tales. Our great challenge is stewarding not only the land, but the narrative, through the generations that follow.

As a veteran rebuilder or formal leader, resist the urge to dominate the storytelling of your enterprise. Instead, encourage emerging leaders and new builders to take the anecdotes and explanations and struggles, and create their own heartfelt versions of the enterprise story. Too many organizations create the conditions for a censoring culture, arguably, to protect the enterprise from cynics and critics. But, as I've explained in this chapter, those constraints are often detrimental to the enterprise's best interests. As a mentor and role model, you must create the conditions for others to speak up and witness their storytelling, thereby breathing new life into the stewardship trajectory. Values of any enterprise are best articulated, and even more powerful, when embodied in the stories we tell.

CHAPTER 7

REBUILD FOR THE STORM AFTER THIS STORM

Most enterprises will not be caught off guard by the next health pandemic. Preparing for more of the same is prudent, but don't squander this rebuilding opportunity. As you transition your enterprise from crisis-survival mode to strategic rebuilding, resist the temptation to simply restore old structures and former ways of doing things. Rebuild for the storm after this storm.

Does your enterprise have the organizational agility to navigate new risks and the curiosity to keep evolving? Do you have the willpower and capacity to keep teaching the dinosaur new dance moves? Think about what could have been possible for BlackBerry if Mike Lazaridis had done some rethinking about how people might want to use their cellphones. Even if you are at the top of your game, you never stop building; there is always something new around the corner. Michele Romanow, Calgary-based star of CBC television's *Dragons' Den* and founder of Clearco, a tech start-up in the e-commerce market, says it best: "We're excited about [reaching unicorn status] but every single day we believe that we are starting from scratch and we have to continue building."

Personal Leadership Element: Adaptive Learning

Adaptive learning is real-time, continuous, lifelong learning. It is creating maps in the middle of navigation. It is both formal and informal. It must be pursued, and it requires humility. Adaptive learning closes the feedback loop by integrating experience gathered and lessons learned. It is knowing that leadership credentials are never "earned," always being earned.

No doubt your enterprise's evolving risk matrix is populated with a long list of storm clouds gathering: climate change, hyperinflation, cyberattacks, protectionism and regionalism, another health pandemic, climate migration, escalating trade war and/or conflict between superpowers, technology replacing human workers, technological dominance, sovereignty challenges in new frontiers like space and the Arctic, competition for fresh water, civil unrest triggered by growing inequality and rising xenophobia, a national disaster and declining trust in institutions.

Maybe your enterprise is even contemplating the consequences of a combination of these crises? In Alberta in 2020–21, we dealt with the triple whammy of a pandemic plus an oil price collapse plus the beginning of a marked shift from hydrocarbons to a carbon-reduced economy.

It's very possible that the next crisis won't even be one we can predict. Large organizations with state-of-the-art risk management strategies did not foresee the COVID-19 pandemic. Knowing what you now know, what can you do to prepare your enterprise for the storm after this storm? Anticipating possible futures in a complex, dynamic and unpredictable world is essential; but devoting your energy to finding solutions to the wrong problem is a waste of resources.

While there are limits to what we can know, there are wise rebuilding actions you can take now with certainty and conviction. You can be explicit about why your enterprise exists, what it values and to whom it is in service. *A Measure of Integrity* is a tool that can guide you in this work. You can tell your organization's unique story in a clear and compelling way and spread it as widely as possible through your own channels as well as through the media (social and traditional) and through the networks of the advocates and even the skeptics and cynics with whom you have engaged to inform your enterprise and its decision-making (applying *The Enterprise Onion* tool to do so).

And then you can rebuild your organization's capacity to walk that talk, whatever storm comes your way. This means building enterprise teams able to prepare for any eventuality, with whatever resources are available, to achieve your organization's desired aims. You don't need loyalists on board as much as you need a diversity of world views and ways of thinking; you need people with different skills, experience and perspectives on your team who can find a way through territory that is not yet mapped.

But before we get to these core rebuilding actions, there are a few weighty questions you need to ask, to rigorously test your enterprise assumptions, namely: What can be left behind? When is more not better? What constitutes "value" (as distinct from "values") for our enterprise?

1. WHAT CAN BE LEFT BEHIND?

The recent pandemic afforded every one of us the rare opportunity to re-evaluate what parts of our enterprise need to be rebuilt and what parts are better left behind. It's convenient to build around existing structures; but to make space for something new, it's often better to clear out the things that no longer serve your enterprise. It may feel like a bit of a contradiction—initiating and releasing—but recall chapter three and the constructive and energizing dynamism of holding seeming polarities.

Letting go of aspects of an enterprise is emotional, and people can feel a sense of loss. When Ontario Hydro expropriated a large chunk of our family farm, our family struggled to understand the premature shutting down of a working feedlot operation. To my parents, who were children of the Great Depression, shuttering a going concern was wasteful. It offended their sense of efficiency. Without daily care and attention, the entire enterprise diminished; there hasn't been a cow in that feedlot since the expropriation over three decades ago.

Personal Leadership Element: Suspending

Suspending is refraining from preconceived notions, recognizing bias and being as neutral as possible. Suspending is clear thinking; parking judgment, ideology or conclusions, and analyzing the data inputs as they emerge. In suspending, we are open to new and adjacent possibilities.

Winding down all or part of a viable business or institution isn't something that comes naturally to many of us. Yet to move forward, there may be parts of your enterprise that need to be left behind. What resources, strategies and, dare I say, values no longer serve your enterprise? Perhaps like LG, once a long-time manufacturer of mobile phones, your corporate strategies have outgrown their useful life. Many of us are familiar with the company's original flip phone, but LG's premium cellphone models, while unique, never caught on, and continuing to invest in the research and development needed to compete no longer made sense for the company. LG made a difficult but strategic choice to exit the smartphone business to focus on TVs and audio equipment; refrigerators, washing machines and other appliances; computer products and other consumer electronics in which they excel.

At a time when disruption is the norm rather than incremental change, there are new challenges and tough choices to be made in almost every enterprise, industry and sector. For example, the delivery of post-secondary education is transforming rapidly and there are even bigger questions bubbling up about the future of elementary and secondary education. With a bifurcated physical-virtual education experience becoming the norm during the pandemic, will we need all the school buildings going forward? And if not, what new investments and supports will be required in education?

The same questions could be asked of cultural institutions: will people become acculturated to virtual reality as an option to in-person visits or experiences, and what would that mean for this sector? And in a carbon-reduced world, even the most highly efficient coal-fired electricity generation plants risk becoming stranded assets. Champions of very ambitious GHG emissions–reduction targets recommend the early abandonment of other hydrocarbon facilities too, including the oil sands.

Before you throw the proverbial baby out with the bathwater, revisit your assumptions. Is there potential in your enterprise that you may have overlooked? Remembering the story of BlackBerry, how do you access different perspectives and see the possibilities your core team cannot see? If BlackBerry had done what LEGO does—reach out to customers directly for insights and ideas—perhaps I would not have replaced my BlackBerry with an iPhone.

The Enterprise Onion is a tool that can build up your capacity for external engagement as a routine and standard operating practice. Reach out to external stakeholders to help you see what your internal team cannot see. For my family, this means talking to neighbours and other family-based companies that have made difficult and inspiring choices about the most effective way to transition a family enterprise from one generation to the next in an ever-changing world.

2. WHEN IS MORE NOT BETTER?

And I encourage you to ask tougher questions, including head-scratching ones like: What happens to our assumptions if we are agnostic about growth? What if we ask what's "enough" rather than how can we get "more?" What if we focus on qualitative growth and not just quantitative growth?

In enterprise, we are conditioned to seek endless growth. Upward trajectories not only reward senior managers, employees and shareholders, but also provide hope and can even ease the tension of wide social inequalities. Though this sounds a little counterintuitive, the idea that economic growth is a given means that poorer citizens (and countries) always have the potential to catch up to richer citizens (and countries). Ever-expanding GDP creates a "positive-sum economy" where everyone's lot in life can improve. This was the rationale of China's Communist Party leader from 1978 to 1989.

Xiaoping Deng famously said that poverty is not socialism, and he interpreted communism to mean it was acceptable for some to become rich to improve the lives of the masses. Deng led China through significant market-economy reforms. The current leader in China, Xi Jinping, supports private business as a way to grow China's economy and create jobs, but he is more ambivalent about personal growth and the widening gap between rich and poor; as a result, billionaires in China face considerable scrutiny.

Can you imagine a world where it is possible for your enterprise to thrive, with or without growth? It's a question that is starting to be asked, by serious people. In the tech world, the idea of not pursuing growth is anathema. No growth or low growth may be okay for some businesses—state-owned utilities and not-for-profit service providers, for instance—but the notion that your for-profit enterprise is operating at "good enough" flies in the face of entrepreneurial ambition and the ubiquitous "grow or die" mantra.

Admittedly, in business-as-usual scenarios, there have been times when growth isn't recommended—for example, new businesses are encouraged to ensure they have profitability before embarking on new growth; established enterprise owners sometimes prefer not to take on new risk or new debt (and additional red tape) and instead, live comfortably within their means; and some smaller entrepreneurs are unwilling to create a layer of management between themselves and their primary workers through expansion.

Beyond these scenarios, though, the idea that growth isn't the primary aim of for-profit enterprise is foreign. Yet, I'm encouraging you to ask the question: Can you imagine a scenario where your enterprise would not treat growth as an imperative for success? This begs the related question: Is green growth possible? (If you think these questions are tricky for private-sector companies, imagine being the leader of a high-income country or jurisdiction where you had to evaluate ways to thrive even without population or GDP growth.) Twentieth-century enterprise builders did not have to ask these questions, but you do. And you can expect to have them asked with more frequency. To keep ahead of the change curve, you might want to broach this topic with people you trust.

Some companies are embracing the opportunity for green growth, and among the most creative of them is Patagonia, a $1 billion manufacturer of high-end outdoor apparel. Company founder Yvon Chouinard believes consumers should "be buying less but buying better." This strategy aligns with Patagonia's corporate values (the company is operating at level +6 of *A Measure of Integrity*, perhaps even at level +7): dedication to the Earth, sustainability, and leaving behind a legacy that gave more than it took. The corporate mission statement encourages the building of quality products, which leads to less consumerism, which leads to less environmental waste.

One of Patagonia's most creative campaigns, launched on Black Friday, told people to stop buying the company's clothing. Here's a short excerpt from their ad: "The environmental cost of everything is astonishing. Consider the R2 Jacket shown, one of our best sellers. To make it requires 135 liters of water, enough to meet the daily needs . . . of 25 people." It's hard to argue against this strategy, unless you are the manufacturer of low-cost, more affordable garments. Ironically, the day of their "Don't buy this jacket" ad, the company sold over $10 million in apparel. Whether or not their approach of appealing to quality reduces consumerism is unknown, but it was a catalyst for Patagonia's growth (and profitability) in the short term.

Beyond the growth-at-any-cost imperative, there are other models available to enterprise rebuilders and new builders. In Canada, many Indigenous friends remind me of their traditional models of "sufficiency" and encourage me to ask: what's too much and what's not enough? As Kate Raworth describes in her book *Doughnut Economics: Seven Ways to Think Like a 21st Century Economist,* the Cree in northern Manitoba defied the profit-motive expectations of European fur traders: "In the hope of acquiring more furs, the Europeans offered [the Cree] higher prices: in response, the Cree brought fewer furs to the trading post, since a smaller number were now needed to obtain the goods that they wanted in exchange." This experience from the nineteenth century may have glimmers of insight for the twenty-first century.

3. WHAT CONSTITUTES "VALUE" FOR YOUR ENTERPRISE?

What constitutes "value" (as contrasted to "values") for your enterprise, and how has this sense of what is considered to have worth or material value changed over time? I admit, it is a tad confusing to talk about value in a book that has focused so much attention on enterprise values (even pointing you to a tool designed for this purpose, *A Measure of Integrity*). However, smarter people than me have written whole books on this question, including Mark Carney, former governor of both the Bank of Canada and the Bank of England and currently the UN Special Envoy on Climate Action and Finance, in his recent book titled *Value(s): Building a Better World for All*.

Carney is exceptionally qualified to address the world of finance, a place where people relate to the perceived material value or worth of things. (Though, it's also worth observing that Carney is becoming a flashpoint for polarized perspectives on climate change strategies.) It's that same thinking that's behind the approach to ESG: encouraging strategic thinking about enterprise "values" by focusing on what values (and their outcomes) will be catalysts for material value to your organization. In other words, how do its values impact the bottom line, and how can your organization demonstrate that connectivity between values and value to key stakeholders?

And while you are thinking about these questions, it's also useful to consider what your key stakeholders value. Again, *The Enterprise Onion* is recommended as a tool to help you with this engagement work. Some of the "material value" questions that are emerging with workers include, for example: Do your employees and contractors value loyalty as much as your organization values loyalty? In an increasingly complex and changing labour market, questions like this are important. Another key stakeholder group to focus on is customers. A case in point: by understanding how Amazon's customers value their time, Jeff Bezos was able to translate that knowledge into a very profitable business model.

What people value can shift, and quickly. Nearly overnight, bitcoin and rare-earth metals became hot commodities. Coinbase (which runs an exchange for digital currency trading) launched in 2021 as the first major cryptocurrency company to list its shares on a

U.S. stock exchange with an initial market valuation of nearly $85 billion—that's more than the market value of long-standing, asset-rich companies like oil giant BP. Access to high-speed internet became more highly valued when people were locked down, and the perceived worth of bricks-and-mortar retail diminished.

Beyond the transition to digital, the value of tangible infrastructure is increasingly being weighed against the value of intangibles. For example, the construction of bridges and highways is being contrasted to the value of improving care for the elderly, children and the disabled. And as the push to a carbon-reduced economy gains traction, "green" becomes more valued: Elon Musk invites you down to a local Tesla dealer to buy your new electric vehicle, and Volkswagen rebrands as Voltswagen (even if only as an April's Fool's product marketing strategy). Afraid of being left behind in this drive on green value, General Motors and Toyota are positioning to move beyond the internal combustion engine, with both companies aiming to make the majority of the vehicles they produce electric by 2035 and 2030 respectively.

Albeit recursive, even the currency we use to pay for things reflects shifts in how we see value. The British pound sterling was the reserve currency pre–World War II; after that, global financial systems were built on the American greenback. What happens if the U.S. dollar is no longer the reserve currency? China's government is re-imagining digital money in ways that could disrupt that status quo. Most people understand the virtual flow of money—tapping our phone to make a purchase or e-transfer funds—but China is doing something different. They are converting legal tender into computer code or digital currency. Bitcoin and other cryptocurrencies already exist, albeit outside traditional financial systems; China's cyber yuan is issued and controlled by China's central bank. This means China's government can take surveillance and data collection to a new threshold, tracking citizens' spending and the financial flows of enterprise, in real time.

Shifts in how we perceive material value are happening all around us. Take the traditional art world as another illustration. In 2021, a computer programmer in Singapore paid $69.3 million at a

Christie's auction for a digital work of art created by Beeple. What the buyer purchased was a non-fungible token (NFT) representing a collage of five thousand cartoonish-styled images titled *Everydays: The First 5000 Days*. The purchaser of the NFT gets the rights to display the full-resolution artwork in a digital museum (but doesn't acquire the copyright), and the NFT allows the artwork to be tracked, based on blockchain technology, hence counterfeiting is prevented. *The Art Newspaper*, a reputable journal for the visual arts world, speculates that "traditional hierarchies of the art market, where values, both monetary and aesthetic, were established and policed by art historians, curators and museums, are being assaulted by a new breed of wealthy new players, with new tastes and 'new' money." Cryptocurrency art purchases are beating out sales of masterpieces by Picasso, Matisse and Van Gogh.

Personal Leadership Element: Sense-Making

Sense-making is like radar, registering strong and weak signals from all levels of one's environment. It is both intuitive and strategic—sensing change, spotting trends, seeing what's happening. It is understanding how the past informs the future. Sense-making requires a deeper understanding of the system one operates in.

What does this all mean for your enterprise? Embedded assumptions about where we place material value need to be challenged. Ask more probing questions. Here's a list of ten to get you started:

1. What is the value of high-speed, reliable, digital capability to our enterprise?

2. What is the value of flexibility in decision-making, in our short-term and long-term planning?

3. What is the value of a dedicated and talented workforce?

4. What is the value of a financial cushion and savings?

5. What is the value of diversity of perspectives, or dissent, in our enterprise?

6. What is the value of open and trusting relationships with enterprise stakeholders?

7. What is the value of an innovative and creative culture, of research and development?

8. What is the value of self-sufficiency to our enterprise?

9. How can we value (or provide value to) all the stakeholders in our enterprise?

10. How can we value different voices and perspectives from employees, customers, skeptics and critics?

WHAT WILL BE DIFFERENT, THIS TIME?

This time, it will be different. That's what we all say as we turn our back on the last crisis and embark, with steely determination, on our forward trajectory. In Alberta, where boom-and-bust cycles are commonplace, a popular bumper sticker for vehicles reads: "Please God, give me one more oil boom. I promise not to piss it all away next time."

This time, what will be different? For one thing, transition to a net-zero carbon world looks like it really will be different. How so? The age of bold promise is over; governments and businesses are implementing ambitious energy-transition strategies, and multi-billion-dollar investments are being made. ESG strategies require fulsome disclosure of carbon risks, cogent emission-reduction strategies and demonstrated actions. For these reasons, the outcomes of the United Nations Climate Change Conference in Glasgow (COP26) will be different than COP21 in Paris. Personally, I hope the delegates who gathered and negotiated at COP26—environmentalists, technology leaders, politicians and financiers among them—will have the courage to go beyond exploring what various shades of green can look like between now and 2030, 2040 and 2050, and make significant concrete change sooner rather than later.

Personal Leadership Elements: Catalyzing and Designing Action

Catalyzing is purposeful disruption of the status quo to provoke fresh momentum or a new direction. It requires the courage to act, even when the outcome may not be clear.

Designing action is knowing the race you are going to run before you start. It is moving from the ethereal to the concrete, from the unseen to the seen. It is creating the intelligent plan and articulating that plan to others.

Getting to net-zero GHG emissions is a game-changer; this time, it really will be different in Alberta and other hydrocarbon-producing jurisdictions. Does that mean fossil fuels are no longer needed? No, we will need hydrocarbons for a while longer to support and accomplish the transition to clean energy, but hopefully we will learn to value these resources in the spirit of Buckminster Fuller's advice from his 1969 book, *Operating Manual for Spaceship Earth*:

> The fossil-fuel savings account has been put aboard Spaceship Earth for the exclusive function of getting the new machinery built with which to support life and humanity at ever more effective standards of vital physical energy and reinspiring metaphysical sustenance to be sustained exclusively on our Sun radiation's and Moon pull gravity's tidal, wind, and rainfall generated pulsating and therefore harnessable energies. . . . We cannot afford to expend our fossil fuels faster than we are "recharging our battery," which means precisely the rate at which the fossil fuels are being continually deposited within Earth's spherical crust.

What's less obvious is how the transition to clean energy will be equitable and fair. Lower-income people spend a larger portion of their household budgets to pay for heat, electricity and transportation. To change behaviours, clean energy must become cheaper to purchase or fossil fuels must become more expensive, or both. These strategies have implications for energy buyers and energy producers.

Another incontrovertible and enormous difference? In the twenty-first century, data is the new oil and digital, one of the pipelines. And unlike oil and other goods and services that are "rival" (meaning they are commodities that can only be used once), data is non-rival, and can be used over and over again and simultaneously by different people without being depleted (for example, think about how cable television functions). Everywhere, artificial intelligence is busy gobbling up data, and connections between people are increasingly mediated by machines. Taco Bell is opening a digital-only restaurant in Times Square, and soon your smart fridge will talk to Amazon to schedule a grocery delivery when you run out of milk and eggs!

Personal Leadership Element: Patterning

Bringing some semblance of order to chaotic situations can only be achieved through recognizing patterns. In natural systems, patterns always emerge. Time and patience are required, together with the deployment of alternative modes of perception. A situation that may seem intractable can reveal new possibilities, and leaders can discern a clear path forward.

COVID-19 forced businesses, social institutions and government agencies to embrace digital to survive the crisis; the upside is that it may have been the catalyst needed to position these organizations for the future and hasten their transition to a digital model. Yet, bumps in the road ahead should be anticipated. After more than a year of working remotely, employees are less connected to their colleagues, their managers and their places of work, and organizational cultures have changed. Talent flight is a material risk: front-line and health care workers who postponed retirement to help with the pandemic are expected to race for the exits. Figuring out ways to offer opportunity to employees—in more remote locations, to re-train for different roles, to access mentorship—can be part of your enterprise rebuilding plan. Your internal enterprise team may feel like "We're all in this together," but some of your stakeholders may not be feeling the same sense of solidarity.

Big Data earned a lot of market share during the pandemic. These companies wield a great deal of power, and their role in solving big issues—like social media manipulation by regimes to suppress human rights, discredit political opposition and drown out dissenting opinions—could be far greater. There are things to be learned from these large technology players, including: how to create the conditions to innovate, how to learn from failure and how to reduce reliance on bricks-and-mortar. Yet it's important to see technology as a tool and to not become a slave to its way of doing things.

In his above-referenced book on value(s), Mark Carney encourages enterprise teams to be digital by design rather than by default: "We shouldn't view technology through the lens of Big Tech, where the role of algorithms is to replace humans, and interactions are organized to feed business models centred on big data." Enterprise teams are instead encouraged to deliberately identify the outcomes they want technology to help achieve and to ask, "What is it we need digital and technology to do for our enterprise?" Don't let technology be the tail that wags the dog; harness its potential to add value to your enterprise, but don't let it compromise your enterprise's lucid and inclusive thinking.

TEST YOUR ENTERPRISE ASSUMPTIONS

Humans are hard-wired to send and receive signals that align to our way of thinking. But to be more effective in enterprise, we need to think omnidirectionally, like an antenna that's able to receive and send signals in all directions. To defy our human temptation to cling to what's known (even contorting our intelligence to see what we expect to see, or what we want to see) and change up our field of vision, it's constructive to engage with people who see the world differently, including marginalized or peripheral points of view. It can be uncomfortable to seek insights from others who may be skeptical of your motives or values. It's also very humbling to say you don't have all the answers to all the big questions. While it can be quite disarming when someone who is knowledgeable admits to uncertainty, people are more apt to pay attention.

Return to *The Enterprise Onion*, frequently, to identify and engage meaningfully with key stakeholders, especially those who aren't like-minded. And remember, this work is dynamic; it's often not sequential, but simultaneous. You can't just schedule a review of key stakeholders and their priorities as an annual event or a task to be taken on by your summer student. Things change quickly, so you need to design your enterprise to have a finger on the pulse of key issues and stakeholders at all times and have the agility to quickly make wise choices based on both judgment and fact.

Evaluate ways to engage internal and external perspectives to help you rebuild your organization better, smarter and more sustainably. Of course, there will be people who see their point of view as an all-or-nothing proposition. For example, climate change is an existential threat and there can be no quarter given, no compromise on anything, and the sooner every vestige of the hydrocarbon economy is eliminated, the better! If you are an energy company or regulator, or a community dependent on energy resources to pay for infrastructure and operating costs, it's going to be challenging to create the conditions for new ideas to emerge through encounters with this kind of non-negotiable positioning. If you are a cattle rancher, it will be daunting to engage with "beyond beef" advocates, including the folks at Epicurious. Unrelenting creativity and curiosity, and a powerful sense of what's possible in dancing a new dance, will be required to find pathways through the barriers.

The single-minded zeal of advocates can be annoying, but the more effective agents of change are to be admired for their ability to unequivocally articulate and pursue what they value. *What could happen if your enterprise thought like an activist?*

When I was in Paris for COP21, there were three parallel platforms for engagement: a stage for governments to formally release statements on their country's climate change commitments; a platform for corporations to rate technical solutions and share enterprise-specific GHG initiatives; and a large tent for NGOs and activists. Each of the three groups reflected a unique tone and culture: diplomatic (the government voices), scientific and fact-based (the companies), and passionate (the advocates). I spent time in all three spaces, sharing the viewpoints of Albertan citizens on climate change and energy policy in our province. By far the most authentic conversations happened in the midst of non-profits and activists—people able to go off-script, explain their values and respond creatively and with agility to changing conditions.

What can an enterprise do to think like an activist? For starters, *The Enterprise Onion* is a key ingredient you need to make this happen, to get your team in the mindset of thinking about how others see your enterprise (its motivation, its values, its aims). And there is more: as a rebuilder or new builder, figure out ways to encourage (and not just condone, or worse, tolerate) people in your organization telling your enterprise story. When an engineer who has worked in the oilfields of northern Alberta stands up, in the midst of environmental advocates, to tell his story of what it takes to ensure that water used in industrial operations is purified before being returned to the river, and to explain why this matters to him (his community accesses water downstream from the plant), it can be powerful.

"WE" KNOW OUR VALUES

Know your enterprise values, or others will try to decide for you. Every person on your team should be able to share your enterprise story, in their own words, and to explain your enterprise values, with sincerity, and not just recite some canned corporate message. Your team should understand what level of integrity your enterprise is aiming to achieve, or at least have a clear sense of whether its target on *A Measure of Integrity* is motivated by compliance or beyond-compliance values. If your enterprise aim is to have positive social or environmental impacts, your team should be positioned to speak to the specifics.

Personal Leadership Element: Storytelling

Storytelling is engaging the hearts of others and bringing a living sense of the destination throughout the journey. It animates a vision, paints a picture, creates a myth or a metaphor. Storytelling paves the long road from the brain to the heart.

Sharing your enterprise values with others—and sometimes thinking like an activist—can be heady stuff. And there's a dark side here that needs to be exposed. Charismatic leaders, like Elon Musk and Steve Jobs, can attract followers to their enterprise and inspire people to help change the world. These followers are enticed to believe they are a part of something bigger than themselves and are drawn to the excitement of doing something differently. But charismatic influence can be abused. For example, the guru-like CEO of WeWork, poster child for a trendy new approach to office space for millennial small business owners and gig workers, raised billions from sophisticated investors and inspired a cult-like following with little of substance to back his brash plan. You can learn more about the rise and fall of WeWork tycoon Adam Neumann in a documentary titled *WeWork: Or the Making and Breaking of a $47 Billion Unicorn*, which was released on Hulu in 2021.

In the non-profit space, the WE Charity organization, led by brothers Craig and Marc Kielburger, attracted celebrities to their charitable cause, including the Duke and Duchess of Sussex and Prime Minister Justin Trudeau's wife (Sophie Gregoire Trudeau) and mother (Margaret Trudeau). Its revenues exceeded $66 million in 2019, and the organization owned a brand-new 43,000-square-foot WE Global Learning Centre in downtown Toronto. An initiative called WE Schools connected students, corporate donors and government sponsors to promote volunteerism among young people. Amid controversy and scandal, WE Charity's Canadian operations were closed in 2020.

These cautionary tales are shared, not to deter enthusiasm for thinking and acting differently, but to reinforce the need for values and purpose to be understood, shared, and lived consistently, enterprise-wide. When one individual becomes the singular flag-bearer of an organization's values, there is vulnerability. And it's very difficult to build and execute a succession plan on that basis. After my grandfather passed, my father was seen as the patriarch of our family enterprise, and with my father's passing, my brother has taken up that mantle. While many family farm decisions have ultimately rested on patriarchal shoulders, there was no sense that other per-spectives or voices required muting. To thrive, through thick and thin, the family farm enterprise benefited from all of us being invest-ed in a shared vision and explicit values. These values were tested, again and again. And like muscles that grow stronger through use, thrashing out tough choices built our collective resolve to protect and steward what we care about most.

SPEAKING CANDIDLY

This book, as you will no doubt be aware by now, is not for every-one. There are enterprise leaders who will insist on trying to sustain their status quo and hope for the best. They refuse to recognize that business as usual is extinct and will remain dinosaurs in an evolving world, stubbornly unwilling to dance to a new tune.

In some organizations, people make bolder statements, as if bra-vado and saying something louder will dispel the uncertainty. Other organizations opt to do the exact opposite, curling up into a safe cocoon until the storm passes. Either way, if you choose to remain ensconced in a world full of like-minded people and avoid listening to the insight of critical friends, you may indeed be able to convince yourself that the world can get back to "normal." Efforts to ignore a changing world and sustain the status quo are, however, likely to generate turbulence—more blaming and finger-pointing, polarized positioning and toxicity, and daily confrontations that accomplish nothing—and the storm after this storm will be daunting to navigate.

Beyond these extremes, this nervousness about the future can also translate into more subtle behaviours; banalities that seem ir-relevant until you realize the extent to which our silent acquiescence and condoning create ideal conditions for the emergence of a different organizational culture, one that we didn't plan for or necessarily want. What am I talking about? Little things—like self-censoring what you say to ensure that you don't inadvertently offend, which leads to a sterilization of dialogue, an over-reliance on scripted messages, and self-imposed limits on genuine and heartfelt story-telling. To fill the void created by self-censoring, and to deflect the vulnerabilities associated with the exercise of discretion and judgment, we adopt rigid and comprehensive approaches to policy- and rule-making. Frequently, these seemingly banal choices are cloaked in righteousness. It is "good" for the organization if we can point to prescriptive rules and policies and codes of conduct; however, in doing so, we often enmesh ourselves in a tangle of constraints that tie down initiative.

There are many who believe that an organization's ability to innovate is its most essential core competency. Piling on layers upon layers of detailed rules, and forsaking difficult conversations for the sake of being able to expeditiously post politically correct policy statements on your website, kills innovation. It's perverse, but we do it all the time. Why? Because it's much easier for an organization to suppress nuance in favour of having one declared way of thinking—the founder's way, the CEO's way, the chair's way—and expecting everyone else to fall in line with that approach. Don't get me wrong; setting clear values for your organization is an imperative for managing and leading from the inside out, a highly encouraged practice. What's troubling is avoiding the conversations required to tease out the meaning of these core enterprise values. For example, when your website banner declares that yours is an organization that respects diversity and freedom of expression, or that it aims to be "sustainable," you need to be able to stimulate and encourage conversations about what that *really* means.

Self-censorship has become an accepted norm within many organizations, and it's causing a suppression not only of voices, but also of ideas and initiative. To pump some much-needed oxygen into boardrooms and shop floors, pay attention to how you solicit opinions from your stakeholders and how you model open-minded, constructive and critical thinking in your enterprise. Speaking honestly about these very important questions affecting the future of your enterprise will give permission to others to do the same. It is not a sign of weakness to not have the answer to every question; humility can be a sign of deep caring. A culture where people are not comfortable saying what they are thinking is stifling.

For those enterprise rebuilders and new builders who accept that business as usual isn't a viable option, I encourage you to focus your energy and resources on re-imagining and redesigning your enterprise in ways that will allow you to thrive in the face of any storm. The decisions rest on your shoulders, but you are not alone in the identification of viable strategies that can work for your enterprise. Reach out to your key stakeholders for ideas, clarify your values and manage to those values, and in this work, give yourself permission to speak candidly.

It's also critical to explicitly acknowledge that we have reached an inflection point where business as usual is no longer a safe or useful strategy. In a fast-paced and highly disruptive era, remaining relevant becomes a prime objective. This fact poses a particular challenge for veteran enterprise builders: How do you mentor new builders, knowing that your guidance to the next generation of enterprise builders must sometimes include advice to *not* do what you did? How do you contribute to enterprise rebuilding efforts in ways that are relevant and constructive? To guide others in your organization, speak candidly about your enterprise story, including the ways that you navigated (or failed to navigate) big changes in the past. Open up the space for fresh thinking. Encourage your colleagues to go deeper, to share stories and nuance, to move beyond self-censorship and scripts. You have more to fear from your inhibitions than you do from your vulnerabilities.

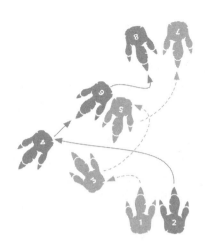

CHAPTER 8

DANCE TOGETHER TOWARD A BETTER FUTURE

G reen is good. Right?
It's 2021 and foreign investors are lining up to finance gigantic renewable energy projects in Alberta. As an early proponent of renewables and one of Canada's first provincial government ministers to be given responsibility for this portfolio, you would expect me to be unequivocally delighted by this scale of investment in green energy. I am watching it all closely, and to be honest, some serious questions are bubbling up about the long-term sustainability of these projects and the true aims of project proponents. Are these champions of green energy really concerned about reducing greenhouse gas emissions, or is this all a smokescreen for making money and burnishing private- and public-sector reputations?

To get a closer look, I signed up as an official observer to the Alberta Utility Commission's review of a mega wind farm being pitched by German green energy supplier ABO Wind on 17,500 acres of privately held farmland near Lomond in southern Alberta. It's an ambitious proposal: eighty-three giant-sized wind turbines (close to 200 metres tall) and a business plan of offsets to be sold to carbon-producing companies that promise to be net-zero by 2030–40 (which is potentially a whole lot of companies).

ABO Wind's megaproject, once given the green light, will produce renewable energy that will compete head-to-head with other wind-generated electricity in the province. Albertans are free-enterprise champions by nature, so competition isn't a big deal. But looking more closely at this business of generating green energy, it isn't as clear or as rosy as one would like to think. ABO Wind has a proven business model that already generates carbon credits for purchase by private-sector companies (like Amazon) to offset their carbon footprint (in places like California). It could be that they are primarily interested in shuffling greenhouse gases on a spreadsheet without actually reducing net emissions in the world.

And this is where it all gets tricky. None of what ABO Wind is proposing is illegal. The provincial government policy encourages this investment—as we are fond of saying, "Alberta is open for business." And several of the filings by affected stakeholders to the Alberta Utilities Commission (the regulatory body that decides on individual projects) reflect support from local landowners and municipal authorities in Lomond, where the project is to be sited. These groups welcome the infusion of new revenue streams into their public and private coffers. And anyone who dares question "green" or inquire about the stickiness of German investment dollars in Alberta, or who raises an eyebrow about the logic of building a standing army of giant turbines as tall and nearly as wide as the Calgary Tower, or who grumbles about the public cost of building out more electricity transmission infrastructure to assure zero congestion on the wires, risks public and personal censure because there is no greater good than green these days in the former petroleum paradise of Alberta.

Yes, green looks great on paper. But looking more broadly, I'm afraid green can be a curse if it's not done well. This isn't just a question of the aesthetics of renewable energy infrastructure, it's far more complex.

The 5,000-year-old Majorville Medicine Wheel lies on a remote knoll within sight and sound range of this proposed super-sized wind farm. Older than Stonehenge, this site is known to the Blackfoot from Treaty 7 in southern Alberta, and to the Blackfeet Tribe in neighbouring Montana, as a place for vision quests. This is sacred territory. So sacred that a gas pipeline was rerouted once the company was informed about the spirit of the place and of the old, big arrangement of stones. Imagine the night sky on this stretch of prairie if the wind farm were to go ahead—flashing air navigation lights that blink, blink, blink from eighty-three gigantic structures. Imagine the sound of swirling turbines that generate standing waves that can be heard well beyond the horizon line. No place for spirits.

How does one reconcile the positive benefits of "greening" Alberta's electricity grid and reducing greenhouse gas emissions with the negative impacts to communities, wildlife and spiritual places? *What's the answer to this sustainability koan?* In my view, it's stewardship. Albertans are stewards of this province; this place is our home, and many of us want to create the conditions for it to have the possibility of being an attractive place for future generations. Sustainability is a lofty aim for any enterprise, as I've explained throughout this book, and is never easy to achieve. And yet, there are rare times when it may not be adequate to simply "sustain" the status quo; it may be necessary to aim higher, to act as stewards and figure out ways to make things better. Thinking like stewards of this place called Alberta, how would we decipher our green energy choices?

Personal Leadership Element: Stewardship

Stewardship is the highest form of leadership. Stewardship requires leaders to think well beyond themselves and be in service to others and the greater good. Stewardship is the art of the long view, a perspective that may span beyond a lifetime and even generations.

As I've pointed out several times in this book, there is a remarkable confluence between the stewardship mindset and Indigenous ways of thinking. First Nations communities in Alberta are signing up to participate as interveners in decisions affecting their sacred territory. It's essential that we invite and hear these Indigenous voices; these communities have survived great hardship, even extinction, and there is much to be learned about stewardship from their experiences. And as articulated in chapter six, it is through storytelling that the pursuit of stewardship aims is best shared. The oral traditions of Indigenous peoples have deeply enriched their ability to tell stories; storytelling reinforces their culture and keeps alive the stewardship values that underpin that culture.

And to be clear, when I speak of stewardship, I'm not contemplating a benevolent "king" or patriarch; stewardship as envisaged by level +7 of A Measure of Integrity is about regeneration and moving forward together toward a better future. Like any powerful dance, stewardship is built upon a foundation of reciprocity—between the enterprise and its stakeholders, between the natural world and humanity, between the individual and the collective. It's the ultimate dance.

A stewardship mindset requires transparency about aims, and durable trust-building between reciprocating partners. In the case of the ABO Wind project, one of the most critical reciprocal relationships is between the citizens of Alberta and this foreign investor. Most Albertans prefer to believe that green energy is good and that investors in green energy care about the environment, but as I wade deeper and deeper into the weeds of this particular proposal, I can't help but wonder: is this company investing in wind generation in our province to reduce emissions or as a way to make money selling carbon credits?

Regulatory watchdogs including the Market Surveillance Administrator (MSA), an independent monitor of Alberta's electricity and retail natural gas markets, also seem to be questioning motives. Tucked into a standard-issue quarterly report, the MSA observes (in very technical-speak): "For wind generation assets, assuming an increasing carbon price in the presence of the current emissions benchmark, the revenue from the sale of environmental attributes [carbon credits] may be sufficient in the future to cover all generation costs without the need for any revenue from the sale of electricity in the power pool." In other words, generating green electricity is not necessarily the primary goal for investments in wind generation in Alberta; foreign investors may be lining up to invest because this province is a very attractive place to generate and sell lucrative and much sought-after carbon credits to companies that need these offsets to meet their emissions targets as set out in ambitious ESG undertakings.

Many Albertans have had enough of foreign corporations walking in and doing what they want. Whether it's Australian coal-mining companies lobbying to carve up the eastern slopes of the Rocky Mountains to sell metallurgical coal to Asia and Brazil, or European renewable energy investors planting gigantic wind turbines to generate carbon credits that can be sold to powerful corporations, very little of the so-called investment is left behind for Albertans who fund the necessary infrastructure and live with the longer-term impacts. Who bears the cost of producing green energy or any eco-friendly product? It's a critical question and one we can't ignore in our quest for climate change solutions. When highly polluting Danish manufacturer Rockwool International wants to plant a pollution-spewing factory in West Virginia (rather than in its own backyard) to manufacture mineral wool insulation as part of its green building-material industry campaign, who pays the price? Similar questions are being asked about other "green" goods that are dirty to make.

There is rarely a "right" or "wrong" answer to questions of stewardship. There is much nuance and there is a need for thoughtful reflection. And in the ongoing process of trust-building required to achieve genuine reciprocity in relationships, shortcuts and superficial approaches won't work. If Albertans and foreign investors are going to be able to move forward *together* to create the conditions for mutually beneficial outcomes, the key stakeholders are going to need to come clean on their motives. Altruistic enterprise aims should be encouraged, but not if they have the effect of undermining the public good.

THINKING DIFFERENTLY

Rethinking enterprise choices requires fresh ideas, an admission that everyone has blind spots and a letting go of some outdated assumptions. That's where diversity in thinking becomes valuable. Some people (and especially Canadians) tend to be polite by nature; while it's nice to be with agreeable people, when it is time to test assumptions about your enterprise, the last thing you need are cheerleaders. A weary enterprise leader can be susceptible to seduction by sycophants, but we learn more from people who challenge our thinking than we do from those who agree with us.

If you accept that "business as usual" thinking won't sustain your enterprise in the storm after this storm, what tools will you deploy to design your way forward? There will be an endless number of novel ideas and problems and stakeholders vying for your attention. Enterprise builders and rebuilders will need to respond to third-party pressure for change and, at the same time, manage organizational strategy, purpose and values from the inside out. And you will need to make these actions flow synchronistically (at the same time, rather than sequentially) and dynamically (constantly checking feedback loops for new information and making necessary adjustments).

Personal Leadership Element: Future-Making

Future-making is birthing something that does not yet exist, initially as an idea and eventually as an extraordinary reality. It is vision and imagination and creativity. It is seeing what others may not yet see. It is the courage to stake out new ground. It is a process that occurs over time, and it is holding the space as that process unfolds.

It may be tempting to reach for commoditized and branded business solutions or to seek outside experts to design your strategy or build your relationships with critical partners, but there is rarely any ready-made recipe that truly fits the unique needs of individual organizations when it comes to something as distinctive and personal as enterprise values, culture and relationships. Avoid analysis paralysis, blind action and slavish mimicry; instead, give yourself permission to try unscripted approaches to design, and create your own models. Tools and concepts shared in this book are intended to stir your curiosity and inspire new approaches to find a creative and sustainable way forward. No one knows your enterprise better than you and your team. To teach your dinosaur to dance, you will ultimately need to choreograph your own dance steps.

Think carefully about who the best people in your organization are to lead this rebuilding work. Whether your enterprise is a for-profit company, an environmental or social advocacy group or a government institution, your employees, managers and leaders and board of directors are likely exhausted and on the verge of burnout after their ceaseless work to put out fires. Inviting colleagues to entertain questions about values and purpose, and to engage with stakeholders who aren't like-minded, is likely to evoke some defensiveness. Talking about philosophical questions is uncomfortable for many, and asking people to engage in enterprise self-examination can make some feel under-appreciated.

In *The Rainforest Blueprint: How to Design Your Own Silicon Valley*, Victor Hwang encourages you to find your boundary-crossers: "Identify people who span boundaries and build bridges between disparate individuals. Real-life linkages are human-to-human, not group-to-group." Do you have people in your enterprise with the motivation and ability to see issues from the perspective of others and who can see how others perceive your organization? Who are the liminal figures who reside, most comfortably, at the edges of your enterprise?

And be adaptive. If you get stuck in your rebuilding work, pause and re-evaluate your approach. Remember, trust is not created by people saying, "Trust me." It's created by people actually doing work together and building rapport through real-life collaboration. And if you open up engagement with others—energetic brainstorming sessions with open-minded allies—proclaim a "great meeting" but then do nothing with the brilliant ideas, expect people to grow frustrated and impatient.

There is no doubt this work of enterprise rebuilding is tough stuff—self-examination, digging deep to define values clearly and opening up to criticism from outside can be uncomfortable—but the work must be done to remain relevant and sustainable to the stakeholders, customers and communities you serve. No organization is perfect, and all can benefit from this exercise, particularly when it's undertaken with a strong vision and motivation to do better.

Although this book has exposed gaps in Amazon's business model (in particular, the company's ruthlessness), Jeff Bezos's unrelenting drive to be original (shared in his final letter to shareholders as CEO) is insightful. In Bezos's own words: "We all know that distinctiveness—originality—is valuable. We are all taught to 'be yourself.' What I'm really asking you to do is to embrace and be realistic about how much energy it takes to maintain that distinctiveness. The world wants you to be typical—in a thousand ways, it pulls at you. Don't let it happen." None of this is easy, cautions Bezos: "Being yourself is worth it, but don't expect it to be easy or free. You'll have to put energy into it continuously."

Personal Leadership Element: Imagining

You can't create the future if you can't imagine it. Imagining is exploring new thinking about what is possible and beyond the norm. Imagining is about the capacity to originate an idea, a concept, a vision for a preferred future. It requires giving up a seat in the knowable world. The spark can be maverick or childlike as one reaches for the ultimate "what ifs."

How does an enterprise build its capacity to "think" differently and be atypical? In one of his lesser-known essays, *Discourse on Thinking*, German philosopher Martin Heidegger describes two ways of thinking—calculative thinking and meditative thinking—each justified and needed in its own way. Calculative thinking "races from one prospect to the next," computing "ever new, ever more promising and at the same time more economical possibilities." Persevering, meditative thinking, while worthless for dealing with current affairs, contemplates the "meaning which reigns in everything that is" by gazing beyond the horizon of what we already know. If there ever was a time to think differently, and more expansively, about how we do enterprise, that time is now. Use your intuition, curiosity and enterprise storytelling to guide your thinking, not just mathematical deduction.

I do not expect that the world will revert to a pre-pandemic status quo once the vast majority of the globe has been inoculated against COVID-19. There is no "back to normal" in these times of social, political and environmental turmoil. Any enterprise that survives the global public health crisis will need to rebuild in order to thrive in a future where stakeholders expect capitalism to do things differently. *Teaching the Dinosaur to Dance* is a road map for renewal, not only in the post-pandemic economy, but also for a better and more sustainable future. Rebuilding success isn't guaranteed if you heed all the insights shared in this book's chapters, but if you don't pay attention to these questions, your enterprise is more apt to fail. Whatever your enterprise pursuit—a social institution, government agency or for-profit company—the world, and your organization, can be a better place if you buckle up your dancing shoes and figure out ways to teach the dinosaur to dance.

APPENDIX

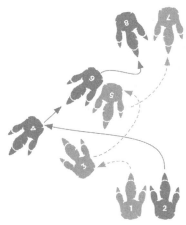

YOUR TOOLKIT FOR
MOVING BEYOND BUSINESS AS USUAL

To remain relevant and sustainable, enterprise rebuilders and new builders will need different approaches to organizational design, stakeholder engagement and personal leadership competencies. To guide you in this rethinking, redesign and execution of enterprise revitalization (and maybe even transformation), three tools and user guides are provided in this toolkit:

1. A Measure of Integrity

2. The Enterprise Onion

3. Essential Elements of Leadership

A Measure of Integrity is an enterprise tool to guide organizations in their alignment of purpose, values, commitments and actions. This tool measures both positive and negative integrity, and it can help your enterprise clarify key values and build organizational capacity to manage in accordance with those values from the inside out.

A Measure of Integrity originated as an Integrity Ladder, first introduced in *Corporate Integrity: A Toolkit for Managing beyond*

Compliance (Kennedy-Glans and Schulz), a book published by John Wiley & Sons in 2005 to guide organizations in their alignment of values, commitments and actions. This specialized tool has been further honed through fifteen years of application, applied research and observation, and I am excited to launch an updated tool—*A Measure of Integrity*—to help organizations walk their talk on core values. The updated tool you'll find in the toolkit reflects both generative and degenerative integrity scales (the original was a positive scale only) and the levels of positive integrity have been refined. In my experience, while compliance with rules and laws is essential, the big reward for enterprise is in the independent choices made possible when you move beyond compliance. Do the work to clarify what values truly guide your enterprise and build the capacity to manage to those values from the inside out.

The user guide that accompanies *A Measure of Integrity* in the toolkit equips enterprise builders with the charts and templates and sample applications needed to guide your organization's discussion about key values, internally and with external stakeholders. Any gaps—between values and commitments and actions—can be quickly identified and managed; the templates will help your enterprise with that essential work.

The Enterprise Onion is a related tool, designed to help organization builders engage more deliberately with others who have a strategic interest in an enterprise and can influence the path forward. It's a stakeholder tool to support organizations in their outreach to, and engagement with, the diverse range of viewpoints required to progress effectively and sustainably on a new path forward.

It's likely that your enterprise does some type of stakeholder influence and interest-mapping, but if you want to generate durable consensus on new ideas and strategies, you will need to reach out to stakeholders who think differently, who ask different questions and who maybe even hold different values. Engagement with a wide range of unique perspectives is encouraged to create the conditions for sustainable change.

The Enterprise Onion is primarily an outward-facing tool, modelling how to recognize and engage with stakeholders outside your own organization, working from the enterprise core to the outer layers of the onion: from the internal enterprise family, to the like-minded, to the open-minded, to the skeptical-minded, and perhaps even reaching the cynical-minded. The user guide for this tool includes mini case studies.

Personal Leadership Elements are referenced throughout the book and shared in their entirety in the *Essential Elements of Leadership* model in this toolkit. Andre Mamprin has been observing and developing leaders for decades, working with organizations to build their capacity, designing leadership learning content and delivering programs to more than 20,000 leaders as Executive Director of the Leadership Development program at the Banff Centre, and as the leader of Knowledge Architecture at The Next Institute. Andre now designs and delivers solutions for an array of blue-chip organizations across North America. *Essential Elements of Leadership* is a distillation of his learnings about the competencies essential for personal leadership, built up through research and application.

WHEN TO USE ENTERPRISE REBUILDING TOOLS

A Measure of Integrity is useful:

☑ When your enterprise team needs to refresh the organization's understanding and execution of one of its long-standing core values (for example, sustainability, privacy, transparency). This refresh may require changes in the organization's level of commitment to integrity on the ascending scale, which ranges from strict compliance with laws (level +1) to thinking about stewardship, regeneration and future generations (level +7).

☑ When your enterprise decides to focus on an emerging expectation—for example, fairness, respect for Indigenous peoples, or diversity and inclusion—and you want to test how that aim aligns with organizational values and actions.

☑ When your organization needs to identify gaps between your organizational talk and its walk on values, and figure out ways to close those gaps.

☑ If your enterprise team decides to move beyond compliance with rules and laws and target higher levels of *A Measure of Integrity*. Level +3 marks the point where organizations move from compliance with laws to a "beyond compliance" strategy.

☑ If your enterprise team decides to move from sustainability to stewardship values. At level +5 of *A Measure of Integrity*, an organization voluntarily chooses to operate at sustainability thresholds, and at level +7, an organization commits to stewardship values.

☑ When your enterprise needs to check in with external stakeholders to understand how they perceive your organization's core values and its alignment of talk and walk on those values.

☑ If your enterprise needs to restore core values and learn from its mistakes. Organizations can slide into failed integrity, situationally justifying decisions to side-step laws and policies that are perceived to be unfair (level −1) or rationalizing a sub-cultural norm to override compliance with laws and policies (level −2).

☑ To avert disaster if your enterprise is spiralling into negative integrity zones—willing to violate rules, or even laws, in response to catastrophic events or to stay competitive and survive.

☑ To guide your enterprise storytelling and its resonance with others.

☑ To prepare your enterprise for the storm after this storm.

The Enterprise Onion is useful:

☑ When your enterprise is evaluating, designing and implementing strategic change—incremental, revitalizing or transformational—to most effectively rebuild the organization.

☑ When your enterprise is potentially or actually constrained by polarized positioning and is evaluating options.

☑ On an ongoing basis, to proactively build durable collaborative capacity with internal and external stakeholders on long-standing priorities and emerging issues.

☑ When your enterprise has prioritized the design and implementation of innovative new ideas or strategies.

☑ When your enterprise is re-imagining your business model, to help you make better decisions, shore up resiliency and deliver value to stakeholders.

☑ To redesign your enterprise model in a way that will increase the number and positive influence of stakeholders with skin in the game.

☑ To guide the telling of your enterprise story and respond to competing narratives.

☑ To test your assumptions and face the future with greater resilience.

Essential Elements of Leadership is useful:

☑ For emerging enterprise leaders who seek to develop and hone foundational leadership skills; for example, sense-making, assessing risk, decision-making and executing to plan.

☑ For experienced enterprise leaders who are starting to break away from the pack and seek to demonstrate incremental leadership elements, including competencies like collaborating, suspending, experimenting and imagining.

☑ For seasoned enterprise leaders who seek to build capacity in emerging leadership qualities, including patterning, stewardship, catalyzing and being able to deal with paradox.

If you don't have clarity in your organization's goals and values, or if your enterprise lacks core competencies, it risks being whipped in different directions by every new wave of change, especially when the status quo no longer holds. You will either end up swirling in directionless flux or wading through molasses. Either way, you will be going nowhere. Use these tools to equip your enterprise team for rebuilding success.

There is no perfect model for enterprise rebuilding and no perfect tool. But there are proven practices for enterprise rebuilders and new builders to follow for putting their own plan in place, and I hope the guidance provided in this toolkit is helpful to you in your own building or rebuilding efforts. Additional resources—tools, conversations, fresh ideas—are available online at **www.teachingthedinosaur.com**.

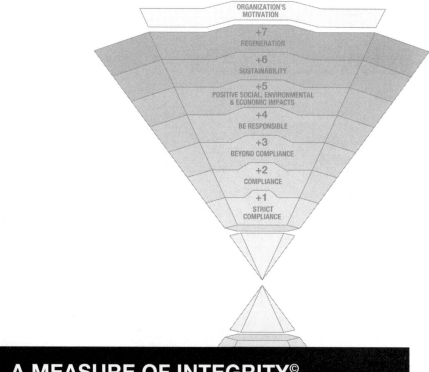

ORGANIZATION'S
MOTIVATION

+7
REGENERATION

+6
SUSTAINABILITY

+5
POSITIVE SOCIAL, ENVIRONMENTAL
& ECONOMIC IMPACTS

+4
BE RESPONSIBLE

+3
BEYOND COMPLIANCE

+2
COMPLIANCE

+1
STRICT
COMPLIANCE

A MEASURE OF INTEGRITY©
A User Guide for Organizations

BY DONNA KENNEDY-GLANS

What Is Enterprise Integrity?

Put simply, it's the full integration of your organization's core values. Walking your talk. Practicing what you preach. Integrity goes beyond honesty to incorporate a wholeness, coherence and alignment that defines enterprise character. Some call it "organizational mindfulness" about the values that matter most to your company.

Most would agree—integrity has always been a critically important value for organizations. Yet in our increasingly complex, globalized and interconnected world, integrity is no longer assumed. It is ironic—our level of connectivity has never been so high, and our level of trust in enterprise has never been so low. Organizations need to learn how to measure, manage and proactively demonstrate enterprise integrity, with greater confidence, credibility and authenticity.

In *Teaching the Dinosaur to Dance*, we are excited to launch an updated tool— *A Measure of Integrity*—to help organizations walk their talk on core values and build the capacity needed to sustain that enterprise culture.

FIGURE 1: A MEASURE OF INTEGRITY

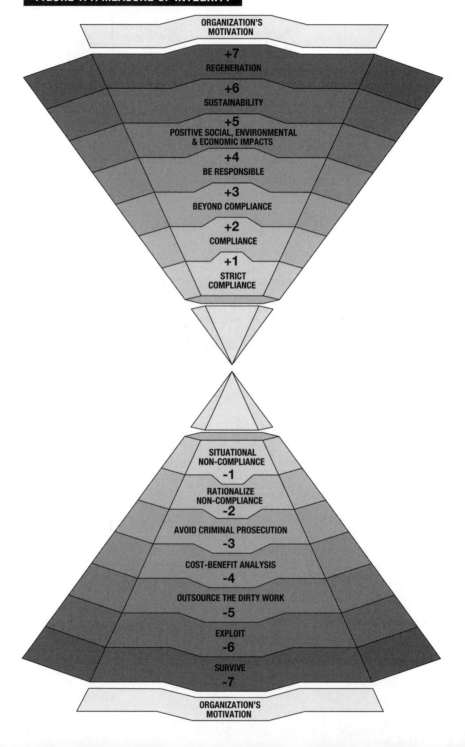

ORGANIZATION'S
MOTIVATION

+7
REGENERATION

+6
SUSTAINABILITY

+5
POSITIVE SOCIAL, ENVIRONMENTAL
& ECONOMIC IMPACTS

+4
BE RESPONSIBLE

+3
BEYOND COMPLIANCE

+2
COMPLIANCE

+1
STRICT
COMPLIANCE

SITUATIONAL
NON-COMPLIANCE
-1

RATIONALIZE
NON-COMPLIANCE
-2

AVOID CRIMINAL PROSECUTION
-3

COST-BENEFIT ANALYSIS
-4

OUTSOURCE THE DIRTY WORK
-5

EXPLOIT
-6

SURVIVE
-7

ORGANIZATION'S
MOTIVATION

WHAT INTEGRITY CHOICES ARE AVAILABLE FOR ORGANIZATIONS?

Ascending Scale

The ascending scale of integrity on *A Measure of Integrity* marks off from level 1 to level 7 the gradients of positive integrity, from strict compliance with laws (level +1) to thinking regeneration and future generations (level +7). Level +3 marks the point where organizations move from compliance with laws to "beyond compliance" strategy. An organization does not necessarily operate at one single threshold. For example, many organizations choose to operate at level +2 (compliance) re: payment of taxes and at level +4 (beyond compliance) re: environmental and sustainability targets.

Descending Scale

The scale of diluting integrity—also marked off from levels 1 to 7—reflects what the demise of integrity can look like, and how these choices are rationalized. Organizations can slide into failed integrity, situationally justifying decisions (on a project, divisional or organization-wide basis) to side-step laws and policies that are perceived to be unfair (level -1) or rationalizing a sub-cultural norm to override compliance with laws and policies (level -2). At the mid-range of this declining scale are organizations willing to violate rules, even criminal laws, in response to catastrophic events or to stay competitive. It can be a bit like a game of Snakes and Ladders! At the very bottom of this scale, at level -7, you will find organizations and individuals who have plunged into full self-absorption: "It's all about me, right now!"

Nesting Layers

Like nesting Russian dolls, each successive level of integrity transcends and includes the previous level or levels on *A Measure of Integrity*. For example, at level +3, organizations are motivated to act beyond compliance with laws and policies. At level +3, that company is also motivated to comply with laws and policies (level +2) and strictly comply with legal requirements (level +1). The same is true in the descending scale. An organization functioning at level -4 (conducting cost-benefit analysis of compliance with laws) would also be motivated: to avoid criminal prosecution (level -3); to rationalize an overriding sub-cultural norm (level -2); and to situationally justify non-compliance with rules and laws (level -1).

Dark Side of Integrity

A Measure of Integrity is unique—this tool looks at the dark side of integrity as well as the positive aspects. Enterprise integrity has a dark side and a light side. The negative scale helps us recognize the dilution of enterprise integrity when it happens in other organizations (e.g., along supply chains, within organizational partners or competitors). And, even the most high-performing organizations can find themselves in negative integrity zones. *A Measure of Integrity* helps the organization's insiders recognize the risks and recover more quickly.

A MEASURE OF INTEGRITY CAN HELP ENTERPRISE ANSWER THESE CRITICAL QUESTIONS:

1. What Are the Enterprise's Core Values?

This tool encourages your organization to take a closer look at its core values. The example shared in Figure 2 on pages 200-01 focuses on the enterprise's commitment to the value of "sustainability." You can replace "sustainability" with any other core value in your organization (for example, transparency, commitment to communities, ethics, respect for human rights, safety, diversity, fairness, etc.).

2. How Do We Talk About Those Values, and How Do We Walk That Talk?

What level is your enterprise on *A Measure of Integrity*? Once you have decided on the core value you want to focus on, think about your organization's reasons for committing to that value, the ways you talk about that value, and your organization's actions. What level of the scale most closely describes your organization's approach to that value?

3. Are There Gaps? If So, How Can You Close Those Gaps?

In any organization, you have many individuals, even divisions and departments, acting on your enterprise's commitment to a value. Is everyone operating with the same assumptions? For example, your organization's legal department may appreciate its commitment to sustainability as a core value but may not understand that your organization wants to act, beyond compliance with rules and laws, at level +4 or +5 on *A Measure of Integrity*.

WHO SETS AN ORGANIZATION'S VALUES?

Whatever your enterprise pursuit—corporate, non-profit, public sector—I recommend that organizations choose their targeted level on the positive side of *A Measure of Integrity*. Not everyone agrees, but I believe that if organizations aren't violating laws set by legitimate and responsible governments or regulators, they get to exercise judgment and decide their values and what "acting with integrity" means for them. (And of course…live with the consequences of those choices.)

Twenty-first-century leaders also recognize that there is growing pressure on enterprise to make capitalism work better for more people. Enterprise that only aims to make profit risks censure in the court of public opinion. Public and stakeholder expectations—of government, social institutions, and capitalism in general—have been shifting for a while and pressure mounting, manifesting in several significant social movements.

Organizations make unique choices about their values. When people have a better understanding of the intentions behind an enterprise's commitments to core values, they can then have meaningful conversations with that organization and make better choices. Do we want to work for that organization, partner with that enterprise, or welcome that investor into our community?

We can also more accurately evaluate how that organization walks its talk. If the CEO says the enterprise wants to "do no harm," and the organization states in its annual report and other public and internal documents that this value is an organizational priority but fails to act in ways that demonstrate this purpose and commitment, stakeholders are better equipped to ask probing questions and demand accountability.

WHY REACH FOR HIGHER FRONTIERS?

Some organizations may be ready to target and move to even higher frontiers on *A Measure of Integrity*. This tool can help you guide your organization in upping your game, moving up a level or two.

Remember, this is not a cookie-cutter exercise. Individual organizations have unique reasons for choosing their core values. Individual organizations will manifest their core values in unique ways. Why do you want to build your organization's capacity to walk your talk on core values?

• To become more resilient

• To build credibility

• To gain competitive advantage

• To stop reacting to crisis

• To improve governance

• To build external trust

• To reduce litigation

• To improve access to capital

• To restore corporate confidence

• To attract and retain employees

FIGURE 2: SAMPLE TEMPLATE—SUSTAINABILITY

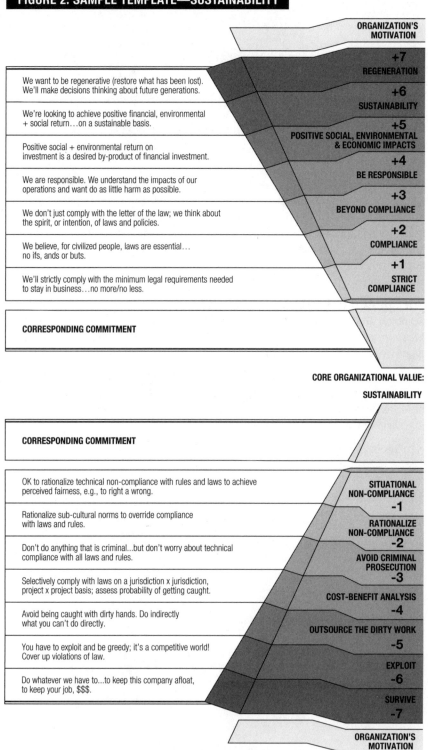

ORGANIZATION'S MOTIVATION

We want to be regenerative (restore what has been lost). We'll make decisions thinking about future generations.

+7 REGENERATION

We're looking to achieve positive financial, environmental + social return…on a sustainable basis.

+6 SUSTAINABILITY

Positive social + environmental return on investment is a desired by-product of financial investment.

+5 POSITIVE SOCIAL, ENVIRONMENTAL & ECONOMIC IMPACTS

We are responsible. We understand the impacts of our operations and want do as little harm as possible.

+4 BE RESPONSIBLE

We don't just comply with the letter of the law; we think about the spirit, or intention, of laws and policies.

+3 BEYOND COMPLIANCE

We believe, for civilized people, laws are essential… no ifs, ands or buts.

+2 COMPLIANCE

We'll strictly comply with the minimum legal requirements needed to stay in business…no more/no less.

+1 STRICT COMPLIANCE

CORRESPONDING COMMITMENT

CORE ORGANIZATIONAL VALUE:

SUSTAINABILITY

CORRESPONDING COMMITMENT

OK to rationalize technical non-compliance with rules and laws to achieve perceived fairness, e.g., to right a wrong.

**SITUATIONAL NON-COMPLIANCE
-1**

Rationalize sub-cultural norms to override compliance with laws and rules.

**RATIONALIZE NON-COMPLIANCE
-2**

Don't do anything that is criminal…but don't worry about technical compliance with all laws and rules.

**AVOID CRIMINAL PROSECUTION
-3**

Selectively comply with laws on a jurisdiction x jurisdiction, project x project basis; assess probability of getting caught.

**COST-BENEFIT ANALYSIS
-4**

Avoid being caught with dirty hands. Do indirectly what you can't do directly.

**OUTSOURCE THE DIRTY WORK
-5**

You have to exploit and be greedy; it's a competitive world! Cover up violations of law.

**EXPLOIT
-6**

Do whatever we have to…to keep this company afloat, to keep your job, $$$.

**SURVIVE
-7**

ORGANIZATION'S MOTIVATION

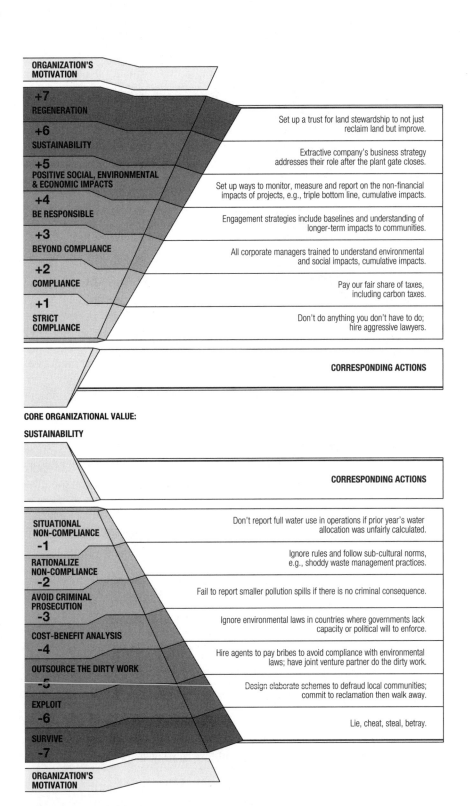

ORGANIZATION'S
MOTIVATION

+7
REGENERATION

+6
SUSTAINABILITY

+5
POSITIVE SOCIAL, ENVIRONMENTAL
& ECONOMIC IMPACTS

+4
BE RESPONSIBLE

+3
BEYOND COMPLIANCE

+2
COMPLIANCE

+1
STRICT
COMPLIANCE

Set up a trust for land stewardship to not just
reclaim land but improve.

Extractive company's business strategy
addresses their role after the plant gate closes.

Set up ways to monitor, measure and report on the non-financial
impacts of projects, e.g., triple bottom line, cumulative impacts.

Engagement strategies include baselines and understanding of
longer-term impacts to communities.

All corporate managers trained to understand environmental
and social impacts, cumulative impacts.

Pay our fair share of taxes,
including carbon taxes.

Don't do anything you don't have to do;
hire aggressive lawyers.

CORRESPONDING ACTIONS

CORE ORGANIZATIONAL VALUE:

SUSTAINABILITY

CORRESPONDING ACTIONS

SITUATIONAL
NON-COMPLIANCE
-1

RATIONALIZE
NON-COMPLIANCE
-2

AVOID CRIMINAL
PROSECUTION
-3

COST-BENEFIT ANALYSIS
-4

OUTSOURCE THE DIRTY WORK
-5

EXPLOIT
-6

SURVIVE
-7

Don't report full water use in operations if prior year's water
allocation was unfairly calculated.

Ignore rules and follow sub-cultural norms,
e.g., shoddy waste management practices.

Fail to report smaller pollution spills if there is no criminal consequence.

Ignore environmental laws in countries where governments lack
capacity or political will to enforce.

Hire agents to pay bribes to avoid compliance with environmental
laws; have joint venture partner do the dirty work.

Design elaborate schemes to defraud local communities;
commit to reclamation then walk away.

Lie, cheat, steal, betray.

ORGANIZATION'S
MOTIVATION

WHO IS RESPONSIBLE FOR AN ORGANIZATION'S INTEGRITY?

The short answer: Everyone! But there are different roles. External stakeholders—including governments and regulators, citizens in local communities, advocacy organizations and watchdogs, industry associations, consumers—set expectations and monitor corporate performance. Inside an organization, enterprise leaders (including the board of directors) are responsible to ensure that overall integrity targets for the organization are set, and may even champion efforts to move the organization up (or down) a notch or two on *A Measure of Integrity*. Managers generally oversee an organization's effective implementation of integrity commitments and actions.

HOW DOES ENTERPRISE INTEGRITY ALIGN WITH PERSONAL INTEGRITY?

This is an important question. Unless you are a sole proprietor, it's unlikely the integrity purpose of your employer will align perfectly with your personal values. If this tension is healthy—and open for dialogue—it can stimulate personal and/or organizational growth. But organizational momentum can be strong. It is not productive when organizations are pulling individuals along in a direction they don't want to go. When enterprise integrity and personal integrity are out of alignment, individuals can become frustrated, disengaged, or cynical.

HOW CAN I USE THIS TOOL?

The best way to use any universal tool, including *A Measure of Integrity*, is to apply the tool to your own situation. Create your own applications. Decide on the core value or values you want to focus on, then get started. Use the blank template in Figure 3 on pages 204-05 to launch this process in your own organization, guided by the detailed explanation below and the example in Figure 4 on pages 206-07, which focuses on the core value of Respect for Indigenous Peoples' Rights.

SAMPLE APPLICATION OF *A MEASURE OF INTEGRITY*

Steps to Guide the Application of *A Measure of Integrity* in Your Organization:

1. Choose a core value of your organization to focus on, and in big bold letters, name that value on *A Measure of Integrity*. For the purposes of our sample exercise (shown on pages 206-07), we will focus on the organization's value of respect for the rights of Indigenous peoples.

2. How do we talk about this value, and how do we walk that talk? Once you have decided on the core value you want to focus on, think about your organization's reasons for committing to that value, the ways you talk about that value, and your actions. What level of the scale most closely describes your organization's approach to that value?

If your company's approach is not obvious, consider the commitment and action columns on *A Measure of Integrity*. Do any of these commitments sound familiar?: "Our enterprise's responsibility is to comply with laws" (level +2); "To be competitive, we're going to be known as the organization that chooses to act beyond compliance with laws on Indigenous rights" (level +3); or "We're a responsible organization that cares; we don't want to do harm to Indigenous communities" (level +4).

Some organizations decide to target more than one level of integrity—perhaps compliance with local laws and policies (level +2) re: payment of taxes, and "beyond compliance" with laws (level +3) for other activities. Organizations may stretch integrity targets to distinguish their organization from competitors; for example, to function at level +5 or +6 re: Indigenous peoples' engagement, by committing to secure the free, prior and informed consent of Indigenous populations before making investments that impact these communities.

3. Are there gaps? If so, how can you close those gaps? As you fill in the commitments and actions columns of the tool for your organization, you will be able to readily identify any gaps. Is everyone operating with the same assumptions? In the sample exercise in Figure 4, there is a wide range of commitments and actions re: respect for Indigenous rights, creating confusion in the corporate commitments. And there are performance gaps between commitments and actions.

4. Setting new frontiers. Finally, if your organization is ready to move up a level or two, use *A Measure of Integrity* as a tool to help you set those new frontiers. What level are you motivated to target on *A Measure of Integrity* for your organization? And what are the corresponding commitments and actions?

FIGURE 3: BLANK TEMPLATE

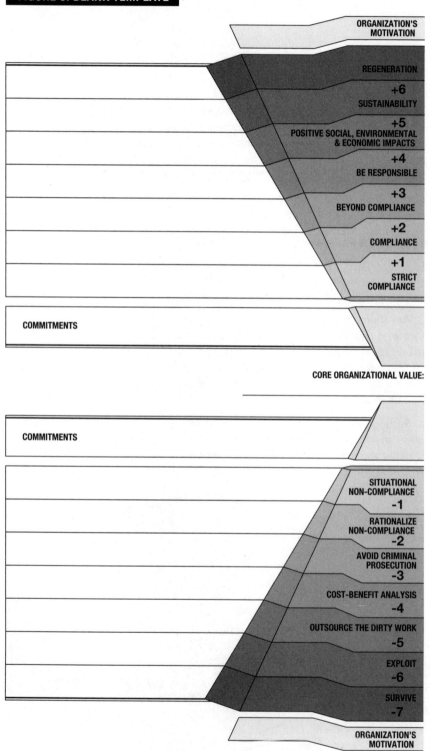

ORGANIZATION'S MOTIVATION

REGENERATION
+6
SUSTAINABILITY
+5
POSITIVE SOCIAL, ENVIRONMENTAL & ECONOMIC IMPACTS
+4
BE RESPONSIBLE
+3
BEYOND COMPLIANCE
+2
COMPLIANCE
+1
STRICT COMPLIANCE

COMMITMENTS

CORE ORGANIZATIONAL VALUE:

COMMITMENTS

SITUATIONAL NON-COMPLIANCE
-1
RATIONALIZE NON-COMPLIANCE
-2
AVOID CRIMINAL PROSECUTION
-3
COST-BENEFIT ANALYSIS
-4
OUTSOURCE THE DIRTY WORK
-5
EXPLOIT
-6
SURVIVE
-7

ORGANIZATION'S MOTIVATION

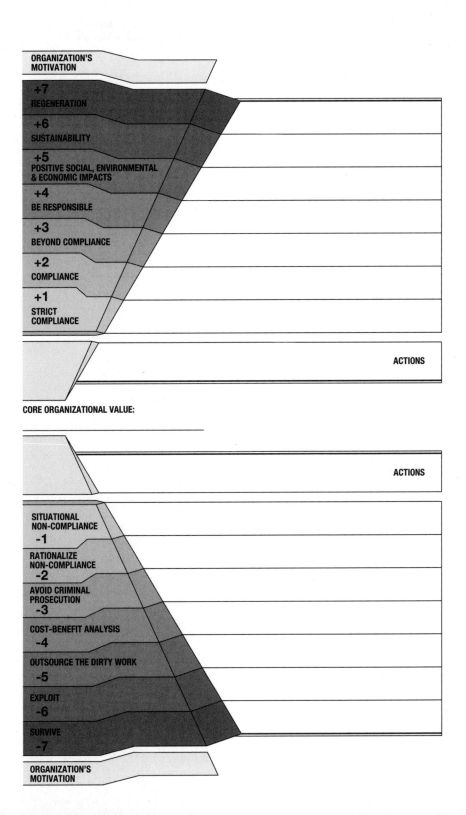

ORGANIZATION'S
MOTIVATION

+7
REGENERATION

+6
SUSTAINABILITY

+5
POSITIVE SOCIAL, ENVIRONMENTAL
& ECONOMIC IMPACTS

+4
BE RESPONSIBLE

+3
BEYOND COMPLIANCE

+2
COMPLIANCE

+1
STRICT
COMPLIANCE

ACTIONS

CORE ORGANIZATIONAL VALUE:

ACTIONS

SITUATIONAL
NON-COMPLIANCE
-1

RATIONALIZE
NON-COMPLIANCE
-2

AVOID CRIMINAL
PROSECUTION
-3

COST-BENEFIT ANALYSIS
-4

OUTSOURCE THE DIRTY WORK
-5

EXPLOIT
-6

SURVIVE
-7

ORGANIZATION'S
MOTIVATION

FIGURE 4: EXAMPLE—RESPECT FOR INDIGENOUS PEOPLES' RIGHTS

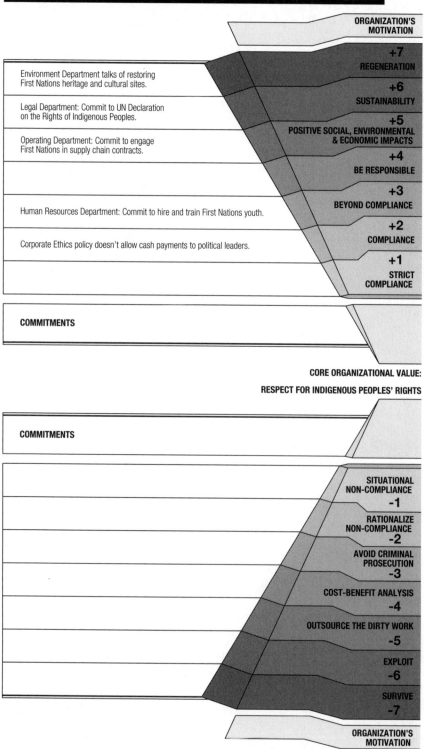

ORGANIZATION'S
MOTIVATION

+7
REGENERATION

Environment Department talks of restoring
First Nations heritage and cultural sites.

+6
SUSTAINABILITY

Legal Department: Commit to UN Declaration
on the Rights of Indigenous Peoples.

+5
POSITIVE SOCIAL, ENVIRONMENTAL
& ECONOMIC IMPACTS

Operating Department: Commit to engage
First Nations in supply chain contracts.

+4
BE RESPONSIBLE

+3
BEYOND COMPLIANCE

Human Resources Department: Commit to hire and train First Nations youth.

+2
COMPLIANCE

Corporate Ethics policy doesn't allow cash payments to political leaders.

+1
STRICT
COMPLIANCE

COMMITMENTS

CORE ORGANIZATIONAL VALUE:

RESPECT FOR INDIGENOUS PEOPLES' RIGHTS

COMMITMENTS

SITUATIONAL
NON-COMPLIANCE
-1

RATIONALIZE
NON-COMPLIANCE
-2

AVOID CRIMINAL
PROSECUTION
-3

COST-BENEFIT ANALYSIS
-4

OUTSOURCE THE DIRTY WORK
-5

EXPLOIT
-6

SURVIVE
-7

ORGANIZATION'S
MOTIVATION

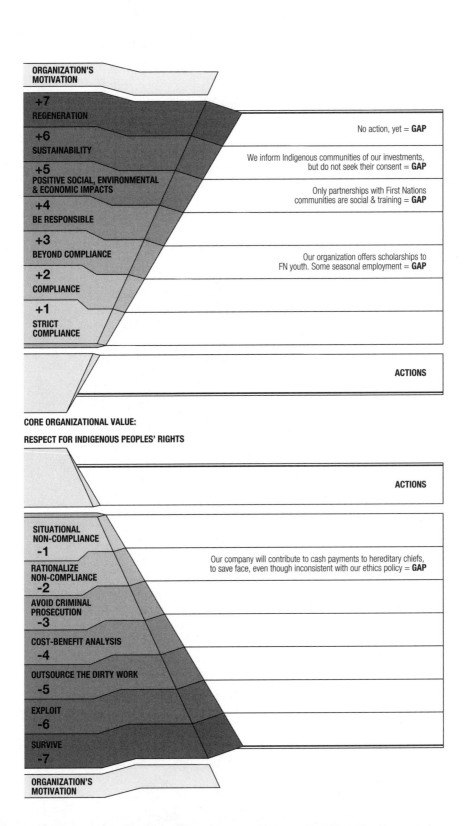

ORGANIZATION'S MOTIVATION

+7
REGENERATION

+6
SUSTAINABILITY

+5
POSITIVE SOCIAL, ENVIRONMENTAL & ECONOMIC IMPACTS

+4
BE RESPONSIBLE

+3
BEYOND COMPLIANCE

+2
COMPLIANCE

+1
STRICT COMPLIANCE

No action, yet = **GAP**

We inform Indigenous communities of our investments, but do not seek their consent = **GAP**

Only partnerships with First Nations communities are social & training = **GAP**

Our organization offers scholarships to FN youth. Some seasonal employment = **GAP**

ACTIONS

CORE ORGANIZATIONAL VALUE:

RESPECT FOR INDIGENOUS PEOPLES' RIGHTS

ACTIONS

SITUATIONAL NON-COMPLIANCE
-1

RATIONALIZE NON-COMPLIANCE
-2

AVOID CRIMINAL PROSECUTION
-3

COST-BENEFIT ANALYSIS
-4

OUTSOURCE THE DIRTY WORK
-5

EXPLOIT
-6

SURVIVE
-7

Our company will contribute to cash payments to hereditary chiefs, to save face, even though inconsistent with our ethics policy = **GAP**

ORGANIZATION'S MOTIVATION

INTEGRITY MINDFULNESS NEVER ENDS

Keep checking for alignment in your organization's intentions on core values, and corresponding commitments and actions. Are there any expectation gaps between your organization's targeted level on *A Measure of Integrity*, and commitments? Are there any performance gaps between your organization's commitments and actions? This alignment requires ongoing management. **Acting with integrity is active work.**

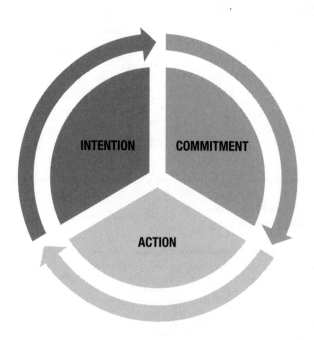

A MEASURE OF INTEGRITY SCORECARD

The scorecard is a companion tool designed to help guide conversations with your key stakeholders about your enterprise values. This template is designed for use with any stakeholder or stakeholder group: internal (e.g., shareholders, individual divisions, investors, board members, employees) or external (e.g., different communities, partners, supply chain, critics). An example of how to use the *Measure of Integrity* template as a scorecard is shown in Figure 5 on pages 210-11.

HOW DOES THE SCORECARD WORK?

First, we encourage organizations to identify a core value to focus on. Maybe it is community investment, sustainability, diversity, environmental protection, or relationships with unionized labour.

Ask the organization: What is your targeted level for this value on *A Measure of Integrity* (Your Target)? And where are you now, regarding the core value in question (Your Reality)?

Then, ask the stakeholder group: What is your perception of this company's target for this value (What Do Stakeholders See)? What are your expectations of this organization regarding this core value (What Do Stakeholders Want)?

Observe any gaps in your organization's targeted level of *A Measure of Integrity*, and your reality. Observe the stakeholders' perceptions and expectations of your organization on this value. Discuss what can be done to close the gaps.

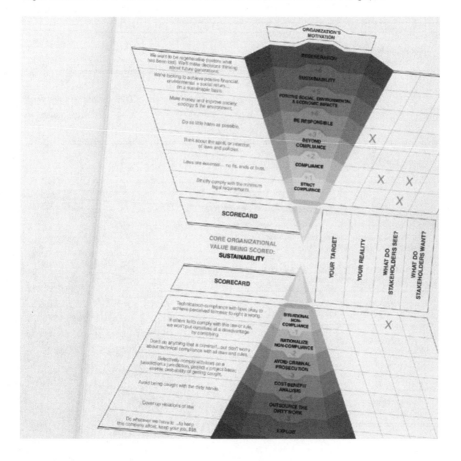

FIGURE 5: SAMPLE SCORECARD—SUSTAINABILITY

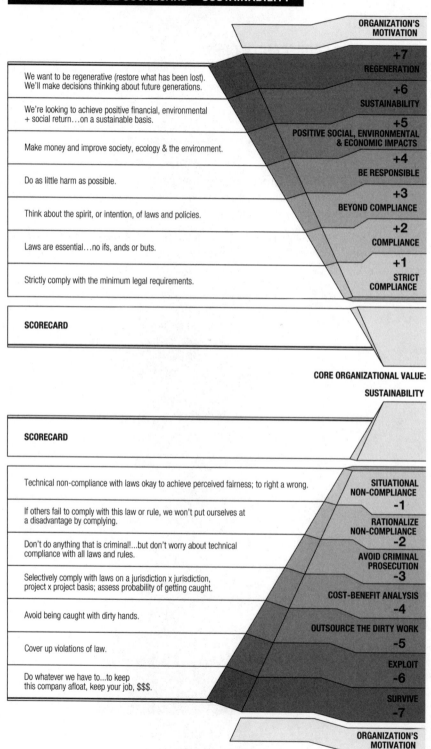

ORGANIZATION'S MOTIVATION

We want to be regenerative (restore what has been lost). We'll make decisions thinking about future generations.
+7 REGENERATION

We're looking to achieve positive financial, environmental + social return...on a sustainable basis.
+6 SUSTAINABILITY

+5 POSITIVE SOCIAL, ENVIRONMENTAL & ECONOMIC IMPACTS

Make money and improve society, ecology & the environment.
+4 BE RESPONSIBLE

Do as little harm as possible.
+3 BEYOND COMPLIANCE

Think about the spirit, or intention, of laws and policies.
+2 COMPLIANCE

Laws are essential...no ifs, ands or buts.
+1 STRICT COMPLIANCE

Strictly comply with the minimum legal requirements.

SCORECARD

CORE ORGANIZATIONAL VALUE:

SUSTAINABILITY

SCORECARD

Technical non-compliance with laws okay to achieve perceived fairness; to right a wrong.
SITUATIONAL NON-COMPLIANCE
-1

If others fail to comply with this law or rule, we won't put ourselves at a disadvantage by complying.
RATIONALIZE NON-COMPLIANCE
-2

Don't do anything that is criminal!...but don't worry about technical compliance with all laws and rules.
AVOID CRIMINAL PROSECUTION
-3

Selectively comply with laws on a jurisdiction x jurisdiction, project x project basis; assess probability of getting caught.
COST-BENEFIT ANALYSIS
-4

Avoid being caught with dirty hands.
OUTSOURCE THE DIRTY WORK
-5

Cover up violations of law.
EXPLOIT
-6

Do whatever we have to...to keep this company afloat, keep your job, $$$.
SURVIVE
-7

ORGANIZATION'S MOTIVATION

ORGANIZATION'S MOTIVATION	YOUR TARGET	YOUR REALITY	WHAT DO STAKEHOLDERS SEE?	WHAT DO STAKEHOLDERS WANT?
+7 REGENERATION				
+6 SUSTAINABILITY				
+5 POSITIVE SOCIAL, ENVIRONMENTAL & ECONOMIC IMPACTS				X
+4 BE RESPONSIBLE				X
+3 BEYOND COMPLIANCE	X			
+2 COMPLIANCE				
+1 STRICT COMPLIANCE		X	X	
			X	

CORE ORGANIZATIONAL VALUE:

SUSTAINABILITY

ORGANIZATION'S MOTIVATION	YOUR TARGET	YOUR REALITY	WHAT DO STAKEHOLDERS SEE?	WHAT DO STAKEHOLDERS WANT?
SITUATIONAL NON-COMPLIANCE			X	
-1 RATIONALIZE NON-COMPLIANCE				
-2 AVOID CRIMINAL PROSECUTION				
-3 COST-BENEFIT ANALYSIS				
-4 OUTSOURCE THE DIRTY WORK				
-5 EXPLOIT				
-6 SURVIVE				
-7				

ORGANIZATION'S MOTIVATION

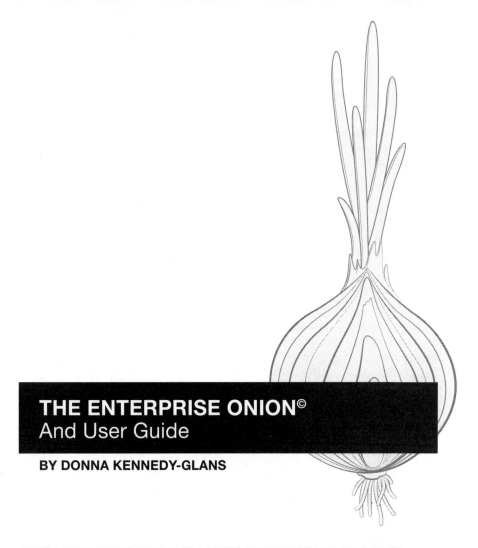

THE ENTERPRISE ONION©
And User Guide

BY DONNA KENNEDY-GLANS

REBUILDING ENTERPRISE: TEACHING THE DINOSAUR TO DANCE

The Enterprise Onion is a tool designed to help enterprise rebuilders and new builders engage more deliberately with others who have a strategic interest in an enterprise and can influence the path forward.

Every enterprise has some understanding of key "stakeholders" (an over-used and sloppy term), and stakeholder influence and interest mapping is common practice, but insufficient if your enterprise wants to build more durable consensus on new ideas, new strategies, and maybe even new values. There isn't a right or wrong way of seeing the world, but when you are rebuilding your enterprise with new ideas and innovation, making complex choices, or are stuck in polarized debate, it's useful to understand how others see an issue and to consider how engagement with these views can aid or inhibit your enterprise's path forward.

Engagement with stakeholders—who think differently, ask different questions, and maybe even hold different values—is encouraged if your enterprise wants to evaluate a big new idea or strategy. And engagement with a wide range of unique perspectives is encouraged to create the conditions for sustainable change in your enterprise values, strategy or purpose.

To be clear, the aim of engaging with a range of stakeholder perspectives is not to merge worldviews into one reductionist, lowest-common-denominator strategy. Watered-down consensus is not helpful to enterprise rebuilding.

Stakeholder and public expectations of government, social institutions and capitalism in general have been shifting for a while and pressure mounting, manifesting in several significant social movements—as diverse as MeToo, Occupy, Divest, Black Lives Matter, Arab Spring, Fridays for Future—pushing for equality, fairness and sustainability. *The Enterprise Onion* is not a model that avoids conflict; it assumes conflict. If an influential stakeholder with a different belief system opposes your enterprise's values, engagement can become polarized and entrenched. This tool will help you move beyond that polarity.

WHERE TO BEGIN?
Engagement with your enterprise's internal team—employees, contractors, shareholders, owners, and directors—is essential. Internal stakeholders will have different ways of thinking, and that diversity is encouraged.

Enterprise Internal Team
The Enterprise Onion is primarily an outward-facing tool, modelling how to recognize and engage with stakeholders outside your own organization, working from the enterprise core to the outer layers of the onion; from the internal enterprise family, to the like-minded, to the open-minded, to the skeptical-minded, and perhaps even reaching the cynical-minded.

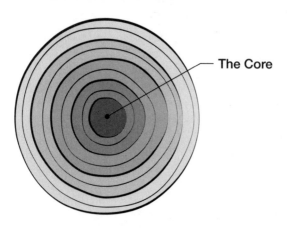

The Core

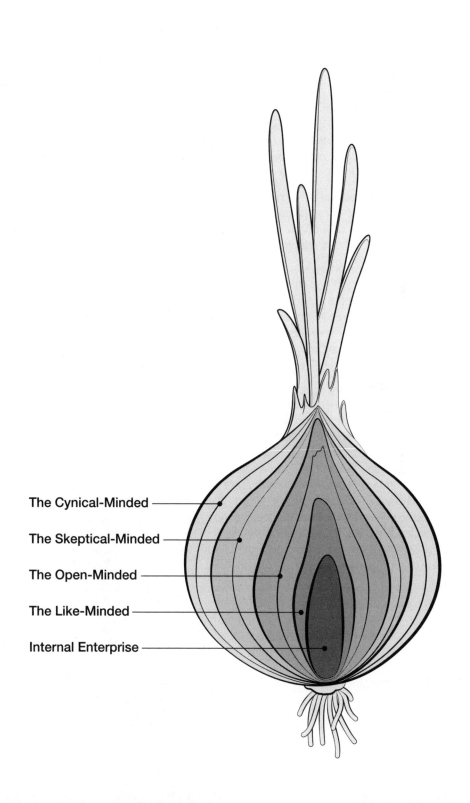

The Cynical-Minded

The Skeptical-Minded

The Open-Minded

The Like-Minded

Internal Enterprise

The Like-Minded

To initiate consideration of an idea or strategy beyond the boundaries of your internal team, enterprise is often most comfortable engaging with like-minded stakeholders. These are people and organizations who see the world in much the same way as you do, perhaps supply chains or partners or independent board members with skin in the game, or local community organizations, media and citizens with interests already well aligned to your enterprise.

You expect like-minded stakeholders to think like your enterprise, and to be positively predisposed to your ideas and strategies. And the more influential your allies, the better for your enterprise. There is often a sense that your enterprise retains a fair amount of control of outcomes when engaging with like-minded stakeholders.

When stakeholder engagement extends only as far as the like-minded, enterprise decision-makers can sometimes presume that a new idea or strategy will be acceptable and effective in wider spheres. When enterprise constrains engagement to the like-minded, seeking feedback or input only from stakeholders expected to confirm your beliefs and values and biases, echo-chambers can be created and monocultures perpetuated.

The Open-Minded

When enterprise moves a little out of its comfort zones to engage more objective (yet interested) stakeholders, new ideas and strategies and possibilities are more likely to be critically assessed. A technical expert may be open to evaluating and analyzing revitalized solutions to a pressing problem; a competitor may be open to collaborating on the design of a reformulated industry standard; a community may be open to exploring the possibility of an atypical development project if their priorities are understood and addressed. The enterprise does not retain control of the outcome of engagement with open-minded stakeholders, yet choices derived from engagement across a more diverse range of worldviews are likely to build consensus and be resilient.

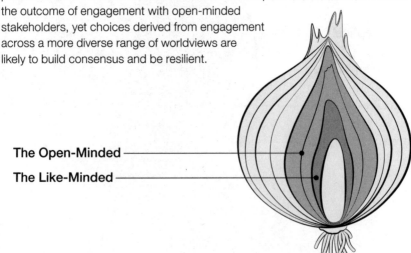

The Open-Minded ——————————————

The Like-Minded ——————————————

The Skeptical-Minded

Your enterprise can no doubt identify stakeholders who, while fair-minded, you also anticipate may be skeptical about your new idea or innovative strategy. Reaching out to stakeholders who are more apt to question or challenge can be uncomfortable; there is a risk that your idea will be rejected.

Engaging the skeptical usually requires trust-building. It's not easy to, for example, win back disgruntled clients with a quality assurance campaign, persuade wary businesses that your government's new red-tape reduction strategy is sincere, or convince climate change advocates to believe that your hydrocarbon company has had a change in values and is committed to renewables. Yet if this engagement across a more diverse spectrum of viewpoints is effective, more creative ideas and strategies can be generated and the outcomes more sustained.

The Cynical-Minded

It can be daunting to reach out to stakeholders with worldviews that contradict or oppose the ideas of your enterprise. But there are times when ignoring antagonistic points of view is neither possible nor recommended. If a negative social media campaign is directed at your enterprise, you can hope it all blows over or you can engage with your critics. If there is a critical incident or crisis in a local community and your enterprise is involved, you must anticipate confrontation. Sometimes, engagement between your enterprise and stakeholders with opposing perspectives becomes a polarized conflict between two belief systems or two cultural trends. For example, the debate between get tough on crime versus restitution, or the pipeline battles. If the power of the parties with the opposing viewpoints is relatively matched, the issue can remain stuck in polarity until a new truth emerges.

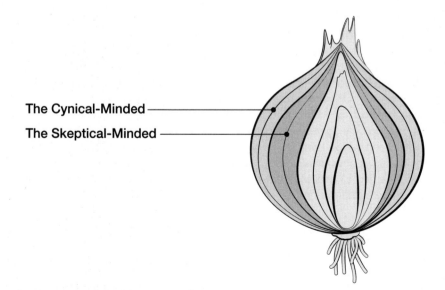

The Cynical-Minded

The Skeptical-Minded

WHAT KIND OF REBUILDING EFFORT DOES YOUR ENTERPRISE REQUIRE?

"An Incremental and Reactive Strategy Is Good Enough."

Your enterprise rebuilding strategy may involve step-by-step incremental measures—responding to issues whenever there is a need rather than working from a design that involves a system-wide strategic shift. A reactive strategy will be heavily influenced by political, technical, cultural, and legal constraints and opportunities in your enterprise's operating environment. Analytical engagement with like-minded and open-minded stakeholders may be sufficient to rationally test an idea or policy against empirical data and foster consensus building.

"We Need a Revitalizing and Proactive Strategy."

If you prefer a more proactive and intentional rebuilding effort, your enterprise creativity and imagination can be stimulated by engagement with a wider range of diverse perspectives. Your aim may be to revitalize a return to your enterprise's core values, or you may decide to advance a new creative idea or innovation that solves a problem, defuses a tension or creates new value.

"Right Now, Transformation Is What's Required!"

Transformational change in an enterprise (for example, the design and implementation of new values and organizing principles) generally requires engagement with all stakeholders—the like-minded, the open-minded, the skeptical and the cynical. This scale of change happens when people and organizations can no longer sustain the status quo. Often, transformational change is driven bottom-up and/or externally, manifesting community or citizen values.

Whatever Path You Choose, Be Intentional

Embarking on a pathway of stakeholder engagement, and then turning back, can leave a trail of distrust, unrest, inertia and cynicism. For example, the Government of Alberta released a new coal policy in the province in 2020, allowing open-pit coal mining on the previously protected eastern slopes of the Rocky Mountains. The government consulted with the coal industry on the new legislation but few others. The new policy triggered a tsunami of public response from angry voices in the skeptical and cynical layers of *The Enterprise Onion* (citizens in local communities rose up, environmental advocates campaigned, and popular country singer Corb Lund emerged to challenge the government policy). The beleaguered provincial government withdrew the offending policy.

CASE STUDIES

Sometimes an enterprise will initiate and lead a revitalization or transformational strategy, engaging with others to understand their perspectives on a new idea or a solution to a problem (for example, Chancellor Angela Merkel's "Green Shift" strategy in Germany).

Sometimes an entirely new way of thinking about an issue will be demanded or imposed by stakeholders (for example, communities in Alberta devastated by Amoco Canada's sour-gas blowout).

And sometimes, engagement between proponents of an idea and stakeholders with opposing perspectives becomes an antagonistic conflict that gets stuck.

The case studies that follow share examples.

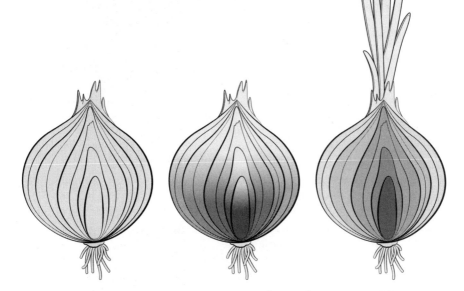

Renewable Energy Integration: Contrasting Germany & Alberta

In 2011, the Fukushima nuclear disaster in Japan shocked German citizens, and reversed the country's position on nuclear power. Then German Chancellor, Angela Merkel, championed the phase-out of nuclear and the integration of wind and solar, while continuing to lead one of the world's largest industrial economies. This "Green Shift" advanced by Merkel is best described as top-down. Beyond the Fukushima nuclear scare, there would be many sound reasons to explain the German government's directed shift to greener energy: Germany is dependent on other countries for hydrocarbon resources and Russia's threats to shut off natural gas pipelined to Europe and oil price volatility create vulnerability. Merkel's ability to align with the values of German citizens on this push to renewable energy enabled scalable momentum, in a relatively short timeframe. Merkel was also able to enlist scientists and researchers, businesses and municipalities in broad-based adoption of this policy.

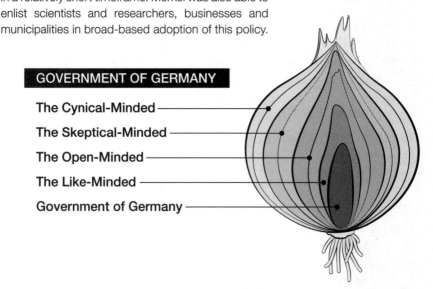

GOVERNMENT OF GERMANY

The Cynical-Minded

The Skeptical-Minded

The Open-Minded

The Like-Minded

Government of Germany

By contrast, the transition to renewables in Alberta, Canada, is unfolding in increments with no single top-down authority leading with a master plan. Alberta is a jurisdiction with significant non-renewable energy resources (abundant oil, natural gas and coal). Over the last decade, the Alberta Electric System Operator improved technical integration of wind into the provincial electricity grid and some regulatory smoothing improved the logistics of solar and micro-generation. In 2014, 55 percent of Alberta's electricity was produced from eighteen coal-fired generators; in 2015, the Alberta

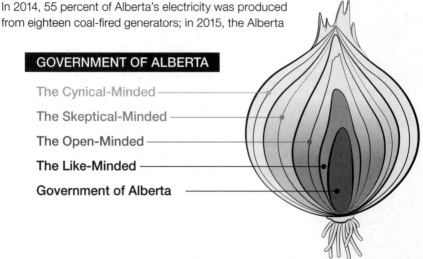

GOVERNMENT OF ALBERTA

The Cynical-Minded

The Skeptical-Minded

The Open-Minded

The Like-Minded

Government of Alberta

government announced it would eliminate emissions from coal-powered generation, by 2030 (and is on track to meet that goal ahead of target). Municipalities and green businesses in Alberta champion renewable energy initiatives (e.g., wind-powered light rail transit system in Calgary; district heat installations; small-scale hydroelectricity) on a project-by-project basis. There is ongoing analysis of renewable energy options by corporate, government and scientific actors, and the full potential and pace for adoption of renewable energy is debated across a full range of stakeholder perspectives with conflicting views on federal-provincial jurisdictional authority for carbon and climate policies.

Gas Flaring in Alberta, as a Model of a Transformational Rebuild

Gas flaring is the controlled burning of natural gas in hydrocarbon production, and the practice has negative environmental, health and climate change impacts. In the 1970s and 1980s, natural gas discovered with oil was often flared in Alberta. Then, there was ongoing dialogue among representatives of the Government of Alberta, the Energy Resources Conservation Board (the provincial energy regulator), energy producers, drilling companies, engineers and scientists, on cost-effective ways to re-inject natural gas into oil wells to boost productivity. Changes made were largely incremental, and came about as a result of analytical engagement between corporate, regulatory and scientific stakeholders.

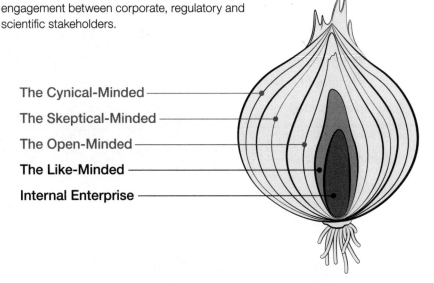

The Cynical-Minded

The Skeptical-Minded

The Open-Minded

The Like-Minded

Internal Enterprise

On October 17, 1982, Amoco Canada (a hydrocarbon producing company) lost control of a major sour gas well near Lodgepole, Alberta. It was the worst sour gas blowout in the province's history, taking emergency responders sixty-eight days to cap and exposing citizens and animals in the local community to deadly hydrogen sulphide. Impacted communities, led by local citizens Rob MacIntosh and Wally Heinrich, forced a public inquiry into the blowout, securing more than eighty regulatory changes from the Government of Alberta and the provincial energy regulator.

Citizens in the affected communities, led by local champions, came together after the crisis to envision a different future state for gas flaring in Alberta. These advocates influenced hydrocarbon companies to incorporate community voice and values in decision-making about gas flaring. And, MacIntosh and Heinrich assertively demanded that government, regulators and companies accept new ideas about how and why to manage gas flaring in Alberta.

In 1985, MacIntosh and Heinrich launched a non-profit advocacy organization, the Pembina Institute, to foster collaboration among scientists, researchers, and communities to ensure impacts of gas flaring were anticipated, evaluated and responded to by governments and investors, in policy and practice. In 1994, the Clean Air Strategic Alliance was created in Alberta, intentionally bringing together perspectives from government, industry, science, communities and environmental champions to collaborate on ways to monitor, measure and minimize the negative impacts of gas flaring in Alberta. Between 1996 and 2010, gas flaring in Alberta was reduced by 80 percent and is on track to be completely eliminated.

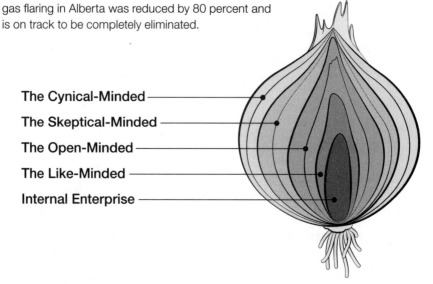

The Cynical-Minded

The Skeptical-Minded

The Open-Minded

The Like-Minded

Internal Enterprise

Keystone XL Pipeline Expansion, as a Model of a Dialectic Pathway

Expansion of the Keystone XL pipeline (a pipeline that crosses the Canada-U.S. border and transports oil produced from the Alberta oil sands to refineries along the U.S. Gulf Coast) is an example of dialectic entrenchment, in this case between companies in support of revitalizing oil transportation capacity in North America and influential environmentalists and political actors vigorously opposing development of Alberta's oil sands.

A decade ago, the American hydrocarbon sector applied fracking technology to accelerate the production of oil and gas resources from shale reserves and transformed the United States from a net hydrocarbon importer to a net exporter. These changes catalyzed significant analysis by policy makers, academics, and business (the like-minded and the open-minded) on the redesign of pipeline hubs and routes, and on the question of transportation safety as shipping crude oil by railway cars became common practice. Citizens in affected communities (the skeptical-minded) are understandably motivated to understand the risks, including potential impacts to water aquifers if a pipeline leaks and the likelihood of crude-bearing railcars derailing.

Approvals to expand the Keystone XL pipeline continued to be refused in the United States, by President Obama in his exercise of Presidential veto and again in 2021 by President Joe Biden. A lineup of celebrities—Robert Redford, Tom Steyer, NASA-trained scientists at Harvard, Stanford and the University of Chicago and a long list of others—press to have Alberta's oil sands shut in. The polarization of viewpoints between pipeline expansion proponents and environmental activists and political actors is entrenched.

Experts, academics and business have tried to break the impasse by quantifying the economic and social upsides of freer-flowing oil routes in North America (for example, safety, efficient utilization of U.S. refineries, royalties and taxes funding education and healthcare, jobs and training, reliability and security of energy supply). Direct engagement with land-owners, unions, local citizens and environmentalists attempts to inject values into these scientific and economic discussions. Yet these efforts, across several worldviews, have not yet broken the impasse. Ultimately, in June 2021, the pipeline proponent, TC Energy, terminated the project.

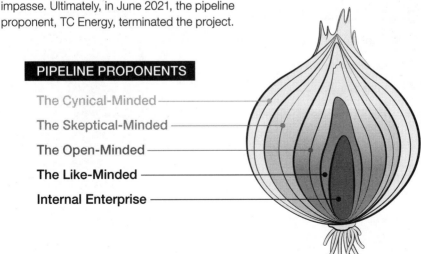

PIPELINE PROPONENTS

The Cynical-Minded

The Skeptical-Minded

The Open-Minded

The Like-Minded

Internal Enterprise

What Does Your Enterprise Onion Look Like?
Shade in the layers of engagement with like-minded, open-minded, skeptical-minded and cynical-minded stakeholders:

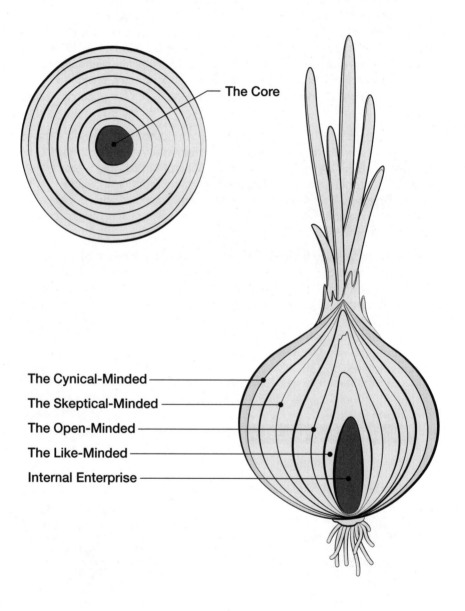

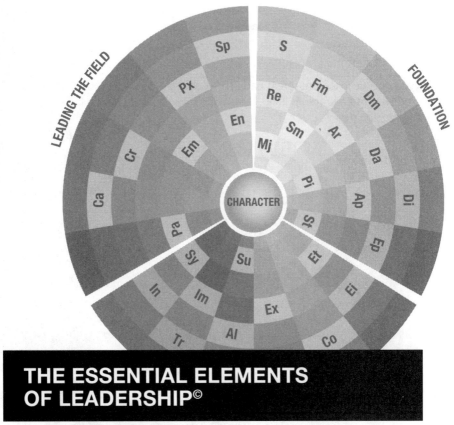

THE ESSENTIAL ELEMENTS OF LEADERSHIP©

BY ANDRE N. MAMPRIN

INTRODUCTION TO *THE ESSENTIAL ELEMENTS OF LEADERSHIP*

The Essential Elements of Leadership originated in 2005 and has been refined over the years through exhaustive applied research, observation and documented evidence of more than 4800 leaders. Originally, there were twelve *Essential Elements of Leadership*. After ten years, 40,000 hours with thirty organizations in twenty-one sectors, each with 100 to 30,000 employees, our observation of changes in the leadership landscape required expanding the elements in 2015.

Leadership

Leadership, which has been studied for centuries, is contextual. What constitutes a leader's success in one enterprise may not ensure their success in another. However, there is a direct correlation between strong and effective leadership and organizational results.

If you can't describe what great leadership looks like, you can't build it. *The Essential Elements of Leadership* is how we, at The Next Institute, define leadership in an organizational context.

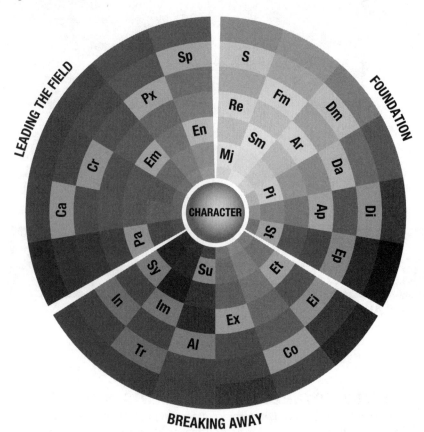

Emerging, Experienced and Seasoned Leadership

To make an ever-growing contribution to the enterprise, leaders must move beyond technical skill, build interpersonal capacity, and operate with confidence in the conceptual and creative realms. The organization that commits to this development generates powerful results for the leader, team, and enterprise.

We have segmented *The Essential Elements of Leadership* into three developmental stages. Historically, we observed that leaders progress and evolve from emerging leaders to more experienced leaders then finally to seasoned leadership. You will be able to identify these leaders when you see them and experience their leadership.

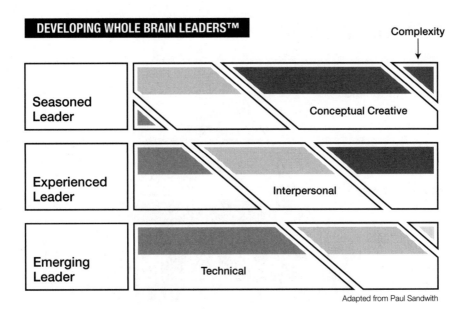

DEVELOPING WHOLE BRAIN LEADERS™

Complexity

Seasoned Leader — Conceptual Creative

Experienced Leader — Interpersonal

Emerging Leader — Technical

Adapted from Paul Sandwith

Effective development meets leaders where they are. The emerging-to-experienced leader relies on "knowing and doing." A leader can know about leadership by study or reading, but at some point, a leader is called into doing the difficult work of leadership. This is where the deep journey of learning and discovery begins. The leadership learning journey continues at every stage.

The primary need for an emerging leader is a more powerful toolbox, used with greater assurance and self-awareness. Over time, the experienced-to-seasoned leader operates from the realm of "being." The primary need at that stage is a deeper understanding and development of character. Seasoned leaders step into their leadership with confidence. Whole Brain Leader™ capacity allows for the skillful and seamless toggling from the analytical, binary and sequential left brain to the conceptual, creative, aesthetic and emotional right side. This capability makes for a leader who can read a situation, discern and apply the skills required.

Leaders become open to different ways of knowing, doing and being as they develop, learning to incorporate new senses and inputs in service to accelerating the growth of their leadership practice and the enterprise in a smart way.

The Essential Elements of Leadership are personal leadership attributes and link to the enterprise attributes in the Intelligent Enterprise Framework.

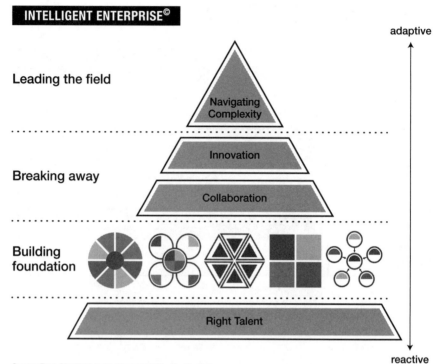

Source: Ross Gilchrist & Andre Mamprin © The Next Institute

The first segment of *The Essential Elements of Leadership* is **Foundational Elements**. In today's environment, these elements of leadership are requisite. If a leader is unable to demonstrate proficiency in these elements, they may not even "be in the game."

The second segment is **Breaking Away.** These elements are somewhat aspirational and not the norm among leaders we researched. These elements line up with a strong capacity for collaboration and innovation. They are higher in creativity and require a more demanding capacity to imagine the adjacent possible.

Finally, the third segment is **Leading the Field.** These elements are the highest order of leadership thinking and action. These elements are witnessed in leaders and organizations that are continuously leading in their respective fields of endeavour and are adept at navigating complexity. This is higher-order leading, and uncommon. Having said this, we observed some that were capable of such leadership. These leaders were gifted and inspiring. These behaviours are worthy of further study and emulation.

The Essential Elements of Leadership are based on observable behaviours. Once a behaviour can be observed, it can be developed. As you develop as a leader, you will begin to, and continue to, demonstrate these behaviours as outlined in the behavioural statements that follow.

Capacity, Character and Cultural Fit

When observing and developing leadership behaviour, context is critical. There are three significant distinctions: capacity, character and cultural fit.

The **capacity** to lead is all about developing and refining the ability to lead.

The **character** of a leader cannot be developed. The attributes of a leader's character include courage, tenacity, integrity, empathy and ethics, to name only a few. A character attribute such as courage cannot be taught; however, we can create the conditions for "discovery" to occur. The character of a leader is a significant factor in the leadership equation and is often the hidden force that is essential in rounding out the leadership mix.

All leaders operate within a specific environment. This is the "context" in which leaders operate and this environment can be considered an ecosystem. Each ecosystem is unique because there are many other humans within the ecosystem.

More than one human within an ecosystem becomes a culture. Culture is extremely sensitive and will either accept or reject the leader (there are many variations of negative reactions to leaders, from mild resistance to outright organized rejection or push-back). A leader's **cultural fit** is instrumental to the leader's success. Leaders significantly influence culture, and often can create culture. Take, for example, introducing a toxic leader into an ecosystem: over time, the entire ecosystem becomes toxic. Conversely, a strong leader can have a positive effect on changing an ecosystem for the better.

Character [C]

Character is the essence of a human and a leader. It is how you behave when no one is looking. It is a settled habit, way of being, nature, or the sum of qualities that define a person. Character cannot be developed but can be discovered and shaped over time during crucible moments.

True leadership comes first from deep within and arises from the continual expression of an individual's unique character. It is distinct personal qualities that underlie the expression of the leader's style and the way one exercises their leadership.

The objective is to lead authentically. Over time an individual grows into the role of leader and grows because of the role of leader. The leader learns to express their uniqueness through increased self-awareness, self-understanding and confidence. This personal authenticity comes from genuine self-expression and is derived from character.

Character is free from circumstances and forms the moral ecology of the leader. Leaders with character are the persons in an organization, culture or society who are seen to demonstrate consistent moral, dispositional and emotional qualities that are expressed in what they say and what they do. Some attributes of character include empathy, humility, grace, integrity, honesty, courage, respect, dignity, love and perseverance.

THE FOUNDATIONAL ELEMENTS OF LEADERSHIP

Self-mastery [S]

Self-mastery is the individual, continuous, lifelong journey to stronger character and higher consciousness. It is the openness to feedback and the willingness to change. It is the understanding of personal strengths and weaknesses, and the choice to learn from experience. It is the rigorous examination of oneself in relation to others. Self-mastery is the starting point on the journey of developing as a leader. It opens the door to significance, and it entices others to follow.

- I understand my values, motivations and intention.
- I demonstrate mature judgment, empathy and restraint.
- I understand my strengths and limitations.
- I can control anger and emotions when others are involved.
- I act with a sense of personal responsibility and accountability.
- I am authentic to myself.
- I am open to and seek feedback to continuously grow and improve.
- I can admit my mistakes and move on.
- I model the way with my leadership skills and behaviour.
- I display an ethical sensibility.
- I am self-aware and realize how I choose to conduct myself has a profound effect on others.

Resilience [Re]

Resilience is the energy and rigour to meet the physically, mentally and emotionally demanding role of leadership. Resilience is the capacity to accept and face reality which prepares us to act in ways that help us endure and survive change, challenges and hardships. Resilience is thinking on our feet and solving problems when the obvious tools and solutions are not there.

- I rely on my values to help me face times of change, turmoil and upheaval.
- Mindfulness and interacting with nature help regulate my reactions to stressful situations.
- Stress, heat and energy that comes my way from others is not about me.
- I am able to apply more "Teflon" and less "Velcro."
- I recharge with activities that energize me, provide fuel and give me perspective.
- I deploy a range of techniques to shield me from and navigate toxic people and situations.

Mature Judgment [Mj]

Exerting mature judgment is knowing and doing the next right thing. It is also being seen to be doing the right thing, whether or not that is popular. It is holding the highest interest of others, and the organization, above self-interest. It is an expression of character. It is what leaders must do.

- I reflect a conscious and consistent commitment to the work.
- I opt for doing the right thing regardless of how difficult.
- I take calculated action towards an ideal end state for all involved.
- I deploy curiosity and inquire deeply to reflect on the best course of action.
- I work in the best interest of the people I lead and focus on the greater good when possible.

Future-making [Fm]

Future-making is birthing something that does not yet exist, initially as an idea and eventually as an extraordinary reality. It is vision, imagination and creativity. It is seeing what others may not yet see. It is the courage to stake out new ground. It is a process that occurs over time, and it is holding the space as that process unfolds.

- I can see a viable future beyond the current reality.
- I continuously strive for relevance.
- I am a pioneer able to chart new paths.
- I am comfortable navigating the unknown.
- I understand the positive and negative impacts of change.
- I consider and work with a range of possible futures.

Sense-making [Sm]

Sense-making is the radar, registering strong and weak signals from all levels of the environment. It is intuitive and strategic, sensing a change, spotting trends, seeing what's happening. It is understanding how the past informs the future. It is translating nuance and complexity into relevance and meaning for the organization. Sense-making requires a deeper understanding of the system.

- I articulate purpose and mission by connecting the "what" and the "why."
- I can quickly read people and situations and create a mental map of the "terrain."
- I am skillful in reading weak signals on the horizon.
- I see beyond the literal.
- I apply alternative ways of knowing and perceiving.
- I construct meaning from a wide variety of sources.

Decision-making [Dm]

Making the optimal decision is foundational to leadership. As the pace and complexity of organizational life increase so do the demands on leaders to make great choices. Our organizations depend on it. Making critical decisions in real-time with minimal data points, in often paradoxical situations, is the hallmark of a great leader.

- I consider all aspects of an issue when appropriate.
- I demonstrate good judgment.
- I do not second-guess my decisions.
- I can make the complex simple when formulating a decision.
- I decide based on the best interest of the whole organization.

Assessing Risk [Ar]

Assessing risk is knowledge, experience and intuition brought to bear on a financial or physical challenge in service of a bold move forward. It is an expression of confidence. Emerging, experienced and seasoned leaders will assess risk differently. It calls on character, sound judgment and openness to input. Reading and minimizing risk are critical to movement without peril.

- I understand the full range of consequences of an action or decision.
- I weigh the cost versus benefit of a decision.
- I incorporate awareness of risk into my decisions.
- I mitigate or minimize risk if and where possible.
- I am aware of the unanticipated consequences of actions or inaction.

Designing Action [Da]

Designing action is knowing the race you are going to run before you start. It is moving from the ethereal to the concrete, from the unseen to the seen. It is creating an intelligent plan and articulating that plan to others. It is a strategy on the verge of tactics and leadership on the verge of management. Designing action is translating a felt sense of the future into getting there.

- I build simple and specific plans that deliver results.
- I ensure that everyone understands the plan and their part.
- I prepare others for performance and provide meaningful feedback.
- I am comfortable challenging habits and assumptions.
- I create plans that work for partners and collaborators outside of the team or enterprise.
- I demonstrate an ability to create conditions of stability, or conversely an ability to create conditions of instability and change as required.

Political Intelligence [Pi]

Political intelligence is accepting that in any organization there are issues of authority, status and power and as a result, politics. It is understanding the political terrain, climate, power structures and pressure points. It is choosing to be aware rather than naive. It is working with this extra layer of complexity and chaos to serve the organization's higher interest.

- I understand the political landscape of my leadership ecosystem.
- I can discern the hidden agenda of others.
- I am adept at managing the political terrain to advance my goal or vision.
- I am skilled at building political alliances that can serve my enterprise.
- I can identify "what's in it for you" to bring others on board.

Developing Other Leaders [Di]

Developing other leaders is committing to the truth that leaders must beget leaders. It is holding oneself accountable for the success of one's direct reports. It is mentoring and coaching and supporting. It is leveraging one's experience by building leadership capacity in others for the present and the future.

- I motivate and inspire others to take positive action.
- I release control and place trust in the ability of others.
- I create succession opportunities and leadership learning for others.
- I support each individual's self-development.
- I hold others accountable for their commitments.
- I delegate responsibility and decision-making.

Aligning People [Ap]

Aligning people is having the right talent in the right roles. It is working to ensure everyone understands where the enterprise is going and is clear on what is expected from them and the situation. It is identifying champions. It is getting people to tell the story in their way. It is inspiring and supportive. It is seeking and enticing the next great hire.

- I am skilled and comfortable with difficult conversations.
- I demonstrate patience.
- I effectively address difficult issues.
- I feature the organization's interests over the interests of individuals.
- I am skilled at anticipating the needs of others.

Executing to Plan [Ep]

Executing to plan is how all focused action happens. It is building the skill and capacity to execute. It is holding oneself and others accountable. It is the pivot point from leadership to management. It is the disciplined, measurable, results-based movement from here to there. It is also knowing when and how to stay out of the way.

- I set clear goals and expectations.
- I marshal resources to help associates achieve their objectives.
- I create a clear plan to achieve the goal.
- I deliver the promised results.
- I create the space and the opportunity for others to step up.

Storytelling [St]

Storytelling is engaging the hearts of others and bringing a living sense of the destination to the journey. It animates a vision, paints a picture, creates a myth or metaphor. Storytelling paves the long road from the brain to the heart. It evokes passion. Individual and organizational dreams are kept alive by stories told over and over again. It motivates action like nothing else.

- I listen first and deeply.
- I make the point simply and succinctly for maximum impact.
- I shift style as needed to really connect.
- I craft impactful stories by using humour, metaphor and relevant examples.
- I use story to inspire others and build understanding.

THE BREAKING AWAY ELEMENTS OF LEADERSHIP

Experimenting [Ei]

Experimenting is adopting the beginner's mindset, connecting imagination to reality, applying and testing new ideas. It requires real tolerance for risk and failure. Letting go of what does not work, and moving on easily, becomes the new norm.

- I create an environment that produces new perspectives and solutions.
- I understand risk and am comfortable with failure.
- I am open to adjacent perspectives, possibilities and approaches.
- I can identify situations that require continuous learning.
- I build on previous knowledge or experience in new ways.

Enterprising [Et]

Enterprising is about finding a way forward especially when confronted by obstacles. Hungry, dynamic and industrious, enterprising leaders are continuously on the search for better or new. Even in the face of insurmountable odds, the most enterprising of leaders can make it happen. Enterprising is having the courage to move to the atypical and unconventional. It is using ingenuity as a default for solving seemingly intractable problems.

- I am comfortable in taking risks and trying new things.
- I use imagination and initiative to create "work-arounds" when necessary.
- I am comfortable with ambiguity and navigate complex situations with seeming grace and ease.
- I am tenacious, indefatigable, relentless and play the "long game."
- I am fierce and bold; driven to "make it happen."

Collaborating [Co]

Collaborating is engaging a diverse range of people to enhance the possibility of traction and a better outcome. It is about genuine curiosity, disparate or divergent points of view. Collaboration is used to solve complex problems or create new value that otherwise may not happen. Collaboration is the relentless pursuit of a better idea.

- I readily engage a diversity of talent, perspectives and styles to achieve a greater result.
- I reach out to people who should be involved or informed, and readily partner with others in and outside the organization.
- I synthesize a range of perspectives, ideas and contributions to solve complex problems.
- I understand and have patience for the collaborative process.

Exploring [Ex]

Exploring is deep and relentless curiosity. It is constantly seeking, the quest for discovery. It is comfort with the unknown and ambiguity. It is the self-confidence to persevere, often through adversity into the unknown, and the humility to admit mistakes. With no stone left unturned, it is getting to the root or essence of a situation. Explorers are agile and adaptive. Explorers face challenges with vision, fortitude and the resilience to explore the impossible and see the possibilities not evident to others. It is maintaining a line of sight to the end goal. It is driven by discovery.

- I am curious about others, my world and how things work.
- I am driven by *better is always possible*.
- I do what it takes to uncover the heart of the matter or situation.
- I am a risk-taker and have an entrepreneur's aesthetic.
- I will find a way, no matter what, to make it happen.

Adaptive Learning [Al]

Adaptive learning is real-time, continuous, lifelong learning. It is creating new maps in the middle of navigation. It is formal and informal, it must be sought, and it requires humility. It is closing the feedback loop by integrating experience gathered and lessons learned. It is knowing that one never arrives, as leadership credentials are constantly being earned.

- I anticipate and understand changing situations and environments and quickly adapt with new approaches and ideas.
- I am agile and responsive to ideas that contribute to a solution.
- I am comfortable with non-conventional ideas and ideation.
- I bring curiosity and new thinking to a complex situation.
- I challenge myself and others to stretch.

Suspending [Su]

Suspending is refraining from preconceived notions, recognizing bias and being as neutral as possible. It is clear thinking. Suspending is parking judgment, ideology or conclusions and analyzing the data inputs as they emerge. In suspending, we are open to new and adjacent possibilities.

- I hold a point of view that is open to other perspectives.
- I am open to letting a situation remain unresolved.
- I do not attach to a pre-determined outcome.
- I refrain from judgment or conclusion when required.
- I can hold more than one truth or construct simultaneously.

Translating [Tr]

Few leaders can take complex situations, problems or strategies and distill the essence to communicate this complexity in a simple way that is easily understood. Translation requires a deep understanding of all the moving parts to connect the receiver to the higher purpose (the why) in a way that can be actioned to achieve the desired outcome.

- I reframe complex ideas and information into relevant messages and simple constructs.
- I can convert ideas and concepts into action.
- I use or blend various communication styles.
- I create meaning for others.
- I communicate with focus, clearly and simply.

Imagining [Im]

You can't create the future if you can't imagine it. Imagining is exploring new thinking about what is possible and beyond the norm. Imagining is about the capacity to originate an idea, a concept, a vision for a preferred future. It requires giving up a seat in the knowable world. The spark can be maverick or childlike as one reaches for the ultimate "what if."

- I can form mental images or concepts of what is not present to the senses.
- I use a range of modalities of perception to create something new.
- I am comfortable with conceptual thinking.
- I use experiences and stored memory to create solutions.

Influencing [In]

Influencing is the convergence of three **Essential Elements of Leadership**: Story-telling, Aligning People and Political Intelligence. Influencing is the art of leading without authority while having the ability to bring others skillfully and subtly to your point of view. Influence is having confidence in your direction and crafting the conditions for others to enroll because your vision has merit. The best leaders are skilled in influence while using it judiciously.

- I am skilled at moving others from a fixed perspective or point of view.
- I can compel others to take actions or decisions they hadn't considered.
- I create a positive effect on the actions or behaviours of others.
- I affect change in someone or something indirectly and importantly.
- I can change a trajectory or outcome based on my trustworthiness.

Synthesizing [Sy]

Synthesizing is seeing, understanding, shaping and naming new patterns critical to future success. It is about distilling metadata, connections beyond the obvious and relevance to the business at hand. Clear and simple communication makes these insights useful. Synthesizing is focusing ideas and applying convergent thinking.

- I collate a variety of inputs to achieve a unified outcome.
- I reduce complex problems into brilliantly simple concepts and solutions.
- I can see patterns and connections and translate them into action.
- I can combine parts or elements into a single unified entity.
- I continuously seek insight and promote knowledge capture and transfer.

THE LEADING THE FIELD ELEMENTS OF LEADERSHIP

Patterning [Pa]

Patterning brings some semblance of order to chaotic situations. It is using an array of sensory means of data collection and knowledge to gain a deeper understanding of a situation or scenario. In natural systems patterns always emerge. Time and patience are required. Deploying alternative modes of perception can reveal new possibilities and a clear path forward.

- I spot weak signals or patterns in chaotic or complex situations.
- I identify subtle shifts in a system or situation before or as they occur.
- I look beyond the non-evident to discern pathways where none are apparent.
- I have a deep capacity for anticipation.
- I skillfully make connections between knowledge and experience to new information perceived in real-time.

Catalyzing [Ca]

Catalyzing is purposeful disruption of the status quo to provoke fresh momentum or a new direction. It is about recognizing the right time, accepting the lack of control and reading the feedback. Catalyzing takes the courage to act when the outcome may not be clear.

- I propel action and inspire momentum to advance meaningful change further or faster.
- I dare to provoke new or different thinking.
- I subtly precipitate an event to compel change.
- I stimulate a substantial change in thinking or direction.
- I act as a provocateur when required.

Creating [Cr]

What can be conceived can be created. Creating is the capacity to originate or bring into form something that is novel and does not exist. In some cases, disparate things can be recombined to form something new. It is the highest form of expression and is the deep understanding that true leadership, in essence, is an act of creation. It is understanding and knowing where value lives and how to create it from scratch, from inception in the mind to the back of a napkin to completion. Creators take every possible opportunity to create relevance by developing and sustaining meaning and value for all parties involved.

- I am at ease coming up with novel ideas.
- I have a strong vision of how things can be.
- I am comfortable with the messiness of creativity.
- I use my creativity as a means of self-expression.
- I seek to connect vision, meaning and purpose to create relevance.

Emerging [Em]

Emerging is holding space for new thinking or better ideas to arise. It requires comfort with tension and ambiguity while waiting for the right direction to become clear. If one does not push too hard for closure, better will come. Emergence requires leaders to "sit in the fire," something that may not be either intuitive or comfortable.

- I actively search for opportunities in uncertainty or chaos.
- I am comfortable with and can leverage spontaneity in situations.
- I am open to ambiguity and hold the space for a new idea to present itself.
- I am comfortable in "not knowing."
- I understand that systems are dynamic and constantly in motion and that order will eventually arise.

Paradox [Px]

Paradox is the ability to hold a split view or two perspectives simultaneously. This requires a higher order of thinking from leaders and the capacity to navigate the "middle space," skillfully blending multiple perspectives and extremes into an "adjacent possible." Holding paradox is the understanding that two contradictory views can co-exist.

- I can hold two distinctly different or even opposing perspectives simultaneously.
- I can manage the tension between two opposing ideas or forces.
- I see and engage in a variety of perspectives as opposed to being steadfast to a single view.
- I work within known or obvious constraints to resolve chaotic and paradoxical situations.
- I skillfully navigate complex environments and situations.

Stewardship [Sp]

Stewardship is the highest form of leadership. It requires leaders to think well beyond themselves and be in service to others and the greater good. Stewardship is the art of the long view, a perspective that may span beyond a lifetime and even generations.

- I think beyond myself and incorporate the view of the greater good.
- I have a deep understanding of the impact and consequence of my actions, decisions, strategies and initiatives.
- I am aware of nature and other species as partners in our long-term existence.
- I aspire to positively impact and benefit communities, the natural world and our environment as a result of my work and actions.
- I am aware of my legacy and what I leave behind.

Enchantment [En]

Enchantment is deep, continuous curiosity and an insatiable quest for discovery that results in new ways of knowing. It is the experience of wonder even in the minute and mundane. Enchantment is our closest link to the wonders and lessons inherent in the natural world. Leaders who understand enchantment can see inter-relationships and connections, understand that everything is a natural ecosystem and organize accordingly to achieve a result. Enchantment goes beyond cause/effect thinking.

- I am curious.
- I have a penchant for the unique and interesting.
- I see the grace, beauty and elegance in small things.
- I am adept at noticing and deploy a heightened awareness of the world.
- I generate interest through thoughtful design, creativity and experiences.

GRATITUDE

To all of the rebuilders and new builders in our midst who struggle day to day to make the world a better place despite harsh setbacks and unrelenting pressure to sustain the status quo, my gratitude to you has no bounds. You are creating our future. You are demonstrating to all of us the power and beauty that are possible when you teach the dinosaur to dance.

Choosing to write a book about enterprise rebuilding in the middle of a pandemic was not something I planned to do; it just happened. As my ever-supportive husband, Laurie, will attest, ideas invaded my waking (and sleeping) hours. If business as usual was extinct, what could fill the void? I dug deep into this question with the many people I know: rebuilders and new builders standing shoulder-to-shoulder in the trenches, doing the heavy lifting of corporate, non-profit and government enterprise. I have learned so much from all of you. Building, and rebuilding to make things work better, is largely a team effort. There are many isolated moments—of questioning, reflection and sometimes anxiety—but the joyful moments, seeing a new idea emerge or a vision realized, are best shared.

Don Hill is a former CBC journalist with a prescient sense of perception and pattern-recognition who joined me in the writing of the blog *Beyond Polarity* in 2018. Don's determination to rebuild a stronger Alberta is unwavering, and his friendship and wise counsel on this shared journey are cherished. Andre Mamprin, a Sherpa to enterprise leaders across North America for decades now, is a fellow Albertan whose values align perfectly with the aim of this book. Andre's work building the capacity of new builders and rebuilders demonstrates his commitment to enterprise that is capable of much more than simply making more money.

Curiosity is a powerful force that drives me across the boundaries that divide: geographical, sectoral, faith, even political. In this way, I've encountered some of the most profound thinking across the globe, including for example, that of community leaders across Yemen; Bohmian physicists and Indigenous elders at the Pari Center in Italy; higher-order thinkers including (the late) Bernie Novokowsky and Lenn Jaskula; governance gurus such as Allan Pedden; and fellow writers, including Kaycee Krysty, who conjured up the book's title. I'm so grateful to have my way of thinking disrupted—sometimes gently and sometimes not.

Finally, I'm grateful to those professionals who made it possible for you to hold this book in your hands (or on your iPad), including and especially Karen Milner, the editor of my earlier book, *Corporate Integrity*, whom I had the good fortune of rediscovering as this manuscript was taking shape nearly two decades later. Karen's professional, creative and constructive approach to the editing and publishing of this book are testimony to the talent we have here in Canada. Many of the larger publishing companies have decamped to the United States, yet significant expertise remains here, in our midst, quietly and diligently rebuilding.

This book is dedicated to my granddaughter, Kennedy, and to her generation. On the cold winter day in late January 2020 when Kennedy arrived in this world, the front pages of newspapers spoke of a strange virus coming our way. Then, we had no inkling of what lay ahead. Kennedy remains blissfully unaware of the pandemic, nurtured by her family and friends in a safe cocoon. Watching this wee child put one foot in front of the other—developing the skills to crawl and walk and run and, yes, dance—fills me with hope, every single day.

ABOUT THE AUTHORS

DONNA KENNEDY-GLANS

Donna is a boundary-crosser, adding value to enterprising projects in over thirty-five countries, in the public, private and non-profit sectors.

Born a farmer's daughter near Tillsonburg, in southwestern Ontario, Donna left the family cattle and tobacco farm to get a law degree at the University of Western Ontario. From there, she headed further west, to Alberta, to work in the oil patch, where she held several unique and pioneering roles in risk management, corporate integrity and sustainability: she became the first female vice-president at Nexen; was an early architect of transparency initiatives in places like Nigeria; and again and again, demonstrated the ability to bring together investors, communities, advocates and governments on values-based issues.

Donna has varied experience across many sectors: founding a non-profit to build the capacity of women in Yemen, serving as an elected politician and cabinet minister, holding leading roles on boards of directors, and participating with her siblings in the stewardship of the family farm enterprise.

She is the lead author of *Corporate Integrity: A Toolkit for Managing beyond Compliance* (Wiley, 2005), and is now a political commentator, community builder, writer and speaker, weighing in on energy, leadership, governance, community and integrity issues.

Collaborating with others to design and implement smart solutions to vexing problems is a passion for Donna. Her goal has always been to make better decisions within organizations, and to help others do the same, with greater agility and intention.

When she is not teaching dinosaurs to dance, Donna can be found hiking in some remote place, camera at the ready, or playing with her granddaughter, Kennedy.

www.teachingthedinosaur.com

ANDRE N. MAMPRIN

Laura Grace Photography

Andre has been a student of both the art and the science of strategy and leadership for more than two decades. As Leader of Knowledge Architecture at The Next Institute and Executive Director of The Banff Centre Leadership Development, he has designed leadership learning content and delivered programs to more than 20,000 leaders.

Adjacent to his role at Next, Andre is currently working on several start-ups, including UpLift Studio Lab,™ a storytelling unit of The Next Institute; and The Next Learner Space,™ a global initiative to develop leadership skills for highly enterprising youth.

Andre is keenly interested in advancing new thinking and applied research in the fields of innovation, collaboration, leadership development and enterprise design. He served as Director, Centre for Innovation, Leadership & Management at Sheridan Corporate in Toronto, Canada, and was the co-architect of The Leadership Lab™ at The Banff Centre, exploring issues of organizational leadership worldwide.

As both a leader and entrepreneur in the oil and gas, manufacturing and banking industries, he gained hands-on, applied experience in growing profitable business driven by solid leadership ecosystems, and he has translated that experience into designing and delivering intricate and often large-scale solutions for an array of blue-chip organizations across North America.

As a creative, trans-disciplinary thinker, Andre has a keen ability to analyze and apply a unique approach to a host of contemporary strategic issues. Placing great leadership at the heart of all individual and organizational success, he believes deeply that leaders can be developed.

Andre is an experienced international traveler, painter, sculptor, student of the martial arts and an avid cyclist. He and his family have built their life in Calgary, Canada.

www.thenext.ca